habnf   HEB

364.60973 SCHEN

Schen  W9-BKS-777
Prison by any other name

33410017106388   04-26-2021

DISCARD

DISCARD

PRISON BY ANY OTHER NAME

Also by Maya Schenwar

Locked Down, Locked Out: Why Prison Doesn't Work and How We Can Do Better

Also by Victoria Law

Resistance Behind Bars: The Struggles of Incarcerated Women

PRISON BY ANY OTHER NAME

THE HARMFUL CONSEQUENCES
OF POPULAR REFORMS

MAYA SCHENWAR AND VICTORIA LAW

WITH A FOREWORD BY MICHELLE ALEXANDER

NEW YORK
LONDON

© 2020 by Maya Schenwar and Victoria Law
Foreword © 2020 by Michelle Alexander
All rights reserved.
No part of this book may be reproduced, in any form, without written permission from the publisher.

Requests for permission to reproduce selections from this book should be made through our website: https://thenewpress.com/contact.

Published in the United States by The New Press, New York, 2020
Distributed by Two Rivers Distribution

ISBN 978-1-62097-310-3 (hc)
ISBN 978-1-62097-311-0 (ebook)
CIP data is available.

The New Press publishes books that promote and enrich public discussion and understanding of the issues vital to our democracy and to a more equitable world. These books are made possible by the enthusiasm of our readers; the support of a committed group of donors, large and small; the collaboration of our many partners in the independent media and the not-for-profit sector; booksellers, who often hand-sell New Press books; librarians; and above all by our authors.

www.thenewpress.com

Book design and composition by Bookbright Media
This book was set in Minion Pro and Knockout

Printed in the United States of America

CONTENTS

FOREWORD

THE BOOK YOU HOLD IN YOUR HANDS REQUIRES YOUR FULL ATTEN-tion. On the surface, it seems to be a book about ending mass incarceration in all of its forms. It is that, but it is also more. At its core, this book challenges us to think more deeply and carefully about what we mean by "justice" and what kind of world we aim to co-create.

We are now living in a moment in which large numbers of people are suddenly paying attention to the United States' astronomical incarceration rate and "alternatives" to incarceration have become a topic of mainstream debate. This was not the case just ten years ago. Much has changed in the world and in our collective consciousness during the past decade—some for the better, some for the worse. Some of the things that seem to be changing for the better might actually be leading us to a place that's even worse.

Prison by Any Other Name investigates the kinds of reforms that initially appear to be a step in the right direction but are, in reality, leading us somewhere we don't ever want to go. Unfortunately, many of the alternatives to incarceration being embraced today will likely worsen the lives of the very people and communities that many reformers aim to help. In my view, most concerning is the rapid spread of technological "fixes" to our supposedly "broken" system. In our zeal to make some progress in the fight against mass incarceration, many well-intentioned reformers are wittingly or unwittingly converting homes, neighborhoods, and entire communities into high-tech digital prisons.

Humanity has reached a stage in its development where our technological capacity has greatly outpaced our moral strivings. This seems especially true in wealthy, grossly unequal capitalistic societies like ours—places where the conditions for wealth accumulation and technological progress have been (and continue to be) inextricably linked to slavery, genocide, and the exploitation of people and resources around the world. As a nation, we've learned how to send people into outer space and how to shrink a powerful computer into a device that fits into the palm of our hand. But have we learned how to face our racial history, or how to tell the truth about the devastation wrought by colonialism and global capitalism? We've learned how to develop powerful surveillance systems and how to build missiles that can reach halfway around the globe. But what, exactly, have we learned about the true meaning of justice?

As we desperately seek solutions to crime and alternatives to incarceration, it's all too easy to be seduced by technology and to imagine that there must be a technical fix to the deep moral and structural challenges we face. Maybe, we wonder aloud, if police officers are forced to wear body cameras, that will help. Maybe if people who can't afford bail are released from jail with electronic monitors strapped to their ankles, that will help. Maybe if people are sentenced to house arrest for ten years rather than three years in prison, that will help. After all, isn't house arrest better than prison? Isn't an electronic monitor

strapped to your ankle better than a jail cell? Won't police behave better if a camera is attached to their vest filming everyone they interact
with? Even if body cameras are more likely to collect evidence against
the people they film than against the officers wearing them, aren't the
cameras worth it if they help to catch even one bad cop? Isn't it progress if some people are able to give birth or raise their kids at home
under house arrest rather than being locked in prison (even if their
kids are now living in a digital prison, too)? This is the logic that is
driving much of the current criminal justice reform debate. But what
does it mean—really—to celebrate reforms that convert your home
into your prison?

As momentum builds for some kind of reform, it's worth pausing
to consider what truly counts as meaningful progress. In this groundbreaking book, Maya Schenwar and Victoria Law invite us to wrestle
with this difficult question and to consider the profound challenges we
must face if we are to do more than simply re-form the system of mass
incarceration into another version of itself. Through interviews with
victims of mass incarceration, criminal justice practitioners, and abolitionists, and drawing on extensive research, they demonstrate that
we can end mass incarceration without perpetuating harm, destroying lives, and controlling entire communities. However, we must be
careful not to embrace every policy advertised as a progressive reform,
since they often contain hidden dangers. In the words of Schenwar
and Law:

> Innovation, in itself, is no guarantee of progress. In so
> many cases, reform is not the building of something new.
> It is the re-forming of the system in its own image, using
> the same raw materials: white supremacy, a history of
> oppression, and a tool kit whose main contents are con-
> finement, isolation, surveillance, and punishment.

This book is especially instructive for new (and old) converts against mass incarceration who are eager to move past condemnations of the current system and begin the work of reimagining what justice should look like in their own communities.

Unfortunately, today, when most people discuss the "growing bipartisan consensus to end mass incarceration" they are typically defining the problem of mass incarceration in the narrowest possible terms, focusing only on reducing the number of people who are currently behind bars. Yet if we limit our field of vision in this way—measuring progress solely by the number of people who are no longer locked in prisons or jails—we inevitably fail to take into account the millions of people who can be found in immigrant detention centers or mental health facilities, as well as the tens of millions of people on probation or parole.

The term "mass incarceration" makes it easy to forget the majority of people who are under some form of carceral control aren't even in prisons or jails. More than twice as many people are currently on probation or parole as are held behind bars. We could cut the number of people in cages in half and still have entire communities under surveillance—placed on probation, parole, or electronic monitors—and perpetually hunted or harassed by the police. They would still be labeled criminals or felons and subject to legal discrimination for the rest of their lives in employment, housing, and access to basic public benefits.

In fact, we could slash the number of people in state and federal prisons but still manage to *increase* the size of the carceral state. We could reduce the number of people behind bars but, at the same time, double, triple, or quadruple the number of people who are on probation or parole. These people who are "free" from their cages may be sentenced to their homes, placed under house arrest for years or even decades, or confined to their neighborhoods through electronic monitoring (EM) devices that will summon the police if they dare to leave their invisible cage even for a minute. In short, we could successfully cut the number of people "locked in," while another caste-like system is quietly born. This is not the stuff of sci-fi fantasy or teen dystopian fiction; this is the world that many of us are co-creating right now even as we claim to be working to end a system of racial and social control.

Some scholars and policy advocates might find it convenient to define "mass incarceration" narrowly because reducing the number of people in cages is an easier problem to solve than ending the history and cycle of creating caste-like systems in America. Thankfully, *Prison by Any Other Name* does not shrink from the task at hand. It reminds us that "mass incarceration" should be understood to encompass all versions of racial and social control wherever they can be found, including prisons, jails, schools, forced "treatment" centers, and immigrant detention centers, as well as homes and neighborhoods converted to digital prisons. This important book forces us to clarify what we are truly fighting against: not simply steel bars, but a system rooted in white supremacy, capitalism, sexism, and violence.

As I was reading this book, I kept a running list of the actors who are implicated in the expanding net of mass incarceration. Lawmakers, judges, prosecutors, parole officers, and police officers leap immediately to mind. But what about those we usually trust to serve us and keep us safe, including social workers, emergency room doctors, and landlords, many of whom are required to surveil and report our most vulnerable groups to a system of severe punishment? This book brings an important new cast of characters into view, as we aim to tell a more complete story of mass incarceration. What about teachers? Pastors who work with police departments to create gang databases? School counselors? Psychiatrists? Scientists who create electronically trackable medication that probation officers can use to track those under carceral control? What about people who run homeless and domestic violence shelters?

The "alternatives" that are put on the table against mass incarceration often include many actors who contribute to incarceration in less than obvious ways—ways that have important implications for reform. When we say things like "We just need more mental health institutions instead of prisons," that may be accurate, but it is a false and dangerous alternative if the mental health institutions actually function like prisons, and if the doctors are concerned primarily with control rather than the healing and well-being of their patients.

To be clear, none of this is to say that efforts to reduce prison populations are unimportant. To the contrary, we can and we must end the practice of putting people in literal cages. But as Schenwar and Law emphasize in the pages that follow, as we dismantle our prison system we must do everything in our power to avoid becoming co-conspirators in the creation of another, equally dangerous system of control.

Through their work as organizers, researchers, and storytellers, Schenwar and Law are radically changing the terms of the debate. They remind us that mass incarceration must be defined to encompass all versions of racial and social control that keep people locked up and locked out. The whole system must go—not just the prisons—and a new conception of justice, one that honors the dignity and humanity of all, must take its place. This will not be easy, but nothing less will do if we ever hope to break the history and cycle of birthing caste-like systems in America.

—Michelle Alexander

PRISON BY ANY OTHER NAME

INTRODUCTION:
EVERYBODY LOVES PRISON REFORM

Colette Payne had been in Chicago's Cook County Jail for a week when she was offered the option of being released on electronic monitoring and house arrest. Payne was eager to escape the jail, where women were crowded into cells in a manner that reminded her of slavery, where breakfast was served at 3:30 in the morning, where many meals consisted of old baloney sandwiches, and where "discipline" often meant being thrown in torturous solitary confinement. Worst of all, in jail, she was separated from her four-year-old and six-year-old children. So Payne chose the monitor—an electronic shackle that would essentially incarcerate her in her home, forcing her to stay within a certain radius, or else the police would be alerted. The monitor was presented as her only alternative to incarceration, and she wanted to be able to live at home so that she could see her children freely.

What Payne hadn't counted on were the extreme restrictions that came with house arrest and monitoring. Every step beyond one hundred feet of her mother's doorway had to be preapproved by her probation officer. Employees from the sheriff's department came to Payne's home to conduct inspections, alerting the entire housing complex that she was being monitored. Payne was unable to take her young children to school or to the store. She knew they were affected by her confinement—her older son began to act out in school, and cried often. Payne missed family barbecues. She couldn't even take the garbage out, since the dumpsters were at the end of the housing complex, beyond where she was allowed to go. In effect, Payne was imprisoned. "You're basically held hostage in your own home," she said of her time on the monitor.

Being tethered to her home didn't help Payne address the reason she had been arrested in the first place—a decade-long heroin addiction. Strong relationships are among the most significant motivators to curb drug misuse, and people with strong relationships are less likely to be rearrested, too.[1] But electronic monitoring does the opposite—it traps people, many times isolating them from loved ones, sometimes making it difficult for them to take care of others and to feel a sense of purpose and meaning. (Think of Payne, barred from even taking her children to school.) Instead, they often spend their days wrestling with boredom and the strain of captivity.

For Payne, that boredom and isolation exacerbated her desire to get high. Her cravings for heroin were ever-present. But neither the court nor the probation office offered resources to support her in confronting her addiction. In fact, she was not granted permission to leave her home to look for or attend treatment. If she attempted to do so, she would be violating the terms of her electronic monitoring and subject to arrest and reimprisonment.

For someone with a severe addiction, quitting heroin use can be an excruciating battle even under the best of circumstances. For many people, it takes multiple relapses and years of attempts before recovery sticks. Such was the case for Payne. While on electronic monitoring, as she struggled with her addiction, she chafed at the limitations of her home confinement. She began to wander out of bounds, sometimes to buy drugs and sometimes just to feel the freedom of walking to the store. Eventually she was arrested for going "out of range" and briefly jailed. Still unable to access treatment to address the underlying causes of her problems, she was eventually arrested on a new charge related to her addiction. Once again Payne was incarcerated and separated from her children.

The severe constraints of her "alternative to incarceration" didn't prevent Payne from ending up back in a cage. In fact, by isolating her from her extended family and community and short-circuiting her attempts to get help, electronic monitoring made her relapse—and subsequent incarceration—nearly inevitable.

Payne's experience is no anomaly. "Alternatives to incarceration" such as electronic monitoring have grown increasingly popular in recent years. In 2005, 53,000 people were on electronic monitoring across the country; by 2015, that number exceeded 125,000—and monitoring is just one of many alternatives to incarceration that have been implemented nationwide.[2] As the number of people locked into jails and prisons has swelled to nearly 2.3 million and government budgets have felt the weight of ballooning costs, politicians on both sides of the aisle have called into question the lock-'em-up zeal of the 1980s and 1990s. Some are alarmed by the fact that the United States has long been the most incarcerated nation in the world, especially because widespread research has proven that more incarceration not only doesn't reduce violent crime, it may even increase it (in addition to the violence that prison itself perpetuates).[3] Others are questioning the deterrent effect of incarceration, because most people who are released are later rearrested, in a dismal cycle: five out of six people released from state prisons are rearrested within nine years.[4] Mainstream conversations are also increasingly challenging the system's racism, pointing to the fact that Black and Brown people are much more likely than whites to be targeted by police and subsequently incarcerated.[5] And across the political spectrum, almost no one seems pleased with the fact that the incarceration system is costing the government and families $182 billion per year.[6]

The cast of characters advocating for prison reform is large and varied. In February 2015, the media and Washington politicians were abuzz with news of what seemed to be a wildly unlikely alliance: the Koch brothers, conservative oil barons who've bankrolled a broad range of right-wing agendas, were banding together with the NAACP (National Association for the Advancement of Colored People) and the liberal think tank Center for American Progress to address mass incarceration, a problem that just a few years earlier had barely squeaked into the headlines.[7] They were forming a new organization, the Coalition for Public Safety. Other conservative groups including Americans for Tax Reform and FreedomWorks were also joining the party.[8] The Right on Crime initiative, a project founded in 2010 that makes a "conservative case for prison reform," was supported by Republican stalwarts such as Grover Norquist, Newt Gingrich, and Jeb Bush. Gingrich and conservative billionaire B. Wayne Hughes Jr. co-wrote a *Los Angeles Times* op-ed denouncing the long-term imprisonment of thousands for nonviolent drug crimes while continuing to call for the imprisonment of "people we are afraid of."[9]

Excitement about addressing mass incarceration was also building among Democrats. In the summer of 2015, President Barack Obama visited a federal prison. It was the first such trip by a sitting president and, given the shifting currents of public sentiment, a widely lauded one. Obama championed changes in sentencing laws, better reentry programs, and an emphasis on rehabilitation for those caught in the legal system. But Obama was far from advocating for a complete and transformative overhaul of the criminal legal system. In fact, like Gingrich and Hughes, Obama made sure to emphasize first and foremost that "there are people who need to be in prison."[10]

Obama took some noteworthy steps, such as ending solitary confinement for youth in federal prisons and granting clemency to hundreds of people incarcerated on long federal drug sentences. Yet, like Right on Crime and the Coalition for Public Safety, Obama never challenged incarceration at its core. He called for rehabilitation. He called for drug courts. He called for releasing those deemed "safe." He also called for continuing to keep a lot of other people locked up.

"Reform" is the refrain of the Koch brothers and Right on Crime. Those on both sides of the aisle call for changes that would shift money away from prisons—and toward mandated treatment programs, predictive and community policing, and data-driven surveillance. Both political camps advocate alternatives including electronic monitoring, house arrest, and extended (and often privatized) probation.

One case in point is the First Step Act, a package of minimal reforms that passed the U.S. Senate in late 2018, geared toward providing a modicum of support for people coming out of federal prison, slightly reducing sentences for a thin sliver of yet-to-be-incarcerated people, and significantly expanding electronic surveillance and risk assessment measures widely known to be grounded in racial bias.[11] In an apparent concession to the National Fraternal Order of Police, an association of more than 300,000 police officers across the country that endorsed the bill, sentence reductions would not apply retroactively to already-incarcerated people.[12] Despite its extremely limited usefulness to criminalized and incarcerated people, the passage of the reform bill—and widespread support among Democrats and Republicans—was hailed as a bipartisan triumph. President Trump signed the bill into law shortly before the end of 2018, tweeting, "These historic changes will make communities SAFER and SAVE tremendous taxpayers dollars."[13]

But listen closely to both conservative and liberal reformers' plans for addressing mass incarceration. They sound a lot like . . . mass incarceration.

A few edits to the system hardly change the larger story. Reforms like the First Step Act and the Right on Crime modifications might allow for some improvements, but they also entrench the underlying principles of the system, and can cause immediate harm to those still ensnared in the carceral web.

Our concerns about these reforms stem not only from our years of reporting and organizing but also from our own interactions with the system. In 2005, Maya's sister was arrested and sent to juvenile detention for a drug offense. Over the next fourteen years, she served seven more sentences in jails and prisons, all for offenses related to her heroin addiction. Clearly, incarceration wasn't solving her problems. Even in the periods between incarcerations, she wasn't free to live her life. Instead, she was pushed into different forms of state surveillance and confinement: electronic monitoring, house arrest, probation, mandatory drug treatment, parole.

Meanwhile, as Maya reported on and corresponded with other people behind prison walls, she noticed how quickly some of them were returned to incarceration after their release, having—often accidentally—broken the rules of a strict post-confinement regimen. From unremitting "treatment" requirements to the stifling protocols of the sex offender registry, many of the structures outside of prison bore uncanny resemblances to the prison itself: control, punishment, and a constant reminder that your body is not your own—that once the system has you in its clutches, you are the state's to manipulate.

Shortly after we began writing this book, Maya's sister was rearrested and sent to a local jail to serve a brief sentence. In a letter, she reflected that in one crucial sense the sentence was a relief: "At least, when I'm released this time, I won't be on probation."

Victoria, or Vikki as she's known to friends, was once on probation—two decades earlier than Maya's sister and with a much different experience and outcome. At sixteen, Vikki was arrested for several counts of armed robbery and gun possession, all of which are violent felony charges. New York is one of two states that automatically charge sixteen-year-olds as adults, but her attorney was able to convince the judge to grant her youthful offender status (meaning that upon successful completion of her sentence, her record would be sealed). She was ultimately sentenced to five years of probation.

Probation kept Vikki out of prison and enabled her to finish high school and college. It also allowed her the opportunity to grow into an adult with a meaningful—and legal—career and, later, to start her own family. If she had gone to prison, she would have been ripped away from her loved ones; she would have risked not finishing high school or attending college; and upon release she would have been saddled with a felony conviction record and a lifetime of collateral consequences.

But Vikki's probation happened more than two decades ago before technology made surveillance easier. In the 1990s, as someone considered at low-risk for reoffending, her only requirement was to report to her probation officer in person once a month. Even that was flexible. One evening, her closing shift at the neighborhood library caused her to report late to her probation officer. She arrived to a darkened (but, curiously, still unlocked) office; everyone had gone home for the day. She left a note on the front desk addressed to her probation officer. The next day, the officer scolded her not for missing her appointment but for coming to the office late in the evening. "This isn't a safe area at night," the probation officer said. "I don't want you coming in this late. If you can't make it earlier, just call and tell me." This attitude probably stemmed from privileges including her ethnicity (East Asian, not Black or Brown) and the prevailing stereotype that Asian women, particularly tiny ones, are submissive and therefore not a threat at all. But it was also a sign of a different time—although incarceration was skyrocketing and growing ever more punitive, non-incarceration surveillance mechanisms did not yet use invasive technology to ensure compliance, and Vikki's probation officer considered her a low priority on her overcrowded caseload. Had Vikki been sentenced now, those stereotypes and privileges might not have saved her from a more punitive and restrictive probation: heavy, binding surveillance, aided by technological advances, is simply woven into the fiber of current practices.

These varying manifestations of the criminal punishment system raise the question of what defines a prison. Is it bars and steel? Bland khaki uniforms? A door that locks from the outside only? Is it the eyes of authority probing you at all times? Is it the hands of authority, manipulating you, hurting you, rendering you "criminal"? Or is it more amorphous: a combination of the ways that the state acts on people—in particular, marginalized people—without their consent? There is unique gravity to an actual prison sentence, the violence of locking a human being in a cage. Yet the system is broader than the buildings called "prisons." Manipulation, confinement, punishment, and deprivation can take other forms—forms that may be less easily recognized as the violence they are.

Working for real freedom, in which no one is under any form of control, surveillance, or threat of state punishment, means resisting not only incarceration but all of its interconnected manifestations. Gender and criminology scholar Beth Richie calls this intersecting mass of structures—from the foster care system to immigrant detention centers to locked-down halfway houses to sex offender registries, plus punitive policies like welfare reform and English-only laws—the "prison nation."[14] This term is important because it embodies both the system's vastness and its embeddedness within the very fabric of this country.[15] We use "prison nation" throughout this book to describe all of these overlapping forces that carry out the removal of people from and the destruction of their communities. We also use the term "prison industrial complex," a term brought to prominence by leading prison abolitionist activist, author, and scholar Angela Davis.[16] This phrase is defined by Rachel Herzing, a co-founder (along with Davis and others) of the anti-prison organization Critical Resistance, as "the symbiotic relationship between public and private interests that employ imprisonment, policing, surveillance, the courts, and their attendant cultural apparatuses as a means of maintaining social, economic, and political inequities." The image of the prison industrial complex brings to light the web of punitive systems targeting people who are marginalized by race, class, gender identity, disability, or immigration status, and who are considered to be simply a surplus to society. It's helpful to keep this concept in mind as we talk about reform, because often, limited reforms—instead of shrinking the web or taking it down—weave in new strands of punishment and control.

As the reform train gains steam around the country, it's important to keep looking at what's happening out the window. We must consider the prison nation as a whole—and who is being captured by it.

Perfecting the Prison Nation

Many conservative and mainstream advocates operate from a framework of personal responsibility: the idea that those deemed "guilty" are caught in the system due to their own moral failings. In order to be redeemed, guilty people must be punished—or at least confined, isolated, and separated from the rest of the world. This emphasis on "redemption" tends to ignore or minimize the prison nation's foundations in structural oppressions such as racism, classism, and ableism. Instead, it suggests that the current brutal form of punishment can be *replaced* in certain circumstances (usually involving people whose crimes are deemed nonviolent) with a less brutal, more compassionate "alternative," while still placing guilt and blame squarely on the individual.

In its statement of grounding principles, Right on Crime proclaims the "conservative case for prison reform": "For too long . . . American conservatives have ceded the intellectual ground on criminal justice. Liberal ideas came to occupy the space, and in many respects, they were misguided ideas. They often placed the blame for crime upon society rather than upon individuals. . . . When the system has real teeth, the results can be dramatic."[17]

This concept of reshaping the system to give it "real teeth"—pushing individuals to take responsibility for their crimes—goes hand in hand with a push to spend fewer public dollars, thus relieving government budgets of the burden of paying for the roughly 2.3 million people now caught in the system. Reforms such as moving people from prison cells to electronic monitoring are promoted as both saving public funds and demanding more from people who've done wrong. People on electronic monitoring are generally required to pay for the equipment that confines them.

Some of the proposed reforms advocated by conservatives change classifications of criminality, tailoring them more to the people who, in the words of Gingrich and Hughes, "we are afraid of." But this determination is fraught with race- and class-based judgments. If someone robs a store as a result of chronic, generational poverty, they're classified as "violent" and therefore feared—more deserving of "teeth" than rehabilitation. Meanwhile, the landlords and property-owning corporations that provide substandard housing or lobby against tenant protections remain undeterred, as do the politicians making policies that perpetuate socioeconomic injustice. The individual who robbed a store is cast into the "criminal" box while the generational poverty goes unchallenged.

For people who've been shoved into that "criminal" category, it's not uncommon to be subject to multiple forms of confinement, one after another. Each time a punishment does not "work," it's attributed to a personal failure—and another punishment is imposed. Colette Payne, for example, served a grand total of eight terms of probation, some of which included the draconian restrictions of electronic monitoring. Although she lived with her children, Payne was cut out of family and community life; she could not fulfill some of the most basic parenting responsibilities such as taking her children to the store or attending parent-teacher conferences. She missed family celebrations and get-togethers with friends. At the same time, nothing in either her probation or her EM sentence helped her find resources to overcome her addiction. Halfway through her last probation sentence, she was arrested on another drug-related charge and sent to prison for two years. Clearly, neither alternative—probation nor monitoring—solved her underlying issues.

In some ways, recent reform attempts prop up and solidify this process of criminalization. They tend to emphasize the importance of changing the ways the most "sympathetic" people in the system, such as nonviolent first-time offenders, are treated. The goal is not to move beyond criminalization but instead to better define who is "criminal" and deal with those deemed criminals in more effective ways. But these efforts to "right-size" prisons—shrink the numbers of people in prisons by diverting people who are seen as less dangerous to less-expensive alternatives—still entrench the prison's place in society while expanding the carceral state into our everyday lives.

Instead of challenging the idea of a person being deemed criminal, today's most prominent proposals simply adjust the punishments brought down upon those who are criminalized. Some of these reforms involve shortening people's sentences—a useful step, because it decreases the number of people in prison. But others only change the look and feel of the sentence: including a component of mandated drug or psychiatric treatment, sentencing people to less-brutal prisons, or sentencing them to a fate besides traditional bars and steel.[18] In other words, the criminalization machine is being adjusted to keep up with the times, but it remains well-oiled and well-functioning.

What does it mean to reform—to improve—a system that, at its core, relies on captivity and control? What are the dangers of perfecting a system that was designed to target marginalized people?[19] Reforms that supposedly improve the current system run the risk of entrenching dangerous, violent, racist, classist, ableist, oppressive institutions—making them even harder to uproot. When captivity is perceived as kinder and gentler, it becomes more acceptable and less of an urgent priority to confront, even though it continues to destroy countless lives.

Prison Is a Reform

It shouldn't be a surprise to be betrayed by reform. The modern prison itself emerged as a reform to a grisly system. Before prisons gained popularity, capital punishment and bodily harm were the preferred modes of punishment. When the United States was founded, the death penalty was routinely imposed for offenses including burglary, counterfeiting, and even stealing horses.[20] In the eighteenth and early nineteenth centuries, prison reformers in the United States and Europe promoted prison as a more humane alternative, a "kinder substitute for the whip, the stocks, and the branding iron."[21] These early reformers were often from devoutly Christian backgrounds, and many envisioned prisons as sites of redemption. They saw the penitentiary—a term that comes from the word "penitent"—as a place where people might, in isolation, come to realize the nature of their sins and emerge remorseful, obedient, and rehabilitated. The experience wasn't supposed to be pleasant—the earliest penitentiaries certainly had teeth, generally calling for either near-constant solitary confinement or silent, ruthless labor—but the system's stated goals were lofty. Abbé Petigny, the warden of an early penitentiary in France, declared proudly, "What is for an irreligious prisoner merely a tomb, a repulsive ossuary, becomes, for the sincerely Christian convict, the very cradle of blessed immortality."[22]

As Angela Davis and others have noted, this reform-driven institution wasn't for everyone. American prisons were designed for people who were recognized as full citizens by the legal system—in other words, white men.[23] Enslaved Africans were not given due process under the law. They were already deprived of their freedom under slavery. While reformers insisted that punishment should shift from a focus on punishing the body to a focus on punishing the soul, Davis reminds readers that "black slaves in the US were largely perceived as lacking the soul that might be shaped and transformed by punishment."[24] Enslaved people were consequently punished by torture, mutilation, and death. Indigenous people were generally not placed in penitentiaries either; rather than penitence, the dominant society's goal for them was genocide, not rehabilitation. For white women, who also lacked full citizenship, punishments were usually meted out in the home by male family members, and these punishments were often brutally physical in nature. The handful of women who were incarcerated were often poor women and/or sex workers, and because the image of the fallen or morally depraved woman ran deep, they were less likely to be considered "redeemable" than their male counterparts. Women in early American prisons were often shoved into attics or basements, where they were subject to chronic rape and beatings.[25]

Prisons didn't adhere to their penitentiary mission for long. The purpose and nature of the new institutions morphed to meet the needs of their society, including the need to establish racialized control. After slavery was abolished, incarceration was quickly deployed as a way to continue enslaving people legally. The Thirteenth Amendment to the Constitution, which outlaws slavery, contains a stark exception: "except as a punishment for crime." Incarceration rates rose precipitously after slavery officially ended in 1865, as African Americans were arrested, many for newly minted offenses like curfew violations or loitering, then incarcerated and sometimes made to perform hard labor without pay.[26] Davis describes how prison became "punishment attached not to crime, but to race."[27] In other words, slavery had always been a type of imprisonment and racial control; now, instead of the individual master, it was the state that had the power to confine, isolate, dehumanize, and dominate Black people and other marginalized communities.

Likewise, in the mid- to later twentieth century, after the fall of Jim Crow and passage of civil rights laws, prison rapidly became the route to legally maintaining what Michelle Alexander, author of *The New Jim Crow*, calls a racial caste-like system.[28] The system ballooned, thanks to the expanded prosecution of drug crimes as well as many other charges. Today, Black Americans are disproportionately surveilled, policed, arrested, and prosecuted; they are five times as likely as white Americans to be behind bars.[29] Racial disparities in drug arrests persist: Black people are 2.7 times more likely than whites to be arrested on a drug-related charge, even though whites are just as likely to use illicit drugs—and more likely than Black people to be selling them.[30]

Prison has also been strategically deployed against Indigenous people. Throughout the twentieth century, incarceration, in a sense, became the "kinder" purveyor of genocide. During the latter half of the twentieth century, increasing numbers of Native people were disappeared into prisons.[31] Native scholar Luana Ross writes of how, as a child, she noticed that "people from my reservation appeared to simply vanish and magically return. . . . I imagined this as normal; that all families had relatives who went away and then returned."[32] Just as racial profiling and racist stereotypes have resulted in Black people being disproportionately policed, prosecuted, and imprisoned, Native people, too, are incarcerated at twice the rate of white Americans— and are killed by police at the highest rate of any racial group in the country.[33]

While race remains a key factor in determining who is incarcerated, other marginalized populations have been swept into prisons at high rates as well: trans and nonbinary people, people with psychiatric disabilities, people with drug dependencies, and poor people of all races. In the twentieth and twenty-first centuries, prisons have become places to put "surplus" people: those who are considered expendable, as activ-

ist scholar Ruth Wilson Gilmore has described in depth.[34] This drive
to disappear certain groups of people—including those who might
otherwise need public aid or services—coincided with the demolition
of the social safety net in the 1980s and 1990s.[35] As corporations began
paying fewer taxes and politicians popularized the notion that social
programs such as health care, education, food and housing assistance,
and the arts were not legitimate expenditures, governments began to
prioritize "defense"—keeping Americans "safe"—as the one true purpose of the state.[36] This focus was used to justify pouring money into
wars abroad, but also to justify the financial prioritization of policing
and incarceration at home.

One arena in which a twisted conception of "defense" has been
prioritized above all else has been immigration. The policing and
physical imprisonment of those lacking citizenship have expanded
rapidly over the past decade. Before 2005, when undocumented immigrants without criminal records were apprehended, they were issued
a summons to attend an immigration hearing, then released to their
family and community to await their day in court. But in 2005, the
Department of Homeland Security announced an end to this "catch
and release" policy and the start of a new policy called "catch and
return." The "return" referred to deportation proceedings, and as the
proceedings dragged on, more and more people were held in detention centers—essentially immigration jails. Jail construction kicked
into high gear and the number of immigration jail beds grew from
18,000 in 2005 to 33,000 in 2011.[37] In 2009, as part of its Department
of Homeland Security appropriations bill, Congress passed a mandate requiring U.S. Immigration and Customs Enforcement (ICE) to
maintain at least 34,000 beds in immigration jails each night, ensuring
steadily high numbers of immigrants behind bars.[38]

This drastic increase was promoted as a reform-minded solution
to a pressing problem: the George W. Bush administration presented
the shift to "catch and return" as part of a strategy for comprehensive

immigration reform—a plan to supposedly decrease the number of illegal crossings from Mexico and the rest of Latin America because prospective migrants would be adequately deterred.[39] The bed mandate was ongoingly justified by a Republican-controlled Congress as a move to ensure that the Obama administration would enforce immigration law. Ironically, Obama's presidency deported more people than any previous administration.[40]

Donald Trump, of course, made no effort to hide his hard-line policies and practices on immigration. From his Muslim ban, which prohibited immigration from seven countries, and his stepped-up immigration raids to his attacks on Deferred Action for Childhood Arrivals (DACA) and his family separation practice of tearing asylum-seeking children from their parents, Trump threw himself zealously into putting his racist rhetoric into action. Under his administration, ICE increased the bed mandate from 34,000 to 40,520 beds, with the federal government shifting $10 million from the Federal Emergency Management Agency (FEMA) and another $200 million from the Department of Homeland Security to lock up an additional 4,000 immigrants per night.[41] Trump's responses represent incarceration-expanding reform at its finest: when outrage spread across the country about his policy of separating families at the border, Trump's solution was to allow families to be together—behind bars, in indefinite detention.[42]

In the two hundred years since its rise as a site for penitence and redemption, prison might have lost its sheen of humane reform—especially since even the most basic offerings of education and other forms of rehabilitation have been removed from many prisons.[43] But many of the worst, most racist innovations of the prison nation were also marketed as progressive changes of their times. Throughout the 1970s, '80s, and '90s, the war on drugs, "tough on crime" politics, and intensified aggressive policing toward communities of color were all spurred forward under the banner of reform. For instance, the 1984 Sentencing Reform Act, which abolished federal parole and imposed mandatory sentence lengths on a number of federal crimes, was initially promoted as a tool to eliminate judicial racial bias. The idea was that if individual judges had less say in sentences they handed down, there would be less discrimination.[44] The law ended parole at the federal level, citing the rationale that because parole boards tend to discriminate against Black and Brown people, no parole would theoretically mean less discrimination.

Of course, these steps did not solve racism within a system built on centuries of racial oppression. Instead, they resulted in even more people—largely people of color—being trapped behind bars, often for longer periods of time.

Innovation, in itself, is no guarantee of progress. In so many cases, reform is not the building of something new. It is the re-forming of the system in its own image, using the same raw materials: white supremacy, a history of oppression, and a tool kit whose main contents are confinement, isolation, surveillance, and punishment.

Replacing One Wall with Another

Prison and reform have gone hand in hand since the beginning, and they will continue to march forward together into the future. Currently, in the age of mass incarceration, conversations about reform often focus on decreasing prison populations, not on releasing more people from state control altogether.

In fact, longtime anti-prison and anti-violence activist Mariame Kaba characterizes the latest reform movement as a drive to find a new "Somewhere Else" to stow away criminalized populations.[45] She points out that for many mainstream advocates, prison reform is palatable only if control and confinement, preferably taking place far from the rest of society, continue to be central. At the same time, these popularly embraced alternatives don't challenge the underlying notion of criminality or racist fears of who constitutes a criminal. Instead, the word "alternative" simply becomes an indicator for another place to put people whom society has deemed undesirable.

One popular alternative to incarceration is the drug treatment center. For people charged with drug-related offenses, treatment is often posed as a neatly sewn-up solution to the question of "What replaces prison?" There's no doubt that many incarcerated people have used illegal drugs, and some are dependent on them, so treatment is increasingly seen as the kinder Somewhere Else. There's also no doubt that some people are grateful to be offered treatment instead of serving a prison or jail sentence, particularly those who are ready and willing to embark on a recovery path. Yet some drug treatment centers, regardless of whether they're mandated by judges as alternatives to prison sentences or entered voluntarily, operate on prison-like principles: they confine people under strict watch, hold them to a fixed schedule, and regulate their movements and what they do with their bodies. Outside contact is often bound by a slew of rules and restrictions. Some treatment centers are straightforwardly locked down—those inside are not allowed to leave unless under intensive supervision. The use of rehab-as-sentence perpetuates the basic structure of the prison nation, the continuation of a process whereby people with dependencies get arrested, branded as both criminals and "addicts," and prescribed an isolative punishment. For many people trapped in these institutions, this branding and isolation actually deepens the psychological pain that led to their addiction in the first place.

It's also a stark example of how pervasive incarceration has become that even many of the alternatives, which are couched in the language of healing, actually rely on forcible confinement, surveillance, and utter control.

Coercive drug treatment is not the only alternative that mimics prisons. In 2016, Los Angeles County proposed a reform to address the high numbers of people with mental health problems behind bars:

start building mental health jails, where people with psychiatric diagnoses would be locked up in an environment with more specialized services.[46] Beyond the paradoxical nature of caring for someone by tearing them from their loved ones, isolating them in a small space, and removing their ability to make decisions about their own bodies, the mental health jail demonstrates the Somewhere Else principle in all its glory. People tagged with the "mentally ill criminal" label, the logic goes, cannot be allowed freedom. They must simply be controlled in a kinder way, or at least in a way that appears kinder to those hearing about it on the outside.

As carceral institutions are repackaged as rehabilitation centers, the question resurfaces: What is a prison? Is it still a prison if treatment is present—or if the stated goal is treatment?

Increasingly, it's not just a locked door that prisonizes a place. The surge in law-enforcement-based electronic monitoring over the past decade—more than doubling between 2005 and 2015—confirms this reality.[47] Today, about 200,000 Americans are chained by monitors.[48] When you're bound by an electronic shackle, the door may not lock from the outside only, but it might as well. Should you take an unauthorized step outside, your monitor will beep—and one possible consequence is that the police may rush your house.

Fueled by the quest for alternatives, the varieties of community supervision are proliferating. Each new innovation raises key questions for anyone concerned with the spread of surveillance and confinement. Even if you're not monitored by a tracking device, what does it mean to have to check in with a parole or probation officer before every life decision? To be bound by stringent curfews, restrictions on internet use, and constraints on whom you spend your time with? To be forced to take domestic violence classes that instruct an abuse survivor in how to avoid angering their partner? To have your parenting practices tightly monitored by an agency that may enter your home at any time? To be tested for drugs and alcohol under threat of jail? All of these innovations are not only entrenching the prison nation but also expanding it—creating new forms by which it can exercise its power and harm people's lives.

This penchant for replacing imprisonment with almost-imprisonment and one kind of surveillance with another type of surveillance crops up across the political spectrum. The Right on Crime platform, the campaign promoting conservative solutions to criminal justice policies, advocates boosting CompSTAT—the data analysis and management process that drove the notorious "stop and frisk" practices of New York and other cities—as well as other data collection technologies that have resulted in the heightened targeting of Black, Brown, trans, immigrant, Muslim, and poor communities.[49] Families Against Mandatory Minimums, a nonprofit that advocates for crucial sentencing reforms, also argues that government must "shift resources from excessive incarceration to law enforcement," bulking up police department budgets with the flawed logic that a larger police presence will deter violence and thus reduce incarceration.[50] The Coalition for Public Safety, the coalition of progressive and conservative groups pushing criminal justice reform, lists as its first two planks "Expand alternatives to incarceration" and "Balance the need to reduce overreliance on incarceration with ensuring community safety."[51] The presupposition is that *some* incarceration must be relied upon to ensure safety and that alternatives—instead of freedom from all coercive and controlling institutions—will fill the gap left by eliminating some incarceration.

Diverting money from prisons to policing is no route to ending mass incarceration. Yet conservatives and liberals alike have been drawn to the seductive rhetoric of "data," "technology," "software," and "innovation," ostensibly designed to prevent violence. These systems don't stop violence, but they do have a significant impact: they impose ever-intensifying forms of control on human beings.

The problem of prisons should not be confronted in a vacuum. Instead, it's crucial to remember Kaba's concept of the Somewhere

Else, which might be prison, but could also be forced drug treatment or house arrest. Locked buildings are being replaced with slightly less menacing-looking locked buildings, brutal surveillance with surveillance that may appear less brutal. Oppressive institutions that bear the name "prison" are being replaced with institutions that do not bear that name but are still Somewhere Else—places and systems designed to cut off marginalized people from society.

When funding, resources, and public support are redirected from incarceration into other legs of the prison nation, such as policing and surveillance, the prison nation sweeps more and more people into its web, as witnessed by the expansion of electronic monitoring to previously unconfined populations, and the surveillance of increasing numbers of people using continually advancing police technologies.

The Freedom Side

Given the roots of the prison nation in white supremacy and oppression, and given that the prison nation oppresses, tortures, disappears, surveils, and controls millions of marginalized people, we believe that it's time to abolish prisons.

Following a vibrant tradition of racial justice and liberation-minded activists, we don't believe that prison and its nicer-looking cousins are necessary to address society's problems.[52] These tools of punishment aren't keeping us safe: they enact violence themselves.[53] A just society cannot exist while people are caged, no matter what those cages look like.

We use the term "prison abolition" to describe the belief that prisons—in all of their manifestations—cannot be reformed to become more humane or to meet people's needs. Instead, the entire system must be ended and replaced with resources and supports that genuinely meet people's needs, as well as strategies that effectively address and reduce harm and violence. As Critical Resistance says, prison abolition is "both a practical organizing tool and a long-term goal."[54] If we're going to approach policy change in a way that doesn't replicate the patterns of the past, we have to keep that long-term goal in our sights.

When evaluating whether reforms are helpful or harmful, a key question should always be: Are these reforms building up structures that we will need to dismantle in the future? It's clear that the new era of reform has already generated some formidable structures—from electronic monitoring and locked-down rehab centers to forced outpatient treatment, mother-child lockdowns, and more—that will be very hard to tear down. These structures are built on the same foundations as prison: slavery, genocide, colonialism, capitalism, and the practice of criminalization, powered by the conviction that society must label, isolate, and dispose of a category of people. They're built on the notion that there must always be a Somewhere Else and that the "criminal" who is placed there must always exist.

Many marginalized people are surveilled from birth—whether the eye that's upon them is that of the police, child protective services, a parent's parole officer, or state welfare agencies.

In the late 1970s, political prisoner Assata Shakur wrote that for a lot of the people she was incarcerated with, prison was simply another racist, sexist, oppressive institution in a long series of such institutions—including the institution of poverty itself. "For many the cells are not much different from the tenements, the shooting galleries and the welfare hotels they live in on the street," Shakur wrote. "Riker's [Island] is just another institution. In childhood school was their prison, or youth houses or reform schools or children['s] shelters or foster homes or mental hospitals or drug programs and they see all institutions as indifferent to their needs, yet necessary to their survival."[55]

Shakur pointed to the decimation of neighborhoods of color, which have been not only abandoned and underresourced but also chopped up by incarceration and policing. She also pointed to all the ways that human beings have been alienated from one another, whether by steel bars or by poverty, hopelessness, and simply the knowledge that the system is designed to keep them caged. Not only were people trapped in these institutions, Shakur was saying, but they were also trapped in a society devoid of opportunities, resources, and routes to a life in which real self-determination might be possible.

Nearly four decades later, this reality holds true. Colette Payne, the Chicago mother on electronic monitoring, echoes Shakur's sentiment. Her predominantly Black, low-income neighborhood lacks even a grocery store, meaning that residents must travel for fresh fruits and vegetables. Her local schools are devoid of counselors but filled with security guards and police. In these schools, the go-to strategy is suspension: punishing students and taking away resources instead of providing them.

It seems that confronting the task of uprooting criminalization—and uprooting the racism, economic injustice, ableism, and gender oppression that generate and fortify it—is not only about dismantling a violent maze of structures. It's also a creative question. In addition to asking ourselves what defines prison, we all need to ask: What is freedom?[56] What is liberation?

Liberation is "the practice of love," in the words of sociologist Bobbie Harro.[57] It is not a passive kind of love, nor a love fixated on a single individual. Liberation is a love that is big enough to encompass all society, and active enough to transform it. It is a love that dismantles oppression, recognizing that our oppressions are intertwined. Harro writes, "[Liberation is] about that force that connects us all to one another as living beings, that force that is defined differently by every spiritual belief system but which binds us by the vision that there can be a better world and we can help to create it."[58]

Most popular prison reforms are not aimed at ending oppression and creating a transformed, interconnected future. Yet there is good news as well. In this historical moment, intersecting movements for

Black liberation, prison abolition, disability justice, trans liberation, and more are rising to challenge the structures that underlie prison and to envision new paths forward. Activists are working hard to both release people from cages and dream beyond the cage, building the framework for a free society. A protest song that has run through the Movement for Black Lives and other recent racial justice struggles—a new version of an old labor standard—asks, "Which side are you on, my people? Which side are you on?" The response: "We're on the freedom side." The movement is calling for a culture-wide shift to the freedom side, a shift toward community, healing, nurturing, celebration, and love. Reaching toward real freedom will be a feat of collective imagination, requiring each of us to challenge some of the most formidable institutions in our society—and the most entrenched assumptions in our own consciousness.

Ending mass incarceration is only the beginning.

1

YOUR HOME IS YOUR PRISON

If I had just done time, I would've been done by now.

—Patricia Howard, under house arrest in Indiana

THE "CRIME" PATRICIA HOWARD, MOTHER OF FIVE, COMMITTED WAS an odd one: she climbed through her best friend's window to retrieve a bottle of her own medication. She and her friend had "open-door policies" and visited each other's homes daily, including when the other wasn't present—but her friend's husband was not on friendly terms with Howard, and one day he called the cops on her. Though all theft and drug charges were dropped (since the medication she took was her own), Howard, who lives in Cass County, Indiana, retained a low-level "felony burglary" conviction—she'd entered a home without the permission of the leaseholder. Her caseworker and everyone involved expressed complete faith that she would never do this again. Nevertheless, the prosecutor charged her with felony burglary, which carries a minimum of ten years in prison. Her lawyer advised her to plead guilty to a lesser charge for five years under house arrest and another five years of probation.[1] When she took the plea, the public defender told her there was a good chance she would be free within six months, saying "They're going to realize you're not a criminal."

Three years later, however, Howard remains under house arrest—trapped in her own home for a "crime" that harmed no one.

Capturing More People
in the Name of "Alternatives"

Howard's predicament may sound bizarre, but it is symptomatic of a growing trend. Consider a 2015 op-ed in the mainstream news magazine *The Week*, which sparked much conversation when it stated, "We can abolish prison—and we must." The author, business writer Pascal-Emmanuel Gobry, suggested that the replacement for incarceration was simple—long sentences spent on electronic monitoring devices, which basically translates into house arrest. "Instead of spending three years in prison, you should spend six years working minimum wage in a tedious job, your wages garnished, stuck at home with no internet or TV, with only a single night out allowed once in awhile," he wrote. "That is real punishment."[2]

This is a common theme running through many of the recent conservative proposals for reducing incarceration: that alternative punishments should be "real" or even "just as bad" as prison, but at a lower cost to the state. House arrest, in many cases, fits the bill for cheap yet harsh punishment, particularly because there's no obligation to provide shelter, food, or medical care to the monitored person who is "stuck at home."

There are two main circumstances in which people are placed on house arrest and electronic monitoring. For some, house arrest is a condition of release pending trial (as a substitute for either paying bail or being confined in jail pending trial). But in jurisdictions that have recently reduced their jail populations—often in response to local organizing—house arrest with electronic monitoring has become a substitute for jail. For other people, house arrest is a penalty imposed after pleading guilty in court. In fact, lawyers and courts often present home confinement as an incentive to plead guilty, rather than go to trial and risk multiple years in prison.

Today's electronic monitoring technology has made house arrest more restrictive than ever. GPS systems enable every movement to be tracked. In other words, EM is a type of prison that rides along *with you*, strapped to your body. If you set foot outside of bounds without permission, your sensor will promptly start beeping and alert authorities.

Under house arrest, a person must stay inside their home unless they obtain preauthorization from the court or probation officer to leave the house for a specific destination that is considered essential. That destination might be work, school, the probation office, the grocery store, or a doctor's appointment. However, that destination is almost never a child's school performance, the movie theater, a birthday celebration, or a friend's home.

There's almost always a stringent limit on the number of hours one can spend outside the house. The Corrections Center of Northwest Ohio's monitoring program, for instance, allows out-of-home family celebrations only on Thanksgiving and Christmas. A trip to the library is allowed only for an employment opportunity (not for storytime or even to borrow books); everyday tasks such as grocery shopping and laundry are allowed only if "no other person in the household can provide this service."[3] If the person deviates from the approved schedule, even by stopping en route to an approved destination, they risk being reincarcerated.

Scheduling proves nearly impossible for some, especially for parents with children. Yet requesting last-minute changes to the schedule can put a person who is under monitoring on their probation officer's bad side, and that doesn't just make for grumbles and tiresome phone conversations; violating the strict terms of house arrest or monitoring often means prison.

Angel Sanchez knows this reality well. In the late 1990s, the Miami, Florida, fifteen-year-old was sentenced to two years of house arrest. After about sixty days, the teenager got sick of not seeing his friends and left his house. Like clockwork, he was "violated" for being out of the house, and was sent to prison—for the maximum term allowed for the crime he'd originally committed. He was locked up for the next twelve years.[4]

Sanchez had thought—and it's a common misconception—that if he violated the terms of house arrest and ended up incarcerated, he'd simply have to serve the remainder of his two-year sentence in prison. No one explained to him that if he breached the terms of house arrest, he'd be staring down the maximum sentence: thirty years in prison (of which he served twelve). Ultimately, opting for house arrest gave rise to a much steeper sentence than if Sanchez had initially opted for prison.

People usually (though not always) prefer electronic monitoring to prison.[5] However, monitoring certainly still fits the bill for a brutal penalty. Many people on house arrest will tell you that being forced to remain inside your house transforms it into a kind of jail, contorting the very definition of "home." Depending on one's housing situation, staying in the house may mean remaining in a single room, day in and day out, with little access to food and basic necessities (especially for those who live in neighborhoods with few local grocery options). In addition to being shackled with an electronic monitor, some must also wear an alcohol or drug monitor, allowing external authorities to gauge their intake from afar. Officers can intrude into the home at any moment to make sure the arrestee remains sealed inside.

Wary of activating the monitor, many house arrestees begin mentally policing themselves, frightened of stepping out of bounds. "Persons watched become active 'partners' in their own monitoring," probation commissioner Ronald Corbett and social studies scholar Gary T. Marx warned in 1991 as the practice of monitoring began to increase around the country. "The home is opened up as never before."[6]

Patricia Howard has internalized her surveillance in this way. She has nightmares about leaving her house without texting her parole officer first and being sent to prison as a result. The knowledge that authorities have free access to her home at any time makes her watch her door, expecting them to show up at any moment, day or night.

Meanwhile, the threat of literal prison always looms. For many on EM, the penalty for violating the conditions of their confinement—or "tampering" with their monitor—is incarceration.[7]

Most of us have, at some point in our lives, committed an act that could be considered a crime, but most such acts go unnoticed. When you're being constantly watched, however, smoking a joint or even failing to buckle your seatbelt could swell your criminal record and inch you closer to the prison gates.

Today, by very conservative estimates, more than 130,000 people across the country are tethered by electronic monitoring.[8] EM for people accused or convicted of crimes grew about 140 percent between 2005 and 2015, with the practice rippling across the country.[9] In California, for instance, after the Supreme Court ruled in 2011 that the state's overcrowded prisons violated the Eighth Amendment and ordered the prison population drastically reduced, the state came up with the idea of "realignment," which, in part, shifted the burden of incarceration and supervision from the state to the county level. Part of that shift included a sharp increase in electronic monitoring.[10] In Oklahoma, which has the country's highest rate of incarceration, the state plans to slap ankle monitors on fifteen hundred people classified as low-risk upon releasing them early from prison.[11] The 2018 First Step Act, widely hailed as bipartisan prison reform, proposed to do the same for people in the federal system, allowing people classified as low-risk an early release from prison—by sending them into home confinement and electronic monitoring.[12]

Electronic shackles are now an accepted component of the criminal legal system, and are also promoted as a money-saver, given that jurisdictions often charge people for the monitors it compels them to wear.

However, EM doesn't function only as prison's replacement. It also widens the net of the criminal legal system, sweeping into its clutches people who otherwise might never be subject to state-sanctioned confinement. A study by the Pew Center on the States, a division of the Pew Charitable Trusts that focuses on state-level public policy analysis, pointed out that EM is now commonly used both as an "alternative" punishment *and* "as an adjunct to traditional community supervision practices."[13] In other words, people like Patricia Howard who once might have been simply assigned to probation are now locked in their homes, on monitors. A 2012 analysis in the *Washington University Journal of Law and Policy* noted that most people on EM haven't been convicted of violent offenses, and if EM was not an option, "at least some of these populations would not in fact be incarcerated or otherwise under physical control."[14]

In Chicago, thanks to a strong grassroots campaign against money bail and pretrial incarceration, the jail population has waned in recent years. In September 2017, Cook County, where Chicago is located, implemented an order stating that people shouldn't be assigned bail (a term used interchangeably with "bond") amounts that they could not afford to pay. This was a landmark rule change that, however unevenly enforced, significantly reduced the jail population. However, since the rule was implemented, electronic monitoring has expanded. For example, in 2016, the vast majority of people charged with gun crimes were assigned high bail amounts. In 2017, with bail reform making headway, bail amounts plummeted. Forty percent of people charged with gun offenses still needed to post bail in exchange for pretrial freedom (down from 96 percent the previous year). But of those who were released without having to pay bail, 22 percent were placed in electronic shackles.[15] (The previous year, only 2 percent of gun defendants had been placed on monitoring.) By February 2019, people on electronic monitoring made up 27 percent of those in Cook County custody, and activists were increasingly mounting campaigns to draw attention to the ill effects of EM.[16]

Along similar lines, Indianapolis, Indiana, has reduced its jail population considerably in recent years—from over 2,500 in August 2018 to less than 450 in April 2019.[17] At the same time, it drastically expanded its pretrial EM program from 2,328 in 2017 to 5,121 in 2018, monitoring over 700 more people than had previously been incarcerated.[18]

In San Francisco, years of advocacy against money bail by grassroots organizers culminated in a 2018 court ruling that released a number of people from the county jail who would otherwise have been held on bail. But they weren't entirely free: many were transferred from jail to house arrest. The number of people released on electronic monitoring increased by three times, from one hundred to three hundred per month.[19]

EM has also expanded to entangle people who have not been accused of any crimes, including immigrants. Until 2003, Immigration and Naturalization Service (INS) had contracted with nonprofit organizations to develop and operate a system of community-based alternatives to detention. Under these alternatives, people facing immigration proceedings were assigned individual caseworkers who would connect them to legal, medical, and housing services. But after immigration enforcement was transferred to Immigration and Customs Enforcement (ICE) and the Department of Homeland Security in 2003, these alternatives were jettisoned in favor of the Intensive Supervision Appearance Program, which relies on EM.[20]

According to conservative estimates, on any given day, an additional 38,000 immigrants are shackled by electronic monitors. That number is growing.[21] Yet the rate of detention has not declined due to the addition of electronic shackles. Instead, it has soared from 34,000 to more than 40,000. EM simply allows for more people to be caught in ICE's net, whether in physical detention beds or sleeping in their own beds with monitors shackled to their ankles.[22] Being caught in ICE's net can have dire consequences: the agency uses data gathered from monitors to plan workplace raids, according to scholar Daniel Gonzalez, who researches ICE's use of GPS devices.[23]

Electronic monitoring's image as a "kinder" alternative—surveillance rather than imprisonment—allows it to be broached in cases where the suggestion of incarceration might not otherwise be considered. In 2016, for example, Rudy Giuliani called for all Muslims on the federal government's terrorist watchlist to be placed on electronic monitors.[24] Liberal reformers have fallen for the hype, too. In 2018, Jay-Z announced his investment in Promise, an app heralded as an alternative to cash bail. But instead of unconditionally allowing people to remain out of jail awaiting trial, Promise utilizes surveillance and GPS monitoring to ensure compliance. It also develops a "care plan," which purportedly refers people to job training, housing, and counseling, though advocates have noted that these types of programs often have long waiting lists—and being referred by Promise does not guarantee a slot.[25]

Meanwhile, the availability of EM technology has resulted in an increasing number of people on parole—people who have already served their court-imposed prison sentence—being placed on monitors and subjected to constant surveillance.[26]

The Evolving Panopticon

Despite its current popularity as an innovative twenty-first-century "prison alternative," house arrest is hardly a new idea; it has a long history preceding the advent of electronic monitoring. St. Paul was

placed on home confinement, as were Galileo, deposed Iranian president Mohammad Mosaddegh, and Burmese politician Aung San Suu
Kyi. The practice has been used to stifle political dissidents: confining rebels and nonconformists to their homes both diminished their
ties to the outside world and allowed authorities to know their where-
abouts at all times.

Since the advent of the modern prison, the concept of full surveillance has always played a critical role. In British prison reformer
Jeremy Bentham's famous late eighteenth-century vision of the Panopticon, prisoners would experience a feeling of being seen at all times;
even if inspectors were not literally always watching them, the archi-
tecture made it *possible* for them to view each prisoner at any moment
while remaining unseen themselves.[27] In most places, Bentham's literal vision of the Panopticon never came to pass, but with today's electronic monitoring and house arrest practices, we can feel its legacy: the
creation of an environment where surveillance is constant and intrusion is an ever-present possibility.[28]

Electronic monitoring made its public debut in 1969, with a *Psychology Today* article by scientist Robert Schwitzgebel, "A Belt from Big
Brother."[29] Schwitzgebel suggested enthusiastically that "behavioral
engineering"—using technological rewards and punishments, such as
electric shocks, bleeps, and alerts to train humans away from "unwant-
ed behavior"—was the wave of the future. He described an "electronic
parole system," in which parolees would receive "mild punishment
for every transgression," including physical or verbal actions, but
also "nervous gestures," "anxiety reactions," and someday even "high
blood alcohol levels." (This last bit has partly come true today; alcohol monitors are frequently imposed as conditions of courts in cases
of drunk driving, domestic violence, and even child custody cases.)[30]
Schwitzgebel also proposed that rewards be granted to people exhibiting positive behaviors—a pizza, a haircut, tickets to a concert—but this
"rewards" aspect has fallen out of the equation as monitors evolved

from fiction to reality.[31] Orwellianly enough, electronic monitoring as a feature of home confinement hit the scene for real in the year 1984. It debuted in Palm Beach County, Florida, as part of a "felon release" program in which eighty-seven people were released from the overcrowded jail tethered to ankle monitors, for which they paid $9 per day. The program was seen as a success: of those eighty-seven people, two were rearrested and one escaped.[32] The sheriff expanded the program, and by 2009, 2,392 were shackled with monitors in Florida. The same factors that propelled mass incarceration—racism, "law and order" politics, the war on drugs, the destruction of the social safety net—also propelled mass supervision.[33] Even more people fell under state control on the outside, whether they were awaiting trial, serving probation, or serving parole after being released from prison. EM provided a handy tool to facilitate that external confinement. Fortified by a boom in satellite technology, the electronic monitoring industry exploded.[34]

Corbett and Marx, who warned against EM in the early 1990s, note that monitoring programs, originally promoted as targeting prison-bound, "high-risk offenders," increasingly end up being used to confine "low-risk offenders." Instead of following a "ready-aim-fire" strategy in deploying EM, the authors wrote, governments tended to abide by a "ready-fire-aim" model: "One fires first and whatever is hit becomes the target."[35]

As with all other incarnations of the criminal legal system, these additional sanctions are disproportionately likely to be imposed on people of color and the poor, literally weighing down their bodies with state control. For example, Black people in Cook County represent 70 percent of people on EM but only 24 percent of the area's population.[36] A 2009 survey showed that nonwhites were much more likely than whites to agree that electronic monitoring "perpetuates a racist judicial system," more likely to see it as discriminating against the poor, and more likely to perceive it as a strategy to turn "the home into a prison."[37]

Now electronic monitoring has expanded beyond the criminal and immigration systems. Companies even tout it as a way to prevent truancy. As the EM company Omnilink eagerly proclaims, "Juvenile courts and school programs are using electronic monitoring technology to help ensure students are in school at the appropriate times. . . . When their peers pressure them to skip, it's easier for them to say 'no.'"[38]

Of course, that choice to say no is not really a choice. It's a response mandated by the "belt from Big Brother," and there's no evidence that being on an electronic monitor elicits any positive mental or psychological transformation that would encourage future attendance—let alone growth, learning, fulfillment, inspiration, or enrichment. Even kids who abide by the monitor aren't necessarily tossing out "bad habits"; they're setting them aside for the time being. Monitors and house arrest aren't rehabilitative or transformative—they don't support people in making changes that would be helpful to their lives, gaining needed resources, addressing harm or violence, or confronting the social forces that have affected them.

That doesn't mean monitors don't have a significant impact on individuals' lives, though. For those swept up into the ever-widening net, monitoring may first appear to be a relatively gentle option—and lawyers often portray it this way when convincing clients to take a plea deal. This was the case for Patricia Howard, the Indiana mother who, in retrospect, wonders whether she should have simply "done time." But in fact, for Howard and many other people on house arrest, the monitor's impact—like the monitor itself—is felt every minute of every day.

"In-Home *Is* a Type of Incarceration"

A 2018 analysis by the mainstream think tank the Brookings Institution found that intensive supervision actually increases, rather than decreases, the chance that someone will be rearrested and reconvicted.[39] This finding is notable because recidivism rates—the rates at which people are convicted of new offenses after previous involvement with the criminal legal system—are a common metric used to evaluate whether a strategy is working or not. Prison reform advocates often cite high rates of recidivism as an indicator that the prison system isn't actually promoting safety or rehabilitating people; it's simply cycling people through the system, again and again. There are problems with the use of recidivism as a metric; many abolitionist activists argue that as long as police continue to target Black, Brown, and other marginalized communities, members of these communities will continue to be arrested regardless of the "effectiveness" of any post-arrest strategy. Still, it's significant that the increasingly popular practice of electronic monitoring fails even by this most basic measure of "success."

In fact, it isn't surprising that monitoring doesn't decrease recidivism. Monitoring and house arrest—and the resulting prison time for failure to comply or violating the terms—often mean that people are unable to apply for or attend school or work.[40] Even those who are granted release to go to work or pursue an education face barrier after barrier. With their time and mobility strictly limited by the monitor (not to mention the stigma attached to it), it's harder to get a job or enter a program than it would be otherwise. Restrictions also impact people's ability to participate meaningfully in society and build relationships—and having strong relationships is among the most significant ways to prevent recidivism.[41]

As with every other aspect of the criminal legal system, electronic monitoring's restrictions overwhelmingly impact people in poor and racially marginalized communities. But as the net widens, even the rich and powerful can't escape. Take Lindsay Lohan, who was ordered to wear a drug-and-alcohol monitor in 2010 after missing a court date for a drug-related charge. She then missed the court-mandated alcohol education classes and was sentenced to ninety days in jail.[42]

Patricia Howard fears she's headed down the path toward jail, too—

though at this point she doesn't know which sentence is worse. "'In-home' *is* a type of incarceration, regardless of the other definitions provided," she says. Life as she knows it has gone out like a flame; she no longer attends her church or takes her children to school activities, their sports practices, or even to the park. In her small, rural town, stigma runs thick. Howard doesn't want anyone to know about the monitor or her "in-home" sentence, so she has mostly stopped seeing people, telling no one but her parents, her husband, her in-laws, and her two best friends. For the first six months of her sentence, she didn't even reveal it to her parents.

For young people in particular, that sense of stigma can cut deep, influencing their lasting self-perceptions. As the American Bar Association's report on juvenile electronic monitoring notes, "When the juvenile wears an EM device, he or she feels like a criminal, and may start behaving as such."[43]

Angel Sanchez points out that although house arrest is often framed as rehabilitation, a tactic to facilitate "reform," it tends to just keep people "stuck"—particularly when it comes to marginalized communities with few resources. "For most of us, there is no rehabilitation; that idea assumes you were on a 'right' path to begin with, and you got off of it," Sanchez says. "For most of us, we need 'habilitation.'" Habilitation would mean better housing, health care, mental health care, childcare, jobs, educational opportunities—all resources that are, in many senses, the opposite of house arrest and monitoring.

In fact, a monitor often actively decreases one's chances of "habilitation." According to a Department of Justice study, even probation officers acknowledged that visible ankle monitors often act as a "scarlet letter": monitored people who are allowed to seek work have trouble getting and keeping jobs.[44] That makes it tough to pay steep ankle monitoring fees—and to live your life. It's common knowledge that a job is one of the keys to avoiding future arrest, but a monitor can make that nearly impossible.[45]

Pat, a young woman from Northern California (and a different person from Patricia Howard) who prefers not to use her last name, experienced stigma and shame during the four months she spent with a monitor tethered to her ankle. She was fortunate to be able to keep both of her service industry jobs and continue attending college while on her monitor, and was grateful to be on EM instead of being incarcerated, but every day was a struggle. Beyond paying for the monitor ($10 per day), the gaze of her classmates and teachers weighed heavily—for example, in PE class, where she had to wear shorts and couldn't hide the monitor. "People don't really understand it," Pat says now. "You're trying to move on with your life but you have this black box around your ankle."[46]

That shame is understandable: society reinforces it at every turn. When Patricia Howard visited the doctor, people in the waiting room whispered about her monitor, saying she "should be ashamed of herself." She walked out. At a dentist appointment, the dentist was rough and refused to finish her dental work. The electronic shackle is "like a license to abuse someone," she says.

Sentencing the Family

House arrest doesn't impact only those saddled with the orders of confinement or with the electronic shackle strapped to their ankle. The tentacles of surveillance extend to families and loved ones, effectively sentencing them as well.

For Howard, the experience of house arrest affected her whole family—although her sentence of house arrest was, according to authorities, intended to allow her to care for her children. Her restricted movement made it impossible to go on family outings or even take her children to community activities.

When she was sentenced to house arrest, Howard's husband had to sign a waiver agreeing not to have firearms or drink alcohol even outside the home. The control over their lives extended to activities it would otherwise be legal for him to do. In addition, caseworkers could arrive and inspect their house at any given time. At first they dropped by two to three times each week, sometimes walking through and inspecting every room in the house. Though Howard's conviction was for a burglary (of her own medicine) and did not involve illegal drugs or alcohol, she has also been subjected to at-home urine tests, sometimes once a month, sometimes several times a month. Each time she was required to pay an additional $60.

At the same time, family members of those on house arrest must also take on even more responsibilities to compensate for their loved ones' lack of mobility, twisting their schedules to assist with basic tasks like running errands. Monitoring colors even minor household interactions, shifting the larger dynamics of how family members respond to one another. Even probation officers acknowledge this impact. In a Justice Department survey, 89 percent of officers reported that "offenders' relationships with their significant others changed because of being monitored." The intense restrictions on movement—even preventing people from taking out the garbage to a dumpster at the other end of their housing complex—forcibly shape the contours of someone's life—and a family's life.

Such confinement becomes untenable when one is responsible for caring for others on a regular basis. What happens when your young kids run into the backyard or down the street and you can't dash out to retrieve them? A study by the *European Journal of Probation* notes that parents on monitoring often feel they can't teach their kids to follow rules, since if the children don't like those rules, they can simply run out of the monitor's range.[47] ("You can't catch me!" becomes an all-too-real truth.)

Even more important, parents on monitors struggle with what their restriction means in the face of family crises, including when a loved one's life could be in danger. James Kilgore, the founder and director of Challenging E-Carceration, a project to confront and challenge the increasingly widespread use of EM, explains that the harm can be truly grave. Kilgore himself spent a year confined to his home on an ankle monitor, and he has since devoted years to researching the use of monitors. "People get reincarcerated for going to the hospital in a medical emergency, and they can't get ahold of their probation officer," he noted. "They have to make a decision: 'Am I going to the hospital to get this looked after, or get my child or my mother looked after? Or am I going to follow the rules and take my chances as to what happens with them?'"[48]

Howard has never told her children about her home confinement and is careful to hide the monitor from them at all times. But her inability to actively participate in her children's lives—to attend their events, to take them on day trips, to drive them to their extracurricular activities—has affected their sense of self-worth. "I have a ten-year-old who doesn't think I want her because our level of activity has changed so drastically from 'mom and daughter all the time' to what can we do from the house," she says. She has never taken her toddler to the park or to the zoo.

The effects pervade children's developing senses of self and normalcy in other ways. One parent in the Justice Department survey described his kid's habit of strapping a watch around his ankle "to be like Daddy." Another said, "When it beeps, the kids worry about whether the probation officer is coming to take me to jail. The kids run for it when it beeps."[49]

Paying for the "Privilege" of Confinement

The boom in incarceration gave birth to the boom in home confinement and electronic monitoring and, when it comes to profit-making, the apple hasn't fallen far from the tree. With the rise in electronic monitoring, there is money to be made. Lots of it.

BI Incorporated (BI) is one of the biggest monitoring companies. Since 2004, ICE has awarded BI more than half a billion dollars in contracts, including, in 2009, an exclusive five-year, $372 million contract to slap electronic monitoring on immigrants awaiting adjudication in asylum or deportation cases.[50] In 2010, BI was bought by GEO Group, the world's largest private prison company, for $415 million.[51] It was a lucrative investment: in 2011 alone, BI pulled in more than $1.6 billion. By 2014, it was tracking more than 75,000 people on electronic monitoring.[52] That year, it also renewed its contract with ICE, this time for $235 million for another five years. In 2018, the company boasted that it produces 200,000 monitors annually (used both in the United States and internationally) and contracts with approximately 900 federal, state, and local agencies.[53]BI and GEO Group are not the only corporations to profit off the move from imprisonment to electronic monitoring. As the political tide has turned toward the prospect of "humane punishment," the profiteers are carving out fresh strategies for transforming confinement into hundreds of millions of dollars.[54] Since 2014, the private corporation Offender Management Services (OMS) has monopolized the realm of electronic monitoring in Richland County, South Carolina.[55] The company charges a setup fee of $179, then $9.25 per day (or approximately $300 per month) thereafter. The cost falls not upon the court or county but on the person shackled to the device. Those who can't afford the cost are sent to jail. Often, whether you qualify for—or are allowed to stay on—"humane" punishment depends on the size of your wallet.

The practice of forcing people to pay for their own confinement isn't unique to OMS. In all states except Hawaii and Washington, DC, those on monitoring are required to fork over fees.[56] This applies not only to adults on monitoring but also to parents whose children are placed under supervision. As the American Bar Association outlines in its study of juvenile electronic monitoring, when a child is sentenced to a monitor, even the most indigent parents are required to pay the associated fees as well as the ancillary costs of house arrest, which can include landlines, random drug and breathalyzer tests, and additional equipment. If they cannot pay, the study notes, the service may be terminated.[57] When the "service is terminated," incarceration often ensues.

EM can also present a financial incentive to cities and counties. Consider Mountlake Terrace, Washington, a suburb north of Seattle, where a one-day jail stay costs the city $61.[58] The city would normally spend $610 to $854 each day to detain ten to fourteen people, or $220,000 to $312,000 each year—but it employs a creative tactic for reducing this price tag.

Mountlake Terrace contracts with a small private company for pretrial electronic monitoring. Those placed on monitoring are, by the city's own admission, "low risk offenders who have little to no previous criminal history."[59] In other words, these are people who, if it weren't for the new technology, might not be placed under any physical supervision at all as they await their day in court.

But thanks to the new gadgets, they are instead assigned to EM— and they are paying for it. The company charges the town $5.75 per person. The town, in turn, charges the person being monitored $20 per day. According to the city's website, the revenue generated from the fees "fully funds the Custody Officer position, the rental of the EHM [electronic home monitoring] equipment, and EHM fees for indigent defendants."

Cities credit EM with cost savings not only because they're making money off people shackled with monitors but also because the programs cost less than jail. For example, in La Crosse County, Wisconsin, monitors cost $6 per day to maintain, whereas a jail bed costs $83 daily.[60]

Monitoring companies aren't targeting only governmental agencies to hawk their wares. In an absurd yet profitable move, the Washington-based company Offender Monitoring Solutions (not to be confused with the aforementioned Offender Management Services) markets directly to potential monitor-wearers, going so far as to offer an online application.[61] Such "private options," while predatory, can have some advantages: for some people, being monitored by a private company is less intrusive—and less costly—than the county-run program. This was certainly true for Etan, a childcare provider, trans man, and co-parent of a two-year-old living in Olympia, Washington.[62] In 2012, Etan attempted to shoplift several pairs of men's underwear, a shirt, and a pair of shorts. Etan was at a time in his transition when he didn't pass as a cisgender man and wasn't comfortable buying men's clothes. A plainclothes security guard, who was a woman, followed him out of the store, hit him, and began choking him with the strap of Etan's bag. Etan hit back.

Ironically, this public fight was the first time that strangers clearly assumed that Etan was a man. When the police arrived, they too assumed that Etan was a cisgender man who had hit a female security guard. They arrested him for second-degree robbery, which is a violent felony and a strike under Washington's Three Strikes law, which mandates life imprisonment without the possibility of parole for a third strike.[63] The prosecutor ultimately allowed Etan to plead guilty to felony theft and misdemeanor assault in exchange for six weeks of home confinement and a two-year suspended sentence, meaning that he could be sent to prison for two years if he violated any of the terms of house arrest.

Etan had initially been told that, as a primary caregiver, he could stay home with his child during those six weeks of house arrest. But because he was not the child's biological parent and did not have legal custody, the jail later informed him that he would not be allowed to stay home. Instead, according to the jail, Etan needed to be employed at a company with liability insurance—a luxury that most of Olympia's small businesses could not afford. Any potential employer was also required to fill out the extra paperwork accompanying a job applicant on home confinement. The only employer willing to do so was a call center that paid on commission and required forty hours per week. This meant that, with Etan gone most of the day, his co-parent would have to rearrange her schedule to care for their child.

In addition, Etan would be required to allow searches of his home at any time, an intrusion his family would feel keenly. If he needed to visit the doctor, he would have to submit a request in advance along with his doctor's contact information. Jail staff would call the doctor's office, inform staff that Etan was on home confinement, and ask that the office confirm that he did indeed have an appointment. After his appointment, jail staff would call the doctor's office again to verify that he had gone.

For Etan, such a call would have had implications reaching far beyond those six weeks. As a trans man, it was already hard to find supportive medical providers and establish a rapport with them. Being notified that their patient was under home confinement would have fractured that rapport.

Etan discovered that under a private monitoring system, he'd be allowed to stay home as a primary caregiver (even without legal custody of his child) and could attend doctor's appointments without informing his provider of his confinement. So he opted for the private route. The trade-off? He'd pay the company $600 to $700 for six weeks of confinement.

Though the restrictions weren't as onerous, monitoring was still no picnic: Etan was not allowed to leave the house to take his child anywhere. He was allowed one hour per week—including travel time—to shop for groceries, and only at one store, with the location submitted to the company in advance. If the family needed supplies from another place, his co-parent or someone else would have to make the trip.

Meanwhile, the private company's fee-related mandates were strict: Etan had to pay a significant portion of his monitoring bill in advance and was required to have paid the entire bill by the day his sentence ended. If, on that last day, he had failed to pay his bill, he would be sent to jail—and upon release from jail would still be required to pay the balance. Fortunately, Etan managed to scrape together the money to pay the full bill.

But, of course, not all people on monitors manage to pull together those funds. In some cases, such as the one that Etan encountered, they can be jailed for nonpayment even after serving their full EM sentence.

Home confinement and electronic monitoring have been proposed as ways to keep people out of jail and with their families. But these sentences still carry the long-term ramifications of being convicted, such as barring people from employment. Felony theft is on the list of convictions that exclude a person from working with "vulnerable populations" in Washington. Before his arrest, Etan had extensive experience working with youth; his conviction closed that avenue of employment. In addition, the two-year suspended sentence, which required that he have no interaction with law enforcement, hung over him, particularly as a trans person. "What if I go to the bathroom and someone calls the cops on me, and they look at my ID and it has an F [female] on it?" he recalls worrying. "That counts as police contact. I'd have to spend the year in jail." In other words, EM may have allowed Etan to stay home with his child, but the collateral consequences of the felony conviction still cast a lengthy shadow over his future options.

"If You're Not Paying, You're Not Being Compliant"

Although some reformers emphasize the supposed humaneness of house arrest, ultimately its most touted advantage is the reduced cost to the county or state. When a person is on home confinement instead of in prison, the county or state is relieved of the obligation to provide for their basic needs, such as food, clothing, shelter, utilities, and health care. Instead, those responsibilities are placed squarely onto the confined person and their family. If the person is unable to meet their own needs while confined (not an uncommon circumstance, given the slew of obvious obstacles faced by those trapped in their homes), well, that's their problem.

In Indiana, Patricia Howard has paid $115 per week over three years for her monitor. It's a steep price, especially since for most of that time she was unable to find employment. That's in part because of her felony record and in part because restaurant and other service industry employers worry that an employee with an ankle monitor might deter customers. The family of seven was forced to rely primarily on her husband's income.

Howard's caseworker told her repeatedly that payments for the monitor had to take priority over her family's basic needs. Her family went through one winter without heat and one summer without air conditioning to afford the monitor. They became unable to afford car payments, and so their car was repossessed. While Howard bought her children's clothes a year ahead of time to take advantage of sales, she and her husband were forced to forgo new clothes, haircuts, and non-emergency health care for themselves. When Howard wanted to enroll her four-year-old son in preschool, her caseworker told her it was "non-necessary" and that she should instead put those funds toward her monitor.

Howard and her family scrimped and saved, cutting painful corners. Nevertheless, in September 2015, she was still nearly $800 behind in her payments. Eleven months later, that figure had more than doubled to $1,900.

Sixteen months into her thirty-month sentence, Howard asked her caseworker about a sentence modification. "My caseworker just kind of laughed and said that while she truly believed that I deserved it, they had a new prosecutor that has refused to consider any modifications of any kind for anyone," she recalled. She feared ending up in jail or simply stuck on monitoring if she was unable to catch up on her payments. "Any life-rebuilding we've done will be back at ground zero," she said.

Nearly a year later, twenty-six months into her sentence, she remained on her monitor. But instead of celebrating the final stretch, she was anticipating a long, rocky trail ahead: if she didn't pay the $1,900 she still owes, she won't see real freedom. At her last meeting, her caseworker told her that, solely because of her debt, the county planned to extend her sentence "indefinitely" until the payments were made. She was required to pay $115 for each week that her sentence was extended.

"It is part of the court order that you continue to pay—so if you're not paying, you're not being compliant," she said. "It doesn't matter your behavior, it matters how much money you have available."

The feeling of being stuck at "ground zero" that Howard describes—stuck in space, stuck in time—is pervasive among house arrestees, who battle the feeling that not only their bodies but also their minds are being held hostage, blocked from making autonomous choices.

In fact, that sense of constant captivity sometimes drives people to forgo the monitor in favor of seemingly more restrictive conditions. In Florida, Harvey Fair was released from prison to a halfway house in late 2013 and presented with the choice of leaving the halfway house with a monitor strapped to his ankle or remaining in the house for several more months. Residents who chose a monitor were required to continue paying the halfway house for a bed, even while struggling to pay rent on the outside. Fair picked option B. He had just emerged from seventeen and a half years of prison; he was done with living in chains.

"Psychologically, I could not live with paying the federal government or the halfway house to fasten on me an electronic shackle that would allow me to be tracked," Fair says, emphasizing how for him, as a Black man, the devices invoke the legacy of slavery. "I saw those black boxes locked to the ankles of others and it reminded me of prison shackles, which I promised to never wear again, forcibly or voluntarily. Ever watch the movie *Roots*? Those chains. No thanks."[64]

Nevertheless, electronic monitoring continues to gain a reputation as the benevolent alternative to prison. Can it ever fulfill this potential?

James Kilgore, the founder of Challenging E-Carceration, is doubtful. For monitoring to be a meaningful alternative to incarceration, he says, it would need to be used in a way that "abandons the punishment paradigm." Recalling his own year spent on monitoring, Kilgore does not think that abandonment is likely to happen. "That doesn't mean that we should never argue to have EM used," he says, "but we should always be trying to push the conditions of EM to be less restrictive, less punitive."[65]

Of course, no matter how many rights are granted, there's no way to strip the "monitoring" out of "electronic monitoring." EM and house arrest will always be forms of surveillance and confinement. Kilgore's pessimism is clearly warranted. Many groups working to reduce incarceration are also challenging electronic monitoring, including Kilgore's project Challenging E-Carceration as well as the National Bail Fund Network, the Chicago Community Bond Fund, JustLeadershipUSA, the National Bailout, MediaJustice, and a host of others. These groups recognize that monitoring is a classic case of Somewhere Else: turning people's homes into containers without challenging the idea that people need to be put in a container in the first place. They are fighting back against the notion that an alternative to incarceration must be another form of confinement.

For many people living in that supposedly humane Somewhere Else, the electronic shackle does not function as rehabilitation or "correction." It functions as a weight on their lives—holding them back and pulling them down, preventing them from moving forward.

"That $10 a day," muses Pat from California. "I could've gone to therapy with that money. Maybe *that* would've been a really good use of my $300 a month."

2

LOCKED DOWN IN "TREATMENT"

*The bed is not there for you to sleep. It's to remind you that
if you don't cooperate, you'll get strapped down.*

—Peg Plews, activist and psychiatric hospital survivor

WHEN STACEY THOMPSON ENTERED SUNLIGHT CENTER, A DRUG
treatment facility in upstate New York in 2002, she was sure she was
headed to a better place.[1] She had just been arrested for a drug charge
after being entrapped by an undercover cop, who followed her down
the street, begging her to buy him drugs until she finally acquiesced.
Luckily, at the time she was arrested, Thompson, who had struggled
with a crack cocaine addiction for nearly twenty years, had already
signed herself up for an inpatient treatment program at Sunlight—and
so the court mandated that she go to the treatment center instead of
jail. She was grateful.[2]

However, Thompson quickly found that Sunlight was not the

healing environment she had hoped for. "I was in the house they called the 'House of Pain,'" she says.

Life in the House of Pain was built around harsh discipline. At one point, Thompson told staff that she wanted to leave. Her counselor responded by telling her to sit on a hard plastic folding chair in the middle of the hallway. "See if you change your mind," she was told. Thompson spent days sitting on that chair as people walked by, staring and whispering.

"They let me off the chair to go eat . . . breakfast, lunch, and dinner," Thompson says, though sometimes she was required to eat meals on the chair. "I had to sit there and wait for somebody's permission to go to the bathroom. That's what made my bladder bad now. I can't hold my water to save my life."

Eventually her counselor permitted her to go to group therapy as well as meals—but after group, it was right back to the chair.

Group therapy wasn't exactly therapeutic either, Thompson says. It consisted of encounter groups, in which staff encouraged residents to yell at and insult each other. Serial abuse from men was one of the factors that spurred Thompson's addiction, but in Sunlight's encounter groups, she faced regular emotional abuse, particularly from men— and from one man in particular, who went as far as calling her a "bitch" during therapy.

Sunlight's primary response to Thompson's emotions was a variety of psychotropic medications. She didn't elect to start taking meds— they were forcibly prescribed when the center's authorities determined that her problem was "depression."

Numerous regulations were imposed on residents, right down to limits on how many pairs of underwear they could own. Residents could not leave the property, and for the first ninety days no phone calls or visits were permitted. "It was just like being in prison," Thompson says.

In some ways, she says, it may have been worse. When Thompson's father became terminally ill, the facility would not allow her to visit him. Her uncle, while in prison, had been allowed to go to his mother's funeral. But Thompson was not allowed to leave at all to see her father.

After six months, she had had enough. She left without seeking permission and returned home to New York City. When she arrived, she called her caseworker, who let her know that the center had reported her absconsion to the court, which had issued a warrant for her arrest. She spent nine days at Rikers Island, the city's island jail complex, before being mandated to another treatment facility.

Thompson's experience at Sunlight raises worrying questions when it comes to the current enthusiasm for the use of mandated treatment to replace incarceration. Mandated treatment is increasing in popularity as a reform for sentencing people diagnosed with substance use disorders as well as a range of mental health issues.

On April 10, 2017, New Jersey governor Chris Christie officially reopened the Mid-State Correctional Facility, a prison that had been closed for three years as the state's prison population dropped. Christie unveiled the renovated complex as the state's first "substance use disorder treatment prison," which would, according to Christie, "help break the costly cycle of addiction, avoid recidivism, and help people reclaim their lives." He proclaimed, "Every person with the disease of addiction deserves the best possible treatment."[3]

That same week, CBS News reported that President Donald Trump would be appointing Pennsylvania representative Tom Marino, a Republican, as his drug czar.[4] The appointment did not transpire, but in the weeks following the reports, Marino's ideas for how to address addiction were widely publicized and, in some quarters, lauded. In 2016, Marino had argued for the creation of "hospital-slash-prisons," in which "non-dealer, nonviolent drug abusers" would be placed in "a secured hospital-type setting under the constant care of health professionals." In other words, "kinder, gentler" prisons.

The recent steep rise in opioid overdoses, particularly in predominantly white communities, combined with the accumulation of overwhelming evidence that four decades of the drug war have not decreased drug misuse, has sparked an interesting political turn.[5] An increasing number of Republicans are now enthusiastically supporting initiatives aimed at combating addiction and aiding recovery, a complete 180 from a time not so long ago, when Republicans were known for calling for the harshest prison sentences for drug users. However, despite being touted as a path to recovery from addiction, many of these initiatives, like the Sunlight Center where Thompson was "treated," are openly based around the principle of confinement and control: they're mandatory, they hold a person's body in a certain space under certain strict regulations, and attempts to escape or diverge from those regulations are punished. But these spaces are embraced as "treatment," not "prison."

Republicans aren't the only ones advocating for mandated treatment. Democrats and progressives also herald it as a clear alternative to prison. As *Newsweek* put it, drug courts—which often prescribe involuntary treatment, whether that means being confined in a treatment facility or within the community under strict surveillance—"seem to be that vanishingly rare thing in Washington: an issue with near consensus."[6] Yet the drug court is a false solution. It was introduced in 1989, at the height of the war on drugs, to deal with the influx of small-time drug cases in criminal courts. Instead of decreasing arrests or prosecutions for drug offenses, the alternate court simply offered a different mode of prosecution, with penalties that purported to be geared toward addressing addiction. Although many of its proponents may be well-meaning, the drug court remains a product of the flawed assumption that the answer to addiction and other substance use problems resides within the criminal legal system.[7]

Addiction is not the only problem for which mandated treatment is posed as the clear solution. Similar locked-down "alternatives" are also being proposed for other mental health diagnoses.[8]

When a mass shooting occurred at a school in Parkland, Florida, in 2018, Donald Trump diagnosed the shooter as a "sicko" and announced that the solution was simple. "Part of the problem is we used to have mental institutions . . . where you take a sicko like this guy," he said. "We're going to be talking seriously about opening mental-health institutions again."[9] One year later, in August 2019, he reiterated that call following the mass shootings in El Paso, Texas, in which a white supremacist gunman killed twenty-two people, and Dayton, Ohio, in which another gunman killed ten and injured dozens. "We must reform our mental health laws to better identify mentally disturbed individuals who may commit acts of violence and make sure those people, not only get treatment, but when necessary, involuntary confinement," Trump stated.[10]

The president wasn't the only one issuing this type of call. The *New York Times* ran an op-ed by a liberal psychiatry professor two years before the Parkland shooting. In the piece, Dominic Sisti argues that "we need to bring back psychiatric asylums."[11] According to Sisti and many of his peers, such "asylums"—state institutions that confine people diagnosed with psychiatric and developmental disabilities while administering treatment—are essential for the "safety" of "vulnerable people." Without psychiatric asylums, Sisti says, people with severe mental-health-related disabilities will continue to be relegated to jails, prisons, and inadequate housing situations. Through this lens, the alternative to prison must be another institution.

Asylums have decreased dramatically since the deinstitutionalization movements of the 1950s, '60s, and '70s.[12] During those decades, activist pressure—especially from groups such as the Mental Patients Liberation Front, led by survivors of psychiatric institutions—called attention to the rampant abuse, neglect, and coercion within those institutions, including the widespread use of electroshock therapy, overdrugging, physical binding, beatings, induced comas, and lobotomies.[13] Physical and sexual violence were commonplace. Asylum survivors and their allies sought self-determination and freedom for those diagnosed with psychiatric disabilities. Organizing within the context of other civil rights movements of the time, from Black liberation to the American Indian Movement to gay liberation to the women's movement to Puerto Rican independence and more, asylum survivors and their allies sought self-determination and freedom for those diagnosed with psychiatric disabilities. Their sustained pressure over these decades resulted in the release of most of those who had been confined in state psychiatric institutions. By the mid-1980s, most people classified as mentally ill were no longer institutionalized. The population of these institutions dropped from 559,000 in 1955 to below 100,000 in 2000.[14] (Today it hovers around 35,000.)

Now, however, Sisti poses new asylums as a solution to the fact that half a million people behind bars have been diagnosed with a serious mental illness. He assures us that these places wouldn't be the "dismal institutions that were shuttered in the past, or settings of gothic fiction," but instead based on principles of actual "asylum." Yet they would nonetheless remain institutions—spaces of confinement.

Around the country, some advocates are pushing for an increase in psychiatric hospital beds, often using the word "care" synonymously with institutionalization.[15] From mandatory, locked-down drug treatment centers to revamped psychiatric hospitals, these institutional "solutions" fall squarely into the category of the Somewhere Else.

They also demonstrate a kind of imprisonment of our imaginations. Activist Rachel Herzing notes that "treatment jails" reflect our inability to reach for something beyond the prison industrial complex, even within our own minds: "In terms of alternatives, the lack of creativity in imagining what else we could have around us is the primary stumbling block," she says.[16]

The popularity of these proposals raises some tough questions: Can you force someone to be rehabilitated? What does it mean to create supposedly kinder, gentler forms of forced isolation and confinement? Would real liberation include the freedom to behave in non-normative, non-sanctioned ways—ways that some might call "mad"?

Drug Courts: Coercive Recovery

There are more than 3,100 "drug courts" in the United States, and the number is increasing.[17] These courts often dole out sentences of mandatory inpatient rehabilitation. They've long enjoyed bipartisan support, from the Clintons and Al Franken to Newt Gingrich and George W. Bush.[18] The assumption behind them is that people can—and, in many cases, should—be required to go into recovery.

Like many alternatives to incarceration, drug court sentences are, on the whole, preferable to prison sentences. Those sentenced to mandatory inpatient drug treatment generally have more liberties and receive better care than those behind bars. Many people express deep gratitude for the chance to enter drug court instead of prison, and some people with serious addictions are able to use the opportunity to pursue recovery. However, drug courts are also widening the net of control and surveillance: people who previously might have seen their charges dropped or been referred to voluntary treatment are now often pressured by prosecutors, judges, and their own lawyers to plead guilty and enter court-mandated programs.[19] Moreover, when drug courts are painted as *the* alternative, their punitive and harmful aspects are eclipsed.

It's hard to make generalizations about what drug court is like, since these courts operate on a local level, and the process varies substantially by court, by judge, and even by individual case. In some cases, a prosecutor and defense attorney can agree to refer a person to drug court after they have already been charged with a nonviolent drug-related crime. Some drug courts are "deferred prosecution" programs, where the person is placed in the program before pleading to a charge. They're then required to complete the program outlined by that particular drug court. If they fail to complete it, they'll be prosecuted.[20] Other drug courts follow a "post-adjudication" protocol: people plead guilty to charges before moving on to drug court. In these cases, their criminal court sentences are deferred or suspended while they're involved in the drug court program. People who successfully complete the program see their sentences waived—but those who don't are then sentenced to a criminal penalty.

Drug court programs may be as short as six months, but many last a year or more. Although these programs vary widely depending on the locality, the court, and the judge, some common requirements include regular drug tests, frequent court appearances, mandated participation in an intensive treatment program (inpatient or outpatient), classes, and support group attendance. Failure to complete the program might involve as minor an infraction as missing a court date, but it carries the threat of a heavier criminal penalty.

Drug court sentences frequently require complete abstinence from drugs, effectively eliminating the use of the medical world's most effective responses to opioid dependency: medically assisted treatments such as buprenorphine and methadone.[21] This means that a drug court sentence can bar some people living with addiction from getting the help they need and which they might be able to access if they weren't mired in the criminal legal system. Moreover, in lieu of medically assisted treatments, many drug courts include requirements for twelve-step programs such as Narcotics Anonymous and Alcoholics Anonymous in their sentences. Forcing a person to attend a twelve-step program has been repeatedly declared unconstitutional, because these programs are grounded in religion and/or spirituality.[22] Yet judges continue to make attendance a requirement: a 2014 Alcoholics Anonymous member survey showed that 12 percent of AA attendees entered the program through the judicial system.[23] Although many of these participants may not have entered against their will, the matter of individual "will" is complicated within the court system, where a deity-based recovery program may be the least objectionable option among many objectionable options.

Mandated treatment generally doesn't take into account the forces that drive drug dependency. Dr. Carl Hart, a Columbia University neuroscientist known for his research on drug use, urges a move away from the "disease model" of drug use. He says that automatically labeling addiction as a disease allows us to discount the social factors—including racism and poverty—that drive it. It also allows society to label drug users as "addicts" and blame their problems on addiction instead of acknowledging those problems' structural roots.

Hart has pointed out that the vast majority of those who use illicit drugs such as heroin, crack cocaine, methamphetamine, and marijuana are not actually addicted to them.[24] Drug use is not inherently problematic—some people can and do use cocaine, opioids, and methamphetamines in ways that do not harm their lives or the lives of others. Of course, some people do struggle with major problems related to drug use—but many do not. Even for those who face serious issues related to drug use, that use is generally not the root cause of their troubles. Hart emphasizes that very heavy drug use is often a reaction to social conditions such as racism and poverty, which are more likely to be the source of the problems attributed to drug use.[25]

The abstinence-only approach, under which mandated treatment and other confinement-based addiction "alternatives" tend to operate, ignores the realities of substance use in society: most people are not debilitated by physical dependence on the substances they use, whether they be alcohol, caffeine, or heroin.

Yet life-endangering substance dependency is also a reality that must be recognized. In these cases, an involuntary and immediate cessation of use generally doesn't lead to lasting recovery—especially when it comes along with surveillance and confinement. A 2016 Boston University Medical Center study found that mandatory treatment isn't effective in reducing drug use.[26] The study also points out that mandatory treatment also violates a person's human rights and, ultimately, "does more harm than benefit to the patient" by coercing them to participate in medical programs that they might not consent to otherwise. Indeed, locking people in treatment often leaves them in a worse position than they were when they came in, particularly when it comes to drugs like pain medication and heroin, for which tolerance is significantly lowered when someone has been abstaining.[27] A lowered tolerance means that people who use certain drugs again upon leaving abstinence-only treatment may well have a higher probability of fatal overdose.

Seventeen states currently permit some type of involuntary commitment for "substance use disorders."[28] Thompson's observation that treatment facilities are sometimes "just like being in prison" rings all the more sharply in light of laws like these.

Widening the Drug War Net

Drug courts not only harm those they claim to help, violating their human rights in the process, but also widen the net of surveillance and confinement. Instead of simply providing an alternative for people who would otherwise be sent to prison, drug courts are trying, sentencing, and confining people who in many cases wouldn't otherwise be incarcerated.[29] Some of these courts won't accept people charged with felonies that require a prison sentence upon conviction, while others exclude people with prior offenses. Drug courts tend to try people charged with the smallest of drug offenses—generally, low-level possession charges. Many of these people would be able to remain in their communities, free of surveillance, if they were not placed in treatment mandated by a drug court. Drug courts are capturing new populations.

In fact, drug courts sometimes fuel actual jail and prison populations, since they tend to drive up the number of arrests in a community.[30] The existence of courts designed to handle minor drug-related charges has been shown to encourage police to make those types of arrests—a kind of "if you build it, they will come" phenomenon. Police know these courts exist to handle an increase in small-time drug cases, and so they are more likely to make small-time drug arrests. As Denver district court judge Morris B. Hoffman stated, "It is clear that the very presence of drug courts is causing police to make arrests in, and prosecutors to file, the kinds of ten- and twenty-dollar hand-to-hand drug cases that the system simply would not have bothered with before."[31]A report by the Drug Policy Alliance, a nonprofit organization that advocates against drug prohibition and for policies that allow self-determination and opportunities for recovery, echoes the judge's analysis, explaining that "drug courts may actually increase the number of people incarcerated for drug law violations due to net-widening, a process by which the introduction or expansion of a drug court (or other diversion program) is followed by an increase in drug arrests."[32]

Racial disparities in incarceration sometimes worsen in communities with drug courts. This is because the presence of drug courts inspires a heightened number of arrests, and arrests disproportionately impact people of color. Moreover, many Black and Brown people who are arrested don't meet the narrow eligibility criteria for drug court (such as extremely low-level charges or a lack of prior offenses) because people of color are targeted more intensively by the criminal legal system.[33] In these cases, they are often funneled into jails and prisons.[34] Even if they do meet the criteria, those mandated to treatment haven't necessarily scored a get-out-of-jail-free card. The consequence for failing to complete a mandated treatment program is very often jail or prison.

Moreover, in drug courts that require a person to plead guilty in order to receive treatment, opting for a treatment deal entails giving up the ability to plead to a lesser charge. This means that drug court participants sometimes end up with a more significant charge than they might have agreed to otherwise—and if they fail a drug test, miss an appointment, or disobey the program in some other way, the resulting jail or prison sentence may be more substantial.[35]

Approximately half of people sentenced to a program through drug court don't finish—and the ones that don't often end up with harsher jail or prison sentences than if they hadn't gone the drug court route in the first place.[36] Additionally, the knowledge that failing to finish a program results in jail time may make people less likely to opt for a treatment-related plea.

Consider Oklahoma, which has the nation's highest rate of incarceration. It also has a 42 percent rate of drug court failure: nearly half of its drug court participants do not complete the court's requirements. The average prison sentence for drug court failure is seventy-four months. Most of these "failures" do not include new crimes; they involve minor missteps, such as failing a urine test or not paying court-imposed fines.[37] This means that after many months of following drug court mandates, a person might still end up in jail or prison.

Perhaps most important, "graduating" from a state-mandated treatment program does not necessarily equal real recovery and healing. Even if a treatment sentence doesn't end in incarceration, there's no guarantee it will transform a person's life. In fact, if the underlying causes behind the drug use—poverty, trauma, the enduring impacts of racism and other oppressions, and so forth—aren't addressed, the recovery may not last.

This is not to say that mandated treatment never has a positive impact. Some say treatment helped them reshape their lives for the better. Of course, there is no real data as to whether voluntary treatment would have served them just as well as—or better than—a mandated program. But the reality is that not everyone who is relegated to treatment confinement says it made their life worse.

After the horror show of her experience at Sunlight and her harrowing week and a half at Rikers, Stacey Thompson was mandated to a different treatment facility, Greenhope Services for Women. There the staff was compassionate, the rules were more flexible, and the all-women environment was more conducive to fostering Thompson's healing from the root causes that led her to drug addiction in the first place.

Thompson is still in recovery today and, years later, returns to Greenhope to visit. "I thank them for my recovery," she says. "I don't thank nobody at Sunlight. It's a big difference."

But, unlike many in her position, Thompson had signed up for treatment even before it was mandated. For someone less inclined toward recovery, even a program as supportive as Greenhope might not have an impact. As numerous studies have shown, people are much more likely to stay in recovery after treatment if they've entered it voluntarily.[38]

"No matter what program, what alternative to incarceration you pick, if that person is not ready, they're going to have reservations," Thompson says. "They're going to go through the whole program with reservations, and soon as they get out, they're gonna get high."

Thompson's assessment should prompt us to ask: What should the goal of treatment be? Is total sobriety the test for whether or not someone should be sent to prison? Should the criminal legal system determine what success looks like in someone's personal struggle with drug dependency? Does success look the same for everyone? Within the criminal system, success is generally determined in an impersonal, mass-produced way. It is equated with normativity, with standard and rigid benchmarks determined by authorities, including total abstinence from the substance in question.

The question of how the system works to enforce normativity is especially relevant when it comes to another, related type of alternative: mandated confinement in psychiatric hospitals.

"Bring Back the Asylums"

The first time Elliott Fukui was confined in a psychiatric hospital, he was twelve years old and had just attempted suicide. Minnesota, like nearly every state around the country, allows medical staff to involuntarily hospitalize a person who is at risk for suicide. He was placed on an involuntary hold in a Minnesota adolescent ward for over a week without his consent, marking the first of twenty confinements in five different hospitals over the next seven years.[39]

Fukui's confinement was not the result of a court order. Instead, it was his parents who brought the twelve-year-old to the hospital after a suicide attempt. They were seeking psychiatric help; what Fukui got instead was involuntary confinement, forced medications, a regimented schedule, and a requirement to attend mandatory programs, in which youth drew pictures and were supposed to be taught different ways to express their feelings, including sadness and anger. If they refused to comply, or even if they cried, they were held down by adult guards, forcibly sedated, and placed in isolation.

Upon being admitted to the ward, the twelve-year-old was strip-searched and immediately placed on a combination of psychiatric medications. His clothes and personal items were taken away and he was given scrubs to wear. He was prohibited from going to the bathroom or taking a shower alone. Throughout the night, the staff conducted "checks," entering the room every fifteen minutes and turning on the lights, making it almost impossible to sleep.

The ward had a "level" system. With good behavior, a person could earn the privilege of wearing their own clothes, eating in the cafeteria, going to the bathroom alone, or sleeping through the night. On the flip side, behavior that did not comply with the facility's rules—for example, oversleeping or refusing to participate in an activity—would result in lost privileges, and sometimes an even greater loss of freedom: placement in solitary confinement. In the ward where Fukui was confined, solitary confinement came in the form of the panic room—a stone room with no windows, whose only furniture was a gym mat.

The panic room was not presented as a punishment. It was presented as a place in which a person could calm down, a room that was empty because it needed to be free of objects with which someone could hurt themselves. But it certainly felt like a punishment to Fukui. The panic room was tiny and always cold. The lights were kept on at all hours, so once the sedatives wore off, sleep was difficult. Sometimes the walls were streaked with the blood of the previous person confined there. Fukui could hear screams emanating from the rooms on either side of his own.

Fukui was placed in the panic room multiple times during his first confinement and in subsequent confinements. The sequence: He would have a panic attack, or cry, or get angry, and the staff would "call code." Security guards would then enter and hold him down, strip him, and tie his legs and arms. Sometimes they'd deploy what they called "the burrito," wrapping him in a gym mat and sitting on him until he either stopped protesting or passed out.

"They'd pull your pants down and they'd give you a shot [of a sedative] in the ass," he says. "And then they would take your clothes, tie you up, and leave you in the room until you calmed down."

Compounding this, Fukui was already dealing with profound alienation: he is a queer, transgender, mixed-race person, and grew up in overwhelmingly white Minnesota. In fact, a significantly disproportionate number of people in the hospitals where he was confined were people of color, including a large number of Native youth. In contrast, the nurses and doctors were almost all white, he recalls. Fukui's experiences of solitary—and confinement more generally—felt like a self-fulfilling prophecy: when he suffered a panic attack or felt suicidal, his parents took him to the emergency room, where he was then involuntarily committed. But confinement simply made him feel more mentally ill.

"It just really drove home what I was already feeling, that there's just something completely wrong with me and that I was crazy and that I needed to be corrected," Fukui says. "And it was very lonely."

That loneliness was compounded by some facilities' policies. While Fukui was locked up the first time, when he was twelve, patients were not allowed to touch each other. Nurses were not allowed to touch patients except to restrain them. So unless a patient was receiving visitors, the only human contact they had was punitive and painful.

That weeklong hospitalization did nothing to address the underlying issues of his suicide attempt. Instead, he continued to experience panic attacks and dissociative episodes, leading his parents to once again bring him to the hospital for another involuntary commitment. In later hospitalizations, Fukui also experienced sexual abuse from both staff and other patients. Fukui was already a survivor of child sexual abuse—in fact, he points to that abuse as the root cause of many of the episodes that resulted in his confinement. The violence he experienced while locked up in the wards was re-traumatizing. He now suffers from PTSD-like flashbacks of the time he spent inside psychiatric hospitals.

Fukui also struggles with agoraphobia—a fear of situations and places that may cause him to feel trapped—due to his experiences of being locked up with no chance to go outside. "It definitely shifted the way that I understood what it meant to be safe—being 'safe' meant being alone in a room," he says.

Confinement in psychiatric hospitals is often seen as a relic of the past. However, these institutions do still exist: at least 35,000 people are currently confined in state psychiatric hospitals across the United States.[40] Often, they're confined against their will. One-third were funneled into hospitals through the criminal legal system.[41] And 5,000 people are incarcerated indefinitely in "civil commitment" psychiatric facilities after completing their prison sentences.[42]

Like drug-treatment-based confinement, psychiatric hospitals are increasingly proffered as a compassionate alternative to mass incarceration. Advocates frequently point to the vast numbers of incarcerated people who've been diagnosed with mental illness: 64 percent of people incarcerated in jails, 56 percent of those in state prisons, and 45 percent of those in federal prisons, according to the Urban Institute.[43] (Often, the way in which prison itself causes trauma that can lead to symptoms associated with mental illness is not noted.) Because the population of state psychiatric institutions has dramatically decreased since its peak—558,922 in 1955—the popular narrative states that many of the people who would otherwise have been confined in institutions are now being incarcerated: prisons have become the "new asylums." Reformers and lawmakers are proposing increasing the number of beds at psychiatric hospitals (the old asylums) and building new locked-down psychiatric treatment spaces as a solution.[44]

Along those lines, in 2018 Iowa broke ground on its first for-profit psychiatric hospital; officials said the new institution would ease pressure on the state's jails.[45]

Iowa joins Texas, South Carolina, and Florida in using psychiatric hospitals operated by GEO Group, one of the two largest private prison companies in the United States. The rise of for-profit treatment centers and psychiatric institutions, marketed as alternatives to incarceration, has become a notable trend. The American Friends Service Committee (AFSC), a nonprofit peace and justice organization, issued a report in 2014 on the "treatment industrial complex," a phrase the organization defines as "the expansion of the incarceration industry . . . into areas that traditionally were focused on treatment and care of individuals involved in the criminal justice system," including "forensic mental hospitals, civil commitment centers, and 'community corrections' programs such as halfway houses and home arrest." A number of the companies that benefit from prisons, jails, and immigrant detention centers have now entered the "treatment" business. Like all businesses, their bottom line depends on expansion.[46] According to the report, "This emerging Treatment Industrial Complex has the potential to ensnare more individuals, under increased levels of supervision and surveillance, for increasing lengths of time—in some cases, for the rest of a person's life."

The goal of these companies is not to get people to a place where they're no longer under supervision. In fact, it's often the opposite, according to the AFSC: "The financial incentive for private prison corporations is to keep people in custody or under some form of supervision for as long as possible at the highest per diem rate possible in order to maximize profits." The key to harnessing these profit opportunities? Promoting these programs as the antithesis of prison—as, in fact, a solution to mass incarceration.

However, private companies certainly did not invent the confined-treatment-as-incarceration-solution approach. They are simply capitalizing on an existing trend that has been gaining steam over the past several years. In 2016, the Pew Charitable Trusts, a nonprofit public policy organization, reported, "By one count, the nation needs an additional 123,300 psychiatric hospital beds," pointing out that this "critical shortage" was resulting in many patients being "boarded" at jails and regular hospitals—a blatantly odious practice.[47] Pew noted approvingly that a number of states are increasing psychiatric beds, but indicated that the increase is not happening fast enough. In Washington State, hundreds of beds were added in 2015, but some officials called for an even higher rate of bed increases.[48] In 2018, Governor Jay Inslee announced a plan to decrease the populations of Washington's two large psychiatric hospitals—but open a number of new smaller psychiatric hospitals throughout the state.[49] The governor's 2019–2021 budget includes an earmark for $30 million to open nine hospitals, ranging in size from 16 beds to 150 beds.[50]

Similarly, a 2017 report by the nonprofit Treatment Advocacy Center suggests that increasing the number of beds in psychiatric hospitals ("the 'old asylums'") is actually the key to "emptying the 'new asylums'"—that is, ending mass incarceration.[51] A fall 2018 reflection piece in the *Los Angeles Review of Books* asserts that asylums are currently unavoidable and essential: "We need places like this, and we'll keep needing them until scientists develop drugs to fix the worst of what ails us—drugs we certainly don't have now."[52] In 2018, the *Wall Street Journal* urged a "new generation" of institutions to "reduce the vast numbers of mentally ill adults in jails and prisons."[53] This concept of a "new generation" of institutions is interlaced throughout all of these assessments—the idea that to address the imprisonment of those deemed mentally ill, we must revive and revise a scourge of the past. The supposed answer to abusive forms of confinement is, yet again, what's perceived as a kinder confinement.

Yet mass incarceration is not directly attributable to the deinstitutionalization movement, many activist scholars say. A widely accepted narrative—propagated over the years by numerous academics and activists as well as by mainstream media outlets including the *New York Times*, *Frontline*, MSNBC, the *Washington Post*, and many more—is that deinstitutionalization led to mass homelessness, followed by the widespread imprisonment of people with mental illness.[54] As the Treatment Advocacy Center notes, there are now ten times as many people diagnosed with serious mental illness living in prisons and jails than in hospitals.[55] However, most deinstitutionalization took place during the 1950s and 1960s, well before the increase in housing insecurity and the advent of mass incarceration, both of which hit in the early 1980s, a fact noted by Liat Ben-Moshe, assistant professor of criminology, law, and justice at the University of Illinois at Chicago and co-editor of the book *Disability Incarcerated*.[56] Increasing homelessness and related incarceration were due not to the drop in institutionalization, Ben-Moshe says, but to the rising era of Ronald Reagan and neoliberal economics, including a $30 billion cut in housing assistance. By the time of the prison boom, people with mental illness diagnoses who were being shuttled into prisons weren't the same people who'd been locked up in psychiatric institutions.[57]

Arguments for bringing back asylums based on the large number of imprisoned people who are diagnosed with mental illness fail to account for the fact that prison is a traumatizing and sometimes torturous space that causes most people significant psychological anguish. Prison *produces* mental health problems.

Many of the practices of prisons and psychiatric institutions—confinement, surveillance, coercion, segregation, and punishment—mirror each other. As with prisons, psychiatric institutions are a fairly new establishment as far as human history goes. Psychiatric and medical confinement-based hospitals grew up alongside prisons in eighteenth-century Europe and the United States.[58] In fact, throughout their earlier history, prisons and psychiatric/medical institutions confined similar populations—mostly poor people, people with disabilities, and people deemed "mad." Most of those confined were white, while people of color, whose lives were viewed as even more disposable, were subject to more brutal consequences, such as physical punishment or death.[59]

In the nineteenth century, prisons and psychiatric institutions became more distinct, and each institution grew.[60] As with prisons, confinement-based psychiatric institutions expanded as a result of the dedication of reformers. These reformers, like Dorothea Dix, argued for more humane treatment of people with disabilities—just as eighteenth- and nineteenth-century prison reformers advocated against killing or maiming people who'd committed crimes.

The abuses that reformers crusaded against were real and vicious: People considered to be mad were caged, chained, locked in attics or cellars or outhouses, and even killed by their family members. In 1849,

Dix described a woman who kept her brother in an eight-by-eight-foot pen. She cleaned the area every week or so by having neighbors tie her brother down while buckets of water were tossed into the pen.[61] Dix also told the story of a Rhode Island "mad man," whose neighbors constructed a six-by-eight-foot stone vault to confine him in. He was forced to sleep on wet straw with only a wet quilt for "warmth"; Dix describes the quilt icing over in the winter.

Confinement became the go-to alternative—a way to ameliorate the most violent abuses while still hiding people with psychiatric disabilities from plain sight and, in some cases, a way to inculcate them into "normalcy."[62] As activist writers Kay Whitlock and Michael Bronski note, people labeled insane were seen to be "helpless individuals" in *need* of confinement.[63] The asylum was the kinder, gentler Somewhere Else. These linked goals—punishment and rehabilitation, confinement and care—echo those of the early prison movement.

The entwinement of the asylum and the prison is an old story. For the past two and a half centuries, the discipline and control of people diagnosed with mental illness has ridden alongside the discipline and control of criminalized people. Very often, those populations are one and the same, and controlled by the same authorities. The solution to their existence was, and often continues to be, confinement.[64]

Peg Plews knows the intertwinement of these issues well. Plews is a longtime anti-prison and mental health activist who has organized in Michigan, where she grew up and now lives. Now in her fifties, she has also been involuntarily confined in hospitals several times.[65] When Plews was fourteen, she was institutionalized after a suicide attempt. Thanks to the trauma of this experience, Plews dissociates whenever people grab her body.

In the mid-1990s, Plews, who is white, worked as a mental health services advocate and served as president of the Alliance for the Mentally Ill of Washtenaw County, Michigan. She recalls accompanying people to the ER seeking emergency mental health services—only to see them treated abusively and locked in the emergency psych ward. Nowadays, the procedure remains the same in the hospitals where she's sought help herself.

On a Friday night in February 2017, Plews was drunk when she went to Walmart to buy cat food. She has a mobility disability, and during the shopping "rush hour," a number of people were waiting for motorized scooters to navigate the giant store. Plews grabbed a regular cart and, as she walked down the aisles, began grumbling, "Why doesn't Walmart have enough carts for disabled people on a Friday night?" She grew louder and louder until security stopped her and threw her out. Plews sat in her car to sober up before driving home. But soon Plews, who has issues with incontinence, needed to use the bathroom. She reentered the store and was tackled by a police deputy, who pinned her down. Her bladder gave out and she began peeing on herself. By then, a crowd had gathered to watch.

Feeling desperate, she asked the spectators to call an ambulance. By then, the deputy had rolled off her, but the deputy continued to keep her legs pinned down until the ambulance arrived.

She was taken to the hospital's "psych emergency" wing—a distinct section of the ER, which contains "secure core" cells that can only be opened from the outside. The entrance is guarded by security. Plews attempted to refuse to submit to a strip search or to give up her clothes, explaining that she was a rape survivor. She was told, "If you don't cooperate, things aren't going to go well for you."

She was then evaluated by a doctor who wrote out a petition for involuntary hospitalization, stating that Plews was experiencing "persecutorial delusions" that the police were out to get her. Plews tried to explain to him that she is an activist who works against policing and prisons, but he ignored this. Staff refused to show her the doctor's petition. Instead, they took away her boots and jewelry.

Plews began to shout, "You are violating my rights!" In response, a nurse shot her up with Haldol, a strong antipsychotic drug and sedative. In the paperwork, staff said that she was disturbing other patients. The nurse offered Plews Benadryl, which she refused, explaining that it makes her agitated. The nurse administered it anyway.

From the doorway of her cell, Plews heard the staff talking to her partner, with whom she has a contentious relationship. "Is she taking her medications? Does she sleep at night?" they asked him. Staff prohibited her from speaking with him; she told the doctor she did not want him speaking with her partner about her. "I can speak to whomever I want in an emergency," she was told. As a security guard guided her back into her cell, she watched the doctor turn to the nurse and tell her they'd be holding Plews overnight because she was agitated.

The cell door was closed; so was the window. All Plews could see was the "bright bright bright white" of the cell walls.

The room had no toilet, or even a trash can. Plews still had to go to the bathroom—she hadn't had the chance since her attempt at Walmart—but staff refused to open her cell door.

"I felt like a child crying for the bathroom," she says. "It was horrible." Her pleas were ignored until she pulled her pants down and began to squat in the corner. Only then did staff allow her to use the bathroom.

Plews was determined not to let them subject her to such humiliation again. After using the bathroom, she stood in the doorway of the cell, preventing staff from closing the door. In response, security picked her up and restrained her on the bed as the nurse administered more sedatives.

"I don't remember anything else except writhing and feeling like I was in fucking hell," Plews says. She was kept for twenty-three hours.

Emerging from the hospital, Plews, a survivor of sexual violence, felt she was reliving the rape she'd experienced as a teenager four decades earlier. After assaulting her, her rapist and his friends had laughed at her, taunting her that she'd never tell. The experience of being severely violated at the hospital while not being taken seriously as a human being was devastating—and only intensified her trauma and despair.

"They do this kind of violence to people, but they don't call it violence," she says. "If you search 'violence in the ER,' it's never about involuntary hospitalization or involuntary catheterization of the patients."

The hospital staff had treated Plews not as a human being but as an intense danger to those around her, a threat that needed to be subdued at all costs, even though she didn't intentionally threaten anybody. This type of official labeling of unusual behavior as a threat is not an uncommon phenomenon. Confinement of mentally ill people against their will is based on the idea that they pose a threat to broader society and aren't competent to make decisions for themselves.

Over the past 250 years, as psychiatric asylums evolved alongside prisons, they served as a place to deposit people thought to be especial dangers. In the nineteenth century, some prisons began to transfer people they determined to be particularly risky or disobedient to psychiatric institutions.[66] As psychiatric populations swelled, staff spent less time with each patient, and the emphasis of institutions shifted more firmly away from care and toward management: Psychiatric journal articles from 1844 to 1900 overwhelmingly center on facility management, with relatively very little attention to therapeutic treatment.[67] By the late 1800s, the idea of "treating" or "curing" mental illness—with the goal of returning people to the community—fell out of favor, replaced by the concept of limitless psychiatric commitment to keep "patients reported as dangerous to their communities" (and sometimes even dangerous to their prisons) permanently behind walls.[68] Psychiatric hospitals began to function as the Somewhere Else for the Somewhere Else—an alternative place to store people thought to be unsuited to both prison and the larger society.

"Treatment" Through Endless Incarceration

Once the notion of a Somewhere Else has been established—as well as the notion that, for some "incurable" people, that somewhere else must be permanent—the extent of confinement knows no bounds. Approximately 22,000 people are involuntarily committed to state psychiatric hospitals and civil commitment centers. This includes thousands who are being evaluated pretrial or treated for incompetency to stand trial, as well as those who have been found "not guilty by reason of insanity" and thus sentenced to a non-prison form of confinement.[69]

No place, perhaps, is so Somewhere Else–like as the post-prison civil commitment facilities designated for people convicted of sex offenses. The concept of confining a person within the civil legal system based on a mental health diagnosis has been around for a long time, as witnessed by the extensive history of asylums. However, the indefinite, involuntary civil commitment specifically created for people convicted of sex offenses is an insidious reform that emerged three decades ago and has since multiplied exponentially. Though they're labeled treatment centers and fall within the civil—not criminal—legal realm, these facilities essentially serve as prisons. They hold people whose prison terms have legally ended but who are mandated to undergo continual monitoring and treatment, frequently leading to a lifetime of confinement.[70] These are places where people are confined because of an alleged psychiatric diagnosis (such as pedophilia), not because of a conviction; punishment for the conviction has already been meted out, but confinement-based "treatment" for the diagnosis could be never-ending.

These post-prison confinement facilities came into existence in the 1990s amid a wave of intensifying laws around sex offenses, which may include anything from sex with an underage partner or public nudity to rape and sexual assault. A few extremely brutal and well-publicized

acts of sexual violence against white middle-class children prompted a cultural panic around "stranger danger" and "sexual predators"
(despite the fact that most sexual violence is not perpetrated by strangers).[71] In 1990, Washington State passed the country's first law allowing indefinite and involuntary confinement of people labeled "sexually
violent predators." Other states and the federal government followed
suit, while a series of Supreme Court rulings made way for the indefinite confinement of anyone deemed a "sexually violent predator" or
"sexually dangerous person."[72] Civil commitment facilities now incarcerate about 5,400 people in twenty states and at the federal level.[73]

Prison and civil commitment have a whole lot in common. It's no
accident that in New Jersey, civil commitment programs have set up
residence in former prisons.[74] New Jersey's "Special Treatment Unit" is
a civil commitment facility that follows many of the same policies as
prisons—similar visiting hours, food, and periods of confinement—
and some of the treatment unit guards also work as state prison
guards.[75]

However, civil commitment is not assigned during criminal legal
proceedings. Instead, as a person nears the end of their prison sentence
and begins to anticipate rebuilding their life, they become entangled
in a civil commitment process that could extend their confinement
indefinitely.

The civil commitment process looks different from state to state,
but in general, a person on the cusp of release from prison is evaluated for whether they are sexually violent or sexually dangerous.
Evaluations tend to utilize standardized risk assessments such as the
Static-99R, which uses information about one's prior offenses, age,
and intimate partner history (among other factors) to supposedly
determine how likely a person is to commit an act of sexual violence
in the future.[76] However, such assessments are heavily based on a person's prior record of convictions—and, thus, are influenced by all the
race-based, class-based, disability-based, sexual-orientation-based,

and gender-identity-based biases that determine who gets convicted of a crime and who does not. Some biases are explicit in the test itself: those being evaluated by the Static-99R receive an extra risk point for having "male victims," based on the logic that "having male victims is correlated with measures of sexual deviance and is seen as an indication of increased sexual deviance."[77] Moreover, these tests allow little room for the fact that individuals are capable of change and one's prior actions are not a lifelong predictor of what they will do in the future. Although the risk assessment is followed by a civil trial, judges tend to base their decisions on the evaluator's determinations, disregarding the testimony of the people whose lives are at stake, according to research by activist and scholar Erica Meiners, who has focused her recent work on civil commitment and sex offender registries.[78] It's the word of the state against the word of someone who has already been judged guilty by a state apparatus. Predictably, the state tends to win.

Another difference between a sentence and civil commitment is that the latter can be never-ending. Questionable methods—such as polygraph testing related to sexual fantasies—are used by civil commitment programs to assess whether people are releasable.[79] According to the J-SOAP-II, one of the most widely used protocols used to evaluate youth convicted of sex offenses in the United States, if a child is determined to have been a victim of sexual abuse themselves, that can be a strike against them and a point in favor of their ongoing confinement; they're deemed more likely to commit another offense.[80] Plus, in Meiners's research on the experiences of people confined in civil commitment centers, many reported that what they share with their therapists isn't kept confidential—making it difficult to engage in deep, transformative therapeutic work if they want to protect themselves against indefinite confinement.[81]

In some states, barely anyone is released from commitment. Minnesota, which has confined nearly one thousand people in its civil commitment center since its establishment two decades ago, has only released one person so far.[82] In Texas, no person has been fully released from the state's civil commitment program for "sexually violent predators," which was established in 1999.[83]

Those who are confined in indefinite civil commitment facilities have been placed in a category for which permanent exclusion from society is deemed appropriate. Although each state and the federal government has its own laws governing civil commitment, they all cluster around that same principle: some people must be kept away, regardless of whether they've already served their time. According to the 2006 Adam Walsh Act, the law permitting civil commitment for "sexually dangerous persons" at the federal level, a person may be released "when the Director of the facility in which a person is placed . . . determines that the person's condition is such that he is no longer sexually dangerous to others."[84] For many in civil commitment, that determination never happens.

Despite these strict subjective criteria, there's no palpable evidence that the programs are actually protecting anyone from sexual violence. Sex offenses have some of the lowest recidivism rates of any crimes.[85] Wide-ranging government studies have confirmed, again and again, that people convicted of sex offenses who have been released from prison are less likely to be rearrested than other formerly incarcerated people.[86] Recidivism statistics certainly do not tell the whole story of sexual violence—most people who are harmed don't call the police, and most of those who cause harm are not arrested. Yet myths of "frightening and high" recidivism rates, a catchphrase used by the Supreme Court in a 2003 decision on sex offender registration and repeated more than a hundred times by lower courts, paint an inaccurate picture.[87]

Moreover, there are no studies supporting the virtues of civil commitment as treatment. Yet those indefinitely confined in civil commitment centers are some of the least advocated-for members of society. They are assumed to be "the worst of the worst": people for whom "treatment," even of the locked-down and indefinite variety, is a mercy—people who many presume are simply better off in a cage.

A Danger to Society?

The presumption that some people are actually better off in cages—that they are unable to live life safely on the outside—courses throughout the logic of treatment-based alternatives.

Peg Plews confronts this notion regularly: each time she's been in the hospital, she's been treated as a "danger." But for her, the real danger comes from the powerful forces she's up against. She's extremely afraid of the authorities.

"I don't feel safe going out into the community," she says in the aftermath of her 2017 confinements. "What if a cop pulls me over and I'm shaking and they decide that, because I'm shaking, they need to take me to the hospital?"

Elliott Fukui, too, connects the dots between prisons and hospitals, police and medical personnel, criminal surveillance and psychiatric surveillance, fear of "criminals" and fear of psychological difference. When he was in the hospital and people had panic attacks or other mental-health-related episodes, the staff dubbed them "brat attacks," equating psychological pain with aggressive behavior. This translation made it easier to justify cruelties such as solitary confinement, physical restraint, and the "burrito."

"It was completely invalidating. It made me feel more crazy, like there was something inherently wrong with me that needed to be corrected, and that it was so bad that I needed to be punished in this kind of way," Fukui says.

"Wrong." "Corrected." "Punished." This is the vocabulary of the prison nation. It invokes assumptions of both the intrinsic danger posed by certain people who are labeled in certain ways and the presumed necessity of a Somewhere Else to store them—and to coerce them into a painfully narrow form of normality.

As with drug treatment, not all stories of psychiatric hospital experiences are solely traumatizing. Sadie Ryanne Baker, a trans woman and mental health activist, has had complex experiences with the system. During her first interaction with the mental health system—which "was not voluntary"—she was told that being trans was a mental disorder, asked invasive questions, and coercively prescribed medications that "ended up harming me a lot," she says. At other times, however, she has sought out hospitalization on her own, determining that it was in her best interest.

Baker identifies as "crazy" and is in a tradition of activists who are reclaiming the word "madness," fighting against the assumption that a person diagnosed with mental illness must be "fixed"—stuffed into a set of psychological norms. Mad movements reclaim the term "mad" to encompass a wide variety of experiences of trauma, distress, and deep emotion, in addition to out-of-the-ordinary experiences of joy, ecstasy, connection, or inspiration—including experiences that might traditionally be categorized under a psychiatric diagnosis.[88]

At the same time, Baker takes medications and sometimes uses diagnostic language to describe her situation "when it's convenient." "I've hated all of my psychiatrists, all of whom have been patronizing and some of whom have been disgustingly transphobic," she says. "But, miraculously, I've loved all of my therapists."

Baker credits her positive experiences in part to white privilege, because race has a major impact on how the mental health system manifests in a person's life. While racism contributes to mental health problems such as anxiety and depression, disparities in services mean that white communities in general have more access to mental health care than communities of color (particularly Black communities). Meanwhile, the mental health care that white people receive is less likely to be punitive.[89] Now a mental health provider herself,

Baker stresses that more people should have access to the kinds of non-confinement-based, individualized, self-determination-oriented care options that are currently seen as "luxuries of the ruling class."

"I believe we need to smash the mental health system as much as any other power structure," she says. "But, unlike systems like prison and policing, we should pick up some of the pieces and rebuild a new system with them. We must examine every individual part of the mental health care system critically by asking, 'Does this specific thing help or hurt oppressed people?'"

Unlike prisons, psychiatric institutions can be entered voluntarily, and people often turn to them in pursuit of treatment. But when used involuntarily as prison replacements, hospitals mimic prisons in eerie ways—and the most oppressed people experience the brunt of the trauma and violence.

Trauma Ignored

Plews's and Fukui's stories illustrate a truth that turns the moniker of "treatment" on its head: their experiences of confinement, supposedly intended to "correct" their problems, did not actually address the root causes of their struggles. For both of them, the pain that led to their episodes stemmed from earlier trauma—but they were discouraged from bringing up that trauma while in treatment.

"We weren't allowed to tell 'war stories,' so we weren't allowed to talk with each other about why we were there, not even in therapy sessions," Fukui says, laughing a little. "The therapy was very much drawing pictures and, 'How do you express your feelings in ways that are acceptable? What do you do to cope when you're feeling sad or angry?' None of it was addressing root causes as to why any of us were there in the first place, 'cause they were worried that telling war stories, as they called them, would be triggering and would mean that we would all act out."

Coloring was a staple activity during Plews's hospitalization. In March 2017, Plews, suffering from PTSD and depression stemming from the trauma of her last ER visit, voluntarily admitted herself to the hospital. During her week in the hospital, she basically colored all day, except for one day when staff brought in nail polish and let the patients give themselves manicures. She just wanted to sleep and access therapy. Instead, she was assigned innocuous activities to pass the time.

Like Fukui, Plews and the others confined at the hospital were not allowed to discuss their underlying pain. During one group session, the facilitator asked everyone, "Why are you here? What are your goals?" One woman said she'd witnessed someone shooting her boyfriend in the head. Another said her brother had also been fatally shot in the head. The facilitator responded to neither woman, simply saying, "Anybody else?" Plews felt completely uncared for. Her trauma—including the trauma inflicted by the hospital itself—and the trauma experienced by those around her was simply dismissed.

Her experience recalls that of Thompson in locked-down drug treatment at Sunlight. Despite the close supervision and mandated group therapy sessions, Thompson's most basic traumas were not taken seriously.

"My first husband beat me with his rifle," she says. "My second husband was very abusive. My boyfriend threw me off a balcony. I was just done with men. I couldn't stand men and there were too many around me." Yet despite this history, she says, "one of my counselors was a man."

The fact that the authorities at Sunlight paired Thompson with a male therapist reveals that for people diagnosed with mental illness, their knowledge and interpretations of their own minds and bodies very often aren't taken seriously when determining their care.

The psychological pain and actions or behaviors that result from past trauma are often formally interpreted with psychiatric diagnoses, as they were for Fukui and Plews. This pertains to both individual traumas and, interrelatedly, larger structures like racism and sexism. In fact, while the trauma of racism and sexism often goes unacknowledged within the mental health system, structural oppressions regularly shape diagnoses. For example, women make up 75 percent of those diagnosed with borderline personality disorder—a label associated with the old concept of "hysteria" and often slapped on women who display aggression that doesn't match their traditional gender role, or self-injury that sometimes results from gender-based trauma.[90] Meanwhile, Black people are often handed a "schizophrenia" label. While in the first half of the twentieth century schizophrenia was regarded as a nonthreatening condition mostly diagnosed in white people, Black people began to be diagnosed with it (and heavily medicated for it) at higher rates during the civil rights era of the 1960s and 1970s. Some white doctors even termed schizophrenia "protest psychosis" and insisted that affected people—specifically, Black people—could be cured by strong medication.[91] The schizophrenia diagnosis disparity persists today: Black people are three to five times as likely to be diagnosed with schizophrenia as white people.[92]

Again and again, psychiatric labels become vehicles for race- and gender-based harm. The use of diagnosis as a tool of structural oppression is not a new phenomenon. Braddock and Parish note that in the 1840 census, all Black residents in some southern towns were classified as "insane." After the end of slavery, between 1870 and 1880, rates of mental illness diagnoses in the United States rose dramatically. This was not because everyone suddenly experienced a drastic shift toward increased psychological pain; it was because of the way "insanity" was tabulated. Amid a push toward measures such as institutionalization and sterilization, census-takers were paid extra for counting someone as mentally ill.[93]

This diagnostic discrimination persists today. As a young trans person of color, Fukui notes that much of his trauma can be traced to racism and transphobia—but in the eyes of the mental health system, the effects of that trauma manifest as "symptoms" that are then diagnosed as severe mental illness.

"I think more often than not, we're not acknowledging the ways that systemic racism or systemic misogyny or patriarchy or capitalism functions to make people literally mad," Fukui says. "You can't win in those systems." Once a diagnosis is pronounced, a person is stuck with that mark on their medical record, a strike that they can't remove and which determines much of their future medical treatment. The impacts of that strike have led some survivors of psychiatric confinement to compare a severe psychiatric diagnosis to a conviction on a criminal record.

Fukui experienced another manifestation of structural oppression in the system: the "rehabilitation" efforts he was offered were geared not toward helping him address his trauma but toward stomping out his "symptoms"—often punitively—so that he could fulfill the roles that society expected of him. Instead of allowing group therapy participants to talk about past traumas or even their current feelings in the group sessions, facilitators focused on drilling them in ways in which they could suppress, redirect, or distract themselves from negative emotions. Meanwhile, the causes of those negative emotions were never addressed. The goal was not to heal the causes of his pain but to make him "functional" so that he could work and fit in in society.

Often, the goal of "treatment" is the elimination of madness—or else the disappearance of those who are determined to be "incurably" mad. But, Liat Ben-Moshe says, "Disability/madness are ways of living in the world, not conditions to be eliminated. They are embodiments with rich traditions of histories and their own cultures."[94] Many types of treatment claim to be about fixing the so-called problem of madness. The real problem is that certain ways of experiencing the world are seen as categorical threats—to normativity, to capitalism, to hierarchy, to the system itself. And our society's answer to a perceived threat is, of course, confinement.

In parallel ways, treatment for drug-related problems generally insists on a goal of abstinence—of completely eliminating use. For some people, this may be a desirable goal. For others, this may feel utterly out of the question or utterly unnecessary. After all, humans have always used mind-altering substances, and not everyone feels they must stop—let alone be shut away in abstinence-based inpatient treatment—in order to live a meaningful life.

In the world of state-sanctioned alternatives to incarceration, state systems enforce psychiatric norms and police those deemed "patients" or service users. County, state, and federal governments erect more buildings and fund more treatment beds. Programs pile more diagnoses upon those subject to their services. Lawmakers and advocates set noble goals—goals of sending the populations of prisons and jails to somewhere better, somewhere kinder, Somewhere Else. The list of Somewhere Elses grows longer—it incorporates treatments, rehabilitations, sites of "recovery." Meanwhile, the cycle of segregation and confinement continues to turn, capturing more and more human beings along its way.

3

CONFINED IN "COMMUNITY"

The largest alternative to incarceration in the United States is simultaneously one of the most significant drivers of mass incarceration.

—"Less Is More," a 2017 report on probation by the
Harvard Kennedy School of Government

AFTER PAT (THE COLLEGE STUDENT MENTIONED IN CHAPTER 1) SERVED four months on electronic monitoring, she had no illusions that she'd be "free" after the electronic shackle was removed. That's because she was sentenced to six full years on probation.[1] Probation is a sentence that is served in the community, as opposed to behind bars. It is sometimes assigned in place of a jail or prison sentence, often for less-serious crimes—40 percent of people on probation were convicted of misdemeanors, such as cannabis possession, vandalism, trespassing, prostitution, and disorderly conduct.[2] Sometimes probation is tacked on as an additional punishment after release from jail, prison, or another type of confinement, and in still other cases it's assigned in combination with electronic monitoring. Probation requires one to comply with a strict set of rules, including regular reporting to a probation officer, avoiding particular places or people associated with the offense one was convicted of committing, abiding by curfews, submitting to drug testing, abstaining from alcohol, and paying fees or restitution, as well as a range of other restrictions and conditions that vary by jurisdiction.

Pat liked her probation officer and was determined to avoid ending up behind bars, but she knew there were no guarantees. Thanks to onerous, punitive restrictions—and sometimes fees—a third of people on probation aren't able to complete their sentences and are then shuttled into jails or prisons.[3] For long-term probation, the odds are even more dismal.

Pat's probation officer reportedly told her, "If you get off probation, you should go out and buy a lottery ticket, because you have a better chance of winning the lottery than getting off probation successfully."

His assessment, however cynical, rings true for many serving this "alternative" sentence. While some people are placed on probation after release from jail or prison, the primary use of probation in the system is to provide an option for a sentence that entirely avoids traditional incarceration. (Probation should not be confused with parole, which is the main avenue of post-prison supervision in most states.)

Probation is not the only non-prison sanction that extends the prison nation. Measures such as mandatory outpatient treatment, the sex offender registry, and sex worker rescue programs—some of which may be assigned simultaneously—are also non-prison sanctions grounded in the principle of confinement in time, in space, in the range of possibilities for how people live their lives—and even how they can attempt to heal.

Probation:
Creating Millions of Carceral Citizens

"Mass probation" may not be a household phrase, but in this country it is a reality. The United States doesn't only lead the world in incarceration numbers; it also tops the international charts when it comes to probation. Despite comparable crime rates in the United States and Europe, the United States' probation rate outpaces Europe's average probation rate by over 400 percent.[4] Probation is by far the most commonly assigned non-prison punishment. According to the Bureau of Justice Statistics, about twice as many people are under "community supervision" (generally parole or probation) than are in jail or prison: 3.6 million people are on probation, compared to almost 2.3 million who are incarcerated.[5]

By the system's logic, probation is supposed to set people on a course to avoid jail or prison. However, as Pat's probation officer observed, probation fuels mass incarceration. Nearly a quarter of state prison admissions across the country are due to probation violations (including new offenses and violations of the terms of probation).[6] People who have previously been on probation amount to nearly 15 percent of the United States' incarcerated population, according to a 2017 report by the Harvard Kennedy School.[7] According to the report, "Ironically . . . the largest alternative to incarceration in the United States is simultaneously one of the most significant drivers of mass incarceration."

Like nearly every other facet of the prison industrial complex, probation disproportionately impacts Black people, who make up 30 percent of those sentenced to it. And while less than 10 percent of the United States' incarcerated population is made up of women, 25 percent of those on probation are women.[8] The number of women under "community supervision"—both probation and parole—has nearly doubled since 1990 (and most of these women are on probation).[9] Plus, women face a higher risk of violating probation, because the restrictions probation sentences impose tend to conflict with the childcare needs and family responsibilities many women have.[10]

When Pat's probation officer compared successfully completing a six-year probation sentence to winning the lottery, he was acknowledging what many people entangled in this system know intuitively: when you're on probation, the system is betting against you.

Over the past couple of decades, the number of restrictions imposed on people on probation has exploded, and the restrictions have become increasingly punitive. Left to the discretion of judges—and influenced by racism, classism, and other systemic oppressions—these conditions often seep into the realm of the prohibitive and even the absurd. On top of stringent reporting requirements, curfews, abstinence from drugs and/or alcohol, and bans on setting foot in certain parts of a city, they may include such restrictions as not sitting in the front seat of a car or not getting pregnant.[11] Conditions also include the payment of fees and fines, including a recurring probation fee in most states, as well as fees for drug testing, court-ordered classes such as anger management, domestic violence, parenting or safe driving, and electronic monitoring.[12] These payments pose a serious hardship for many people on probation, who are disproportionately low-income: 66 percent of people on probation earn less than $20,000 annually.[13] Pat had to pay fees for her probation and shoulder the cost of her electronic monitor. It was, she says, "a racket."

On average, a person on probation now has to comply with a list of conditions that numbers in the mid-teens, and it's not uncommon to be saddled with more than twenty conditions.[14] When people are weighed down by onerous requirements and offered few resources for support, sometimes a future behind bars can seem inescapable.

After violating the terms of his house arrest, Angel Sanchez was sentenced to twelve years in prison followed by ten years of probation. At age twenty-eight, he emerged from a Florida state prison and, instead of moving home to Miami, moved to Orlando to live in a homeless shelter, leaving behind everything he knew in hopes of a fresh start.

However, no matter where he moved, he would be on probation, and so his fresh start still involved grappling with a familiar system. Sanchez needed to cope with the intrusion of probation authorities into his everyday life in ways that threatened to hinder his path forward, such as when his probation officer showed up at his job—where co-workers didn't know he had been incarcerated—with his badge hanging around his neck.

Nevertheless, Sanchez was determined to not only keep his job but also earn a bachelor's degree. After thirty-six months on probation, he applied to the University of Central Florida in Orlando. He'd already earned two associate's degrees from Valencia College in Orlando, graduating with straight A's and delivering the commencement address. He seemed like a shoo-in for acceptance—but the University of Central Florida didn't think so. The school's policy required that applicants with felony convictions who were still under community supervision (i.e., probation and parole) complete half of their probation sentence before their application could be considered.[15] Although a number of Valencia College faculty members supplied letters of support—and Sanchez's success story at Valencia gained media attention—his application for enrollment was denied.

But Sanchez challenged the decision, appealing to the court and asking that his total sentence be decreased to six years so that he would be able to enroll at the university (already having completed half the sentence). The judge not only agreed but terminated his probation completely because of his exemplary record over the previous three years. Sanchez entered the University of Central Florida's honors program not long afterward. He went on to study at Harvard Law School. Though he is enormously grateful for this triumph, Sanchez is quick to point out that very few people are able to access these kinds of opportunities. No one should have to be a top-of-the-class student to be considered worthy of an education, he says.

Sanchez's insight illustrates the ongoing problem of discrimination against formerly incarcerated people, but it also reveals a larger issue: on probation, you're marked as a person who, while not caged, should not be allowed to fully participate in the world at large. Instead, a smaller, confined world is mapped out for you, and you are compelled to stay within its bounds.

Law scholars Amanda Alexander and Reuben Jonathan Miller call those subject to the stringent conditions of probation and parole "carceral citizens"—people who live alongside free people but cannot legally access that freedom for themselves. Carceral citizens aren't simply "second-class citizens"—their discriminatory treatment doesn't result from their constitutional rights being cast aside. Instead, they just don't *have* the same rights as other people.[16]

Moreover, unlike their incarcerated counterparts, carceral citizens on the outside are not guaranteed their most basic needs, such as food and shelter. Like electronic monitoring, probation is lauded as "cost-effective": a way to control people without paying for their housing, meals, health care, and other survival needs. In addition to paying fees and fines, people on probation are tasked with funding their own survival while serving their sentences.

Adding to the financial hardships of probation, in more than a thousand court systems around the country, probation is run by private companies.[17] Florida began to allow privatized probation in the 1970s, followed by Tennessee and Missouri in 1989; now ten states allow the practice.[18] Although the prison system is made up of only about 8 percent private prisons, privatized probation has become increasingly common in the United States—sometimes to the benefit of the same corporations.[19] These companies require regular payments from probationers. Although people on probation are generally convicted of minor offenses they wouldn't otherwise be incarcerated for, failure to pay probation fees can land them in jail, further fueling the cycle of incarceration.

Municipalities see private probation as a cost-saving measure. Private companies often don't charge county governments; instead, people on probation are expected to pay—and that expectation becomes a condition of their probation. For example, Thomas Barrett, who stole a can of beer from a store, was charged a fine of $200 and sentenced to one year of probation. Barrett, who struggled with addiction, immediately spent a month in jail because he couldn't pay a "start-up fee" required by the probation company. Finally, his Alcoholics Anonymous sponsor footed the fee. Barrett was released—and promptly faced a slew of probation and monitoring fees, totaling $260 per month. His income, meanwhile, was $300 per month, acquired by selling his blood plasma. To save money, he tried going without food, but that weakened him too much to donate plasma, curbing his income further. Finally, Barrett's probation was revoked for nonpayment and he ended up back in jail.[20]

Longtime anti-prison activist Kay Whitlock sums up the guiding principles of "offender-funded probation": "This industry is built upon disdain for poor and low-income people, and a determination that their wretchedly limited resources should not only support the illusion of administration of justice but simultaneously provide private business owners and courts with new revenue. Moreover, it is a system that, presuming guilt, exerts greater punishment—escalating fees and sanctions, including incarceration—as time goes on. This is the meaning of 'widening the net.'"[21] Low-income people entrapped in offender-funded probation face an impossible choice: pay for their punishment or pay for their survival. As Barrett's story shows, often either choice paves a path back to jail.

"Rescuing" Sex Workers

On a Friday night in May 2013, Monica Jones, a Black trans woman and social work student at Arizona State University, was walking to a bar about a mile from her home in Phoenix when a man pulled his car over near her. After chatting, he offered her a ride to the bar, asking if she'd like to have drinks with him. Jones accepted. A minute after she'd gotten in the car, though, the conversation changed tone: the man propositioned her for sex—and asked how much it would cost.[22]

Jones was shocked—she thought the man was just going to give her a ride. She quickly realized the man was an undercover cop. She urged him to let her out of the car, but he refused, driving past the bar. Jones attempted to get out, but the door was locked.

Soon after, the officer handcuffed Jones, charging her with "manifesting prostitution." But instead of being taken to a police station, he brought Jones to a church. At that point, she knew she'd been caught up in a sting operation for Phoenix's Project ROSE: a prostitution "rescue" operation that purports to "save" sex workers by threatening them with jail. The project was a joint effort by the Phoenix Police Department, Catholic Charities, and the School of Social Work at Arizona State University. Project ROSE founder and ASU social work professor Dominique Roe-Sepowitz has described the project as a "prostitution diversion" program, which allowed sex workers to be diverted from the traditional criminal court system. But Project ROSE actually worked with police to target and arrest people who they assumed were sex workers. Twice a year, police conducted "rescue" operations—police sweeps specifically targeting people suspected of engaging in sex work, who were rounded up, handcuffed, and taken to a church.[23] There, without access to legal counsel or any type of due process, they were issued an ultimatum. Their first option was to accept their "rescue" and its requirements, including up to six months of day-long classes that vilified sex work and encouraged participants to find other ways of earning money. Project ROSE did not provide childcare, bus passes, or substitute income for that period. The second option for those rounded up by Project ROSE was to submit to the court process, which would include the threat of incarceration. Those who had previously been arrested for sex work, as well as those who had previously been through Project ROSE's program, were automatically deemed ineligible and sent through the traditional court system on prostitution charges, which carry a jail sentence of 15 days for a first conviction, 30 days for a second, and 60 days for a third. Any subsequent conviction is a felony with a mandatory minimum of 180 days in jail.[24]

Those who did qualify for Project ROSE's diversion program had to quit their jobs, even when they were the sole providers for their families, and many were left without the ability to care for their children. Their lives were upended in the name of being "saved."

Jones knew Project ROSE well. As an activist, she had been organizing a campaign against Project ROSE, posting warnings on Backpage .com and other online outlets about upcoming roundups and organizing a protest outside the church where Project ROSE was detaining sex workers. After the officer charged Jones with "manifesting prostitution," he brought her to the same church where she had protested less than two days earlier.

At the church, Jones and other women were confronted by prosecutors and more police. She insisted she hadn't done anything against the law—she'd been entrapped. The prosecutors threatened that she would be taken to jail, where she would have to stay over the weekend until court reopened on Monday. When she refused, police took her to one police station, then another. Jones continued to assert her innocence and insisted on her right to an attorney.

Ultimately, Jones's prior arrest disqualified her from admission to the rescue program. She then spent a year and a half going to court, fighting "manifesting prostitution" charges, and spreading the word about Project ROSE's entrapment practices along the way.

Like many alternatives, Project ROSE was a net widener: it ramped up police efforts to target sex workers, with the goal of bringing more people into its program, thus mandating more people to some sort of state control. Although Project ROSE is positioned as a "diversion" program—diverting people from jail—if it weren't for Project ROSE, some enrollees wouldn't have been in jail or under any form of supervision.

Project ROSE was suspended in 2015 because of a lack of "officer availability," according to those organizing the program. Advocates note that it's no coincidence that the program was put on hold after Jones publicized its harmful tactics.[25] However, as of May 2016, sixty-one similar rescue programs existed in more than twenty states. All are grounded in the assumption that those engaging in sex work must be forcibly "saved" from their work. In reality, these programs increase surveillance and incarceration while decreasing due process protections afforded to people in the criminal legal system.[26]

New York State has eleven human trafficking intervention courts, which exclusively focus on people arrested for prostitution. Despite their "trafficking" name, these courts adjudicate many people arrested for sex-work-related offenses, such as loitering. Many sex workers are not trafficked and fight against misconceptions that conflate sex workers with trafficking victims. Instead of jail time, defendants are mandated to a set number of sessions with a designated service provider—sessions that might take place far from their homes and require an enormous sacrifice of time, including unpaid time off work. These services include counseling, case management, crisis intervention, and referrals.[27] Their charges are dismissed only upon completion of these services.[28] While "services" may sound like a straightforwardly positive thing, these mandated programs are happening within the confines of the criminal legal system, and they come with strings attached. In some jurisdictions, such as Manhattan and the Bronx, a guilty plea is required to enroll in the services. Noncooperation with these mandated services could result in jail time.

Even when prostitution diversion programs portray themselves as an alternative to prison, they actually grow the reach of the prison nation. They heighten surveillance and policing by encouraging police to arrest people suspected of sex work in order to "save" them through diversion programs.[29] They place even more power in the hands of the criminal legal system by allowing it to be the dispenser of social services.[30] And, as Jones's story illustrates, they increase the risk of incarceration when those apprehended for sex work either are ineligible for or don't complete the program.[31] Diversion programs can also push participants into other arms of the prison nation. For example, in many states, "safe harbor" programs are used to divert youth from jail when they're arrested for sex work. But often this diversion results in young people being funneled into the child welfare system, ending up in foster homes.[32]

The odds are certainly stacked against those forced to choose between sex work diversion programs with onerous, expensive, and restrictive requirements or incarceration. Jones knew these odds well. After a year-and-a-half-long court fight and legal assistance from the ACLU, she was initially found guilty. She appealed, and in January 2016, citing an unfair trial, the judge vacated both her conviction and her thirty-day jail sentence.

Yet throughout the legal fight, Jones could barely leave the house. As a Black trans woman, Jones had already been a target of police harassment. But throughout her fight against Project ROSE, police targeted her even more; frequently when she walked down the street, she was stopped by the cops. In addition, her employment opportunities were—and continue to be—limited by her charge. She'd like to work with trans youth but can't do so because, although the conviction was vacated, the arrest remains on her record, barring her from many social work positions.

Jones is a carceral citizen, for whom certain opportunities are summarily forbidden and for whom regular invasions of privacy are considered legitimate. For a Black trans woman, the bounds of this form of citizenship are even narrower.

The cloud of carceral citizenship hangs over the whole range of court-mandated alternatives to incarceration, always reminding us that an "alternative" is fundamentally different from freedom.

Nevertheless, rescue programs like Project ROSE depict themselves as saviors, nobly pushing their help onto sex workers, regardless of whether this help is wanted. Project ROSE self-describes as a program that "provide[s] an opportunity for medical and social services, as well as an evidence-based intervention to assist in helping them exit the life of prostitution if they choose."[33] But the "choice" and "help" on offer at Project ROSE eerily echo the offerings of mandatory drug treatment centers, forced psychiatric hospitalizations, and ceaseless civil commitment sentences—except that there are no physical walls, just the threat of imprisonment.

Project ROSE illustrates, once again, that an alternative cannot be both "community-based" and coerced. The program did not physically lock people into a building; instead, it precipitated mass arrests—350 people were arrested through Project ROSE's partnership between 2011 and May 2013. These arrests forced hundreds of people (mostly women and people of color) to choose between entering a demeaning program or spending weeks, if not months, in jail.

Project ROSE is now closed, but in dozens of programs around the country, the project of "saving" sex workers through criminalization and coerced diversion programs is still very much alive.

The Oxymoron of Compulsory Treatment

Another increasingly popular form of forced "help" is court-ordered programs for people diagnosed with mental illness, otherwise known as assisted outpatient treatment (AOT). In these involuntary programs, a judge mandates that a person who has been diagnosed with a serious mental illness follow a specific treatment plan. These plans vary according to the state, the court, and the individual case. People placed in AOT programs remain at home (or "in the community") rather than being confined within a psychiatric institution.

Humanitarian arguments for mandatory outpatient treatment point to the reality that it's always preferable to provide community-based treatment instead of forcing people into incarceration-like institutions. Advocates across the political spectrum have embraced the "cost-saving" virtues of AOT, which is enforced under a civil—as opposed to criminal—court order.[34] AOT doesn't provide people with housing, meals, or other basic needs (costs the state must pay when someone is mandated to a hospital).

A spring 2017 *Psychiatric Times* article announced that "assisted outpatient treatment has finally entered the mainstream."[35] Indeed, 2016 saw a rush of federal funding for AOT programs, after a push led by congressional Republicans with Democratic support. The initiative was cheered on by the American Psychiatric Association, the National Alliance on Mental Illness, the International Association for Chiefs of Police, and the National Sheriffs' Association.

Forty-seven states and Washington, DC, have now authorized the use of AOT.[36] Compulsory outpatient treatment is quickly becoming a bipartisan darling.

However, as with so many elements of the prison industrial complex, it's not clear that AOT "works," even by the system's own standards. Research published in the medical journal *The Lancet* finds "no support" for compulsory outpatient treatment, and asserts that there is no justification for limiting a person's freedom in this way.[37] Meanwhile, a study of several programs in the United States and England concluded that mandated treatment produced no advantage over voluntary treatment in terms of "service use, social functioning or quality of life."[38]

If mandatory outpatient treatment does not, on the whole, improve people's quality of life or capacity to participate in the world around them, what does it do? Like probation, rescue programs, and other purportedly compassionate alternatives, it often functions as another method of social and racial control.

Sadie Ryanne Baker, the mental health provider who has also had significant experience as a service user, briefly worked for a mandatory outpatient program, established as her city's diversion program for people convicted of prostitution-related misdemeanors. Participants could avoid jail if they complied with a requirement to undergo life skills counseling and drug-tested clean for a certain period. Like Project ROSE, the program was initially operated by Catholic groups, but, says Baker, "the city realized that all of the trans women were choosing jail over the diversion program!"

The agency that Baker worked for, which largely employed people with some involvement in sex work, then made a decision to work with the courts to establish a diversion program specifically focused on trans women. However, it quickly became clear that diversion was still a half step away from incarceration at all times. If clients didn't attend classes mandated by the program, service providers were required to report them to the court, knowing they would be sent to jail; this was not a dynamic that was conducive to a trusting relationship.

"Yes, I'm trans and a former sex worker. I was explicit about my abolitionist politics with them, and that helped with our rapport a lot. But I was still another white lady who could send them to jail," Baker says.

Moreover, as Baker saw it, the "treatment" component of assisted outpatient treatment was being lost in the mix because people were not voluntarily coming to the program. Baker noted that counseling that isn't collaborative isn't actually counseling—and forcing someone into treatment under threat of jail is the opposite of collaborative. "From what I've seen and experienced, it will do more harm than good by compounding the client's sense of powerlessness, which is one of the primary causes and consequences of trauma," she says.

When mandatory psychiatric drugs are part of the treatment requirement, that sense of powerlessness is often intensified. Erick Fabris, a psychiatric confinement survivor and scholar, refers to forced psychiatric medication as "chemical incarceration."

"Though [court] orders are considered a less restrictive option than incarceration, over several weeks or months they achieve the same goals as incarceration," Fabris writes, noting that psychiatric drugs are often part of the required protocol for patients who are court-ordered to treatment. "Drugs control the nervous system to restrict bodily movement and communication with others, which are two basic conditions of incarceration."[39]

Similarly, in the periods of his adolescence when he was not in psychiatric confinement, Elliott Fukui was subject to other types of control, particularly in the form of required drugs. Over seven years, he was on a combination of over thirteen different medications. He doesn't have clear memories of his teen years, he says, because of all the medications he was taking without his informed consent.

There was no court order mandating Fukui's treatment, but state law allowed doctors to place him in involuntary commitment—and as a minor, he had very little say in extended treatment. When he turned eighteen, his parents tried to force him to let them maintain control over his medical treatment, but he refused, desperate to finally have autonomy.

The point is not that medication is never useful or that science is unhelpful when it comes to mental health—medication often serves life-saving purposes.[40] Instead, the question is one of consent, agency, and self-determination. The person who will be using the medication should make the decision whether to take it and under which circumstances. This is particularly important when it comes to heavy antipsychotic drugs that significantly alter the human experience for people diagnosed with "serious mental illness," often in ways that move them toward compliance with rigid social norms.

Now, control over medication may be assuming an even more invasive form: over the past several years, internet-based medication tracking technology has emerged. In 2017, the FDA approved the first digitally tracked pill, a psychiatric drug equipped with a digital sensor that tells doctors—or whoever is programmed to collect this information—whether the patient has taken it. The drug, Abilify (called "Abilify MyCite" in its tracked form), is classified as an antipsychotic and generally used to treat bipolar disorder and schizophrenia. Such medical tracking raises alarming questions about the encroachment of social control into our bodies and minds.

David M. Perry, a journalist who covers disability rights, has emphasized that the MyCite pill is "literally tracking whether someone has altered their innate modes of thought." Digitizing the surveillance of medication takes it to a new, more pervasive level: "MyCite makes it easier to demand that people surrender their privacy in order to conform to some artificial idea of normal."[41] Indeed, the use of such intimate forms of surveillance to determine whether someone has ingested a pill that will alter their thinking and behavior opens the door for a whole new level of Big Brother–style surveillance. Surveilling a person's intake of medication is a way of surveilling their thoughts and potential behaviors—and when used with a psychiatric medication, the implications are troubling.

When a person is court-mandated to psychiatric treatment, the question of what the patient wants is largely taken off the table from the very beginning. In these circumstances, the word "treatment" becomes almost meaningless.

One notable way that coercive treatment is harmful is the effect it has of making those subjected to compulsory treatment lose all trust in the medical system, even when it might be useful to them, because they've been so traumatized by the coercion they've been subjected to.[42] Many survivors of coercive treatment say that "mandatory treatment" is an oxymoron: real care, real healing cannot be forced. That's why the legal system—whose modus operandi is forcing people to do things—should never be the arbiter or purveyor of treatment.

Moreover, as the prison creeps outward into our homes and communities, it's time to take a hard look at the concept of "community-based" care. Compulsory outpatient programs are lauded for "keeping people in the community," but they rely on systematically imposing coercive control, raising questions about what "community" truly means.

When "treatment" is synonymous with "control," remaining controlled is often a prerequisite for remaining in the community, or outside of an institution. This can create a wall-less institution where physical freedom is based on adhering to restrictions and norms.

This is true not only for people diagnosed with a psychiatric disability but also for anyone saddled with drug-treatment mandates, or forced into a sex worker rescue program, or constrained by stifling probation restrictions "for their own good." In this way, even "inclusion in the community" can morph into yet another form of social control.

Restrictions at Every Turn: Life on the Sex Offender Registry

In 2009, Robert Suttle, a Black, gay, HIV-positive man from Shreveport, Louisiana, was convicted of "intentional exposure to AIDS virus" after ending a consensual relationship with a partner. The court never determined that he'd transmitted the virus to another person, but Suttle decided to accept a plea bargain for probation instead of risking a decade in prison. However, on his first day at the probation office, he learned that, under Louisiana law, he was required to register as a sex offender for the next fifteen years. He returned to court, where the judge acknowledged his mistake—on top of assigning Suttle to probation and the registry, he was also required to send Suttle to jail for six months.[43]

The worst punishment was being placed on the sex offender registry upon release, Suttle says. Part of the toll was financial: once out of jail, in addition to probation fees and fees to the sheriff's and police departments, Suttle had to pay for the expenses the state incurred by sending out yearly "community notifications"—cards distributed to all people living within a certain radius of his home, notifying his neighbors that he was a "sex offender." Suttle was also ordered to pay for ads in the local newspapers alerting people that a person convicted of a sex offense was living in their town, which displayed his name and photo. Suttle had lost his job as a court clerk because of his arrest, making it almost impossible to cover the costs of being on the registry.

The registry seemed designed to brand and shame Suttle at every turn. Once he registered, Suttle's driver's license proclaimed "SEX OFFENDER" in large red letters under his photo. He dreaded needing to go to the doctor because he'd have to show his ID. He also began to shy away from social situations, like going out to bars with friends.

Stranger restrictions emerged, too: for example, Suttle was not allowed to leave the house on Halloween, to wear a Halloween costume or even a hoodie, or to have a light on outside his house on the holiday.

Suttle was living "in the community," but being on the sex offender registry meant never feeling like an actual *member* of that community.

Registries exist in all fifty states and Washington, DC, as well as on the federal level. Those on the registry, though not incarcerated, are excluded from fully participating in society via stringent restrictions and regulations. The penalty for violating these rules is incarceration. One's presence on the registry is public. Registrants' communities are notified about their presence—so policing and surveillance aren't only enacted by the government but also encouraged among community members.

Overwhelming evidence shows that sex offender registries don't prevent sexual violence. In fact, an article in the *American Journal of Public Health* notes that registries "result in more harm than good," depriving people of their human rights and creating a false sense of protection in communities.[44] While most sexual violence is perpetrated by people known to the victim, registries rely on the myth of "stranger danger," pinning the bulk of the blame on shadowy figures lurking by the side of the road instead of acknowledging the pervasive sexual harm happening within people's homes and social circles.

Placing people on sex offender registries doesn't reduce recidivism or reoffense.[45] Some studies have shown that registries can actually fuel crime by blocking people from obtaining legal jobs and stable housing.[46]

Nevertheless, with the rise of "community-based" surveillance and social control, registries have been expanding over the past three decades. In 2018, the nationwide total of registrants topped 900,000 for the first time.[47] Predictably, the people most impacted are those already living on the margins. For example, Suttle's race and sexual orientation made him a much more likely target of the system.

During his two years on probation, Suttle had to secure permission to travel. On one instance, when he notified his probation officer that he'd be traveling out of state to visit someone he had reconnected with, the probation officer, without telling Suttle, called his friend and told him that Suttle was on the registry for HIV non-disclosure, thus informing him of his status.

"This person did not know," Suttle says. "I was planning on telling him myself in my own way." But the intrusion was par for the course: registrants are subject to frequent and often unpredictable invasions of privacy, and travel is a prime opening for those invasions.

Those on the registry who want to travel out of state often need to request permission. International travel is even more onerous—they must not only obtain permission but also submit to a special designation on their passports, alerting authorities (as well as anyone in the airport who happens to be standing nearby) of their status. The International Megan's Law, which was signed in February 2016 by Obama and went into effect in 2017 under Trump, compels the government to mark the passports of each person on the registry.[48] Though the Obama State Department pushed back on the bill, arguing that there was little evidence that people on the registry are traveling to engage in sex offenses abroad and that there are already avenues for the government to refuse to grant passports to people convicted of certain sex offenses, the law went through.

Since registering, Suttle has moved several times. He is now off probation, but his "sex offender" status continues to travel with him. In 2012, Suttle moved to Milford, Pennsylvania, to become assistant director of the newly established Sero Project, which aims to end HIV criminalization. Upon arrival, he headed to the state troopers' office to register in his new state. He was pleasantly surprised to find that no fees were required and that he didn't need to take steps toward a label for his driver's license. Maybe, he thought, things were different up north. But a few days later, the other shoe dropped.

His colleague was visited at home by the town's police chief. In his hand was a flyer with Suttle's face—and information about his sex offender status. The police were bringing flyers to every resident and business owner to notify them about Suttle, his conviction, and his status on the registry; each resident and business owner had to sign an acknowledgment that they had received the flyer. The flyer disclosed Suttle's identifying information—and his HIV status. Even the police chief himself didn't like this requirement, Suttle recalled, but he had to follow it.

Suttle was devastated. The town was very small, with virtually no Black people; he already stood out. And now the fact that he was living with HIV—and on the registry—was glaring public knowledge.

In an attempt to counter the effects of this mass disclosure, Suttle and a colleague wrote two articles, published in the local newspaper, providing the facts of Suttle's case and exploring the larger issue of HIV criminalization. Writing these gave Suttle a sense of empowerment. "We were able to tell the narrative, versus it being told by someone else," he says. "I had never done anything like that. I felt good about that."

Next, Suttle moved to Washington, DC, to live with his partner. Before the move, his partner notified the landlord of Suttle's status on the registry, attempting to preempt any background-related questions. However, the landlord was not willing to continue renting to him if Suttle moved in. His partner ended up having to leave the home he'd lived in for a decade.

Suttle's predicament recalls that of so many carceral citizens on probation, on parole, or simply living the consequences of an always-present criminal record—people who are restricted and marginalized not only by official laws but also by rampant, legal discrimination.

Housing restrictions create a formidable barrier to a livable life for many people on the registry. In thirty states and hundreds of municipalities, laws bar people labeled sex offenders from living within a certain proximity to schools, playgrounds, churches, and other places likely to attract groups of children.[49] As a result, options for housing range from limited to nonexistent. For example, in 2014, the city of Milwaukee banned a number of people on the registry from living within two thousand feet of a park, daycare center, or school. The ban left people on the registry with only fifty-five addresses where they could legally live in the city.[50] The number of homeless "sex offenders" multiplied by thirteen times in two years. In California, a similar law, passed in 2007, displaced 2,700 people, many of whom ended up on the streets.[51] In Miami-Dade County, about a quarter of people on the registry are homeless. But a 2018 county ordinance has even criminalized that: police are now authorized to arrest sex offenders for camping on public property. The law also prohibits them from seeking housing in homeless shelters.[52] In New York, nearly two hundred people were held in prison past their maximum release dates because they could not provide a residential address that complied with existing regulations.[53]

No research has shown that residency restrictions reduce sexual violence. In fact, study after study, including research from the Justice Department, has shown that they don't do anything good.[54] A Florida study noted that living near children had no effect on whether a person committed another sex offense.[55]

Regardless of the overwhelming evidence showing they don't prevent child sexual harm, registry restrictions often carry a special emphasis on proximity to children. Even Suttle, whose offense is considered "low risk" and has nothing to do with children, is prohibited from helping his sister by dropping off and picking up her kids from school.

For many registrants, these types of policies interfere with their ability to care for their own children. Some people on the registry are forcibly separated from their kids. Others are prohibited from taking them to the park or to school, from attending their events, or from being with them in any place other kids might "gather."

LeeAnn, a Florida mother who asked to be referred to by first name only, is on the sex offender registry for "sex trafficking." It's a conviction that arouses fear and concern—but LeeAnn's story, like many others, is complicated and nuanced. Before her arrest, she regularly engaged in sex work. At one point, she held another sex worker's money—$40—while the other woman was with a client. It's not an uncommon safety tactic among sex workers, but this time the other woman turned out to be fourteen years old. One year later, LeeAnn was arrested for trafficking and handed an eighty-seven-month prison sentence, five years on probation, and a spot on the registry.[56]

LeeAnn recalls her immediate reaction upon finding out, at her sentencing, that she'd be on the registry: "The first thought that really popped into my head was, 'I'm not going to be able to be around my daughter.' Because that's the first thing you think. 'I'm going to have to

register as a sex offender. I'm not going to be able to be around kids.' . . .
And that did it for me. I lost it. . . . I was crying so hard at sentencing
that when the judge asked me if I had anything to say, I couldn't even
speak, I was crying so hard."

LeeAnn is now out of prison and facing the challenges of the registry in combination with the restrictions of probation. For instance,
LeeAnn's sister, who cared for LeeAnn's daughter while she was incarcerated and with whom her daughter still lives, asked LeeAnn to help
out with her daughter's softball team. But LeeAnn's probation officer
refused to allow it—not because LeeAnn was any danger to kids but
because of the risk that one of the other parents might find out about
her registry status and cause a confrontation that could land LeeAnn
back in prison.

An Oppressive Legacy

As a sex worker and a working-class person, LeeAnn was a particular
target of the criminal legal system. And a combination of racism and
homophobia paved a path to the registry for Suttle—a harsh sentence
consistent with the racist legacy of the system that handed it down.
That legacy is often still enacted even when the state actors are Black
as well—Suttle notes that his prosecutor was a Black woman and his
judge was a Black man.

"There is a Confederate monument which stands right outside of the
[Louisiana] court where I was prosecuted," Suttle recounts. "If anything, that should tell you a lot about the history."

Along with racism and classism, homophobia is etched into the registry's history. Scholar and activist Erica Meiners explains that some of
the first "registries" kept were listings, in the 1930s and 1940s, of men
who slept with other men.[57]

In the 1980s, registries began to extend beyond individual police
departments. In the wake of a blitz of high-profile media coverage of

a few prominent cases of victimized white children, state-based registries began to emerge. Race also figured deeply into the construction of the registry. Meiners points out that no such measures were taken in response to a series of missing Black children in Atlanta, whose bodies were later found with evidence of sexual harm. But the media spotlight on the victimization of white youth sparked a wave of national anxiety that, Meiners says, "propelled legislation that people knew was fact-free," including state registries.

Embedded in the concept of the registries is the idea of "stranger danger"—the assumption that the typical sexual perpetrator is an unknown person who snatches children on the street. The image of that stranger, of course, is sculpted by preconceptions around race, sexuality, and class.

In reality, the main danger is not strangers. Children are most likely to be abused at home by family members or other people they know.[58] Ninety-three percent of sexual assaults on children involve family members or acquaintances of the child.[59]

State-based registries became the norm in the late 1980s and early 1990s (all states now have registries) and were followed by a national sex offender registry in 1994. In 2003, the Supreme Court affirmed that the addresses, names, and photographs of those labeled sex offenders could be posted on the internet, making the registries entirely public.[60] Additional bans and requirements, such as Obama's International Megan's Law, have piled on since.

While some efforts have been made to curb the burgeoning registries, they have had a limited impact. The registry continues to grow. In 2016, Texas was adding about twelve new names to its registry every day, despite minor "deregistration" efforts. Notably, the deregistration process cost registrants $2,900 each to undertake, so most never initiate it. The expansion led Texas's *Austin American-Statesman* newspaper to wryly note, "The registry is like a cemetery: Because many offenders are placed on it for a lifetime, or at least decades, it only expands in size."[61]

Growing, too, is the number of restrictions for people on the registry. Many social networks now completely ban people on the registry from having accounts, and individual registrants are often subjected to a host of mandates that make it difficult to use the internet at all—and, therefore, difficult to live a normal life.[62] Some are prohibited from any internet use, while others must effectively make everything they do online public.

LeeAnn hasn't had to give up the internet, but she is required to turn over all of her passwords to her probation officer. If she doesn't, she'll be charged with a third-degree felony. Also a third-degree felony: failure to disclose her status as a "sex offender" to a potential employer. She struggles with this notion that her label is her identity—a marker of who she really is—and that failing to inform someone of it is against the law.

When she first got out of prison, LeeAnn spent her days filling out job application after job application online with no results. Depression began to set in. Finally, she asked her dad for his own boss's phone number. She called and pleaded with him to let her work, saying she'd even be willing to start by working for free. He offered her a chance, and now she works construction, building swimming pools. The job is not ideal—the homes where she's working are usually not very accessible without a car, which she doesn't have, and it's very difficult to get to her legally mandated programs, which occur during the workday—but she is deeply grateful for the opportunity, one that many people on the registry will never have, thanks to disclosure requirements.

In a world of public registries, disclosure takes on new meanings. It's not just about employment: for anyone who takes a moment to check the internet, the status of those labeled sex offenders is easily accessible. This leads not only to discrimination but sometimes also to outright vigilante violence.

Roy Matagora, a sixty-two-year-old California man, opened his door one night in 2015 and was shot twice by a neighbor, who said he shot Matagora due to his "sex offender" status. In a lawsuit filed along with another targeted person, Matagora pointed out that his offense was committed decades ago, but the registry doesn't display that date.[63]

In 2013, Charles Parker, who was on the registry, and his wife, Gretchen Parker, were shot and stabbed to death by a couple claiming they'd been chosen by God to kill all people who'd committed sex offenses.[64] Thanks to the registry, with a couple of clicks, the names, photos, and addresses of potential victims in their area were right there.

At this point, the registries have become so sprawling and so dangerous that even some of the original advocates of sex offender registries are speaking out against them. Patty Wetterling is the mother of abducted child Jacob Wetterling, after whom the Jacob Wetterling Crimes Against Children and Sexually Violent Offender Registration Act—which first established a national sex offender registry—was named. She now condemns public registries. "What we really want is no more victims," Wetterling told American Public Media in 2017. "So, how can we get there? Locking them up forever, labeling them, and not allowing them community support doesn't work. I've turned 180 [degrees] from where I was."[65]

Moreover, it's not only registrants themselves who are labeled and cut off from community support. As Gretchen Parker's death shows, the registries punish many people beyond those who are registered—particularly registrants' families, who, according to sociologist Emily Horowitz, are often "humiliated, shunned, targeted and ruined (financially, socially and psychologically)."[66] The organization Women Against Registry notes that when someone is placed on a public registry, their family can face employment discrimination, violence, and harassment from neighbors and police, as well as displacement and homelessness. They also often experience an ongoing and pervasive sense of fear.[67]

Children whose parents are on the registry describe never being able to have their friends over, constant calls to the police by neighbors for no reason, and an inability to participate in activities. As one grandmother whose son is on the registry stated, "All this has taken a toll, more than anybody, on the children. They can't have friends."[68]

If LeeAnn, whose daughter lives with her sister, were to stay with her sister for more than five nights a month, her sister's house (and therefore, her daughter's current home) would need to be registered.

LeeAnn has tried to protect her daughter from the registry's damaging effects, but sometimes those effects crop up where she's not expecting them. For example, she's required to report any phone numbers associated with her name. When she bought her daughter and little brother cellphones for Christmas, she had to report those numbers to her probation officer as well.

Meanwhile, LeeAnn's treatment requirements are arduous. She's required to leave work frequently for meetings and individual therapy, and since she doesn't drive, her dad must leave work to drive her. The group sessions are held with other women on the registry, but because "none of the women are predators," the therapy is mostly focused on drug addiction—a type of treatment that LeeAnn no longer needs.

LeeAnn's situation raises the issue, again, of whether real therapy can be mandated: whether forcing someone to "get help" is any kind of help at all. If it is not, should the criminal legal system, a system built on force, even pretend to provide help? Or would real care—the kind of care that leads to healing and transformation—necessitate a complete break from any system of coercion?

It's important to note that LeeAnn and others languishing on probation, on the registry, in mandated outpatient treatment, in rescue programs, and in other forms of out-of-prison confinement are considered to be "in the community." This refrain raises the question of what it means to be part of a community. In the vocabulary of the prison nation, being "in the community" simply means not being in prison and occupying the same physical space as others. But community has a deeper meaning—a common bond, a sense of mutual care and responsibility—and it is this meaning that disintegrates in the face of constant surveillance and restrictions.

The prison nation often twists words to mean their opposite— "rehabilitation" becomes endless punishment, "corrections" becomes the maintenance of a destructive cycle. The current crop of alternatives to incarceration attempts to translate the word "community" as its opposite: isolation and confinement. It's crucial to push back against this linguistic manipulation—both in the culture and in our own minds. The prison nation, including non-prison manifestations such as probation and the registry, functions by breaking down connections between people and dismantling the building blocks of community. As we wade through the quagmire of alternatives to incarceration, we must always keep this truth in our sights: rehabilitation does not come via punishment. And confinement is no route to community.

4

POLICING PARENTHOOD

I called for help and they turned it against me.

—Angela Willard, domestic violence survivor
and mother of seven, whose kids were taken by the
Department of Human Services

IN THE NAME OF PROTECTING, HELPING, OR EVEN "SAVING" CHILDREN, the prison industrial complex has invaded family life. This invasion is happening via the expansion of locked-down mother-baby institutions, the increasing reliance on foster care, and the expansion of mandated reporting. As these practices intensify, the dual systems of criminalization and child welfare are pulling more and more families into their webs of surveillance and confinement and, in many cases, tearing them apart.

In locked-down mother-baby institutions, mothers are confined along with their young children and must attend parenting classes where they receive instruction on child development and child-rearing practices. Even if their charges have nothing to do with the ways in which they parent their children, mothers are required to take these classes. These institutions have been promoted as a compassionate alternative to standard prisons that address the very real problem of family separation wrought by the prison system. In reality, however, this supposed solution amounts to more incarceration: to "solve" the issue of incarcerated moms being separated from their babies, they're simply locking up the babies, too.

A similar principle governs the rapidly expanding foster care system. While foster care is not an alternative to prison, it is an expansion of a control-based system that's entangled with the prison industrial complex. It has grown in recent years under the guise of rescuing victimized children and helping marginalized parents when someone reports suspected neglect or abuse. But instead of offering material resources and support to vulnerable families, foster care punishes parents by taking away their children. At the same time, child welfare agencies promote the expansion of mandatory reporting laws, which require ever-broader groups of people to report parents' minor infractions (even common practices such as children sharing a bed), as an intervention that's universally helpful for children. In reality, though, these function as a form of "kinder, gentler" policing—subjecting poor and marginalized families to even more intensive surveillance and putting them at a greater risk of being separated.

These efforts to surveil and control motherhood and caregiving are punitive systems that dig us deeper into the trenches of the prison nation. Like prisons, they grew from inherently racist roots, operating on the premise that women of color, particularly Black mothers, as well as women who are poor, disabled, or struggling with substance use, are unfit parents and that their children would be better off in more affluent white households. These notions continue in today's systems of parenting surveillance and control, which disproportionately impact families headed by mothers of color, mothers in poverty, and disabled mothers. Foster care and related systems are an often-ignored path by which we see the prison nation bleeding into other realms of public life by assuming different forms, serving expanded purposes, and targeting new and ever-growing populations—under the guise of "care."

Imprisoning Families

Tabitha Minson has a year and a half left on her sentence with the Illinois Department of Corrections. She is serving it alongside her one-year-old daughter.[1]

But Minson is not in prison—or at least, she's not in a place *called* prison. She lives in a residential treatment center in Chicago for women with drug addictions. The center is not part of the prison system. Many of the patients have not been arrested or convicted, but the center also partners with the Department of Corrections to allow certain mothers with nonviolent drug convictions to spend the last two years of their prison sentences with their children.

Minson was six weeks pregnant when she was arrested. At first she feared it would be years before she'd be able to see her baby again. Her conviction on drug charges led to a three-year prison sentence, which would have caused her to miss her daughter's entire infancy and toddlerhood—first smiles, first words, first steps.

Searching for a way to stay with her daughter, Minson applied to and was accepted to Illinois's prison nursery program. There are seven prison nurseries across the country, allowing women who give birth while imprisoned to keep their babies for the first twelve to twenty-four months. Expectant mothers must meet certain criteria, which vary state by state. In Illinois, a woman is ineligible for the eight-bed nursery if she has a conviction for a violent crime or if a background investigation reveals past child welfare involvement.

For Minson, being in the prison nursery meant being subject to all of the prison's rules and regulations. She had to give birth with only a prison guard watching, rather than family members holding her hand or encouraging her to push. Still, instead of being separated hours after birth, Minson was able to take her baby "home"—though home was inside a prison.

Even in the nursery program, Minson's three-year prison sentence would have meant being separated from her daughter for the last year. And so, after her daughter's birth, she applied to the treatment center in Chicago. When her daughter was nine months old, her application was approved and the two transferred from the prison nursery to the community alternative. Minson was grateful to be able to keep her daughter with her for the rest of her sentence, and, at least in theory, to be raising her outside of prison walls.

But for the first three months at the treatment center, Minson and her child were not allowed to leave the building at all. After that, she was given a curfew, but that didn't mean she could leave at will within the allowed hours. Each week she had to fill out an activity sheet and obtain permission from the center's authorities, clearing her destinations with them and returning promptly at designated times. Communication in the center was—and continues to be—drastically limited. Residents can have phones but must turn them in to staff at night. They're not allowed computers or tablets at all.

Perhaps the worst aspect of the center is that it doesn't address Minson's most pressing need: to parent all of her children. Although her baby lives with her, she's still separated from her two older children, ages ten and twelve: the cutoff for kids at the facility is age five. Minson's baby is separated from her siblings, and Minson's family is still broken up. In other words, the prison alternative looks an awful lot like a prison.

The center where Minson is confined is part of the country's growing number of residential alternatives to prison specifically geared toward mothers of young children. In contrast with the seven prison nursery programs located inside women's prisons, these institutions are located on the outside. While the programs might partner with the state to serve as non-prison alternatives for select mothers, and may sometimes operate similarly to incarceration, they are not technically called prisons.

These mother-child programs are multiplying, popping up in new states each year—eleven states and the federal government have already adopted them.[2] Their rise is the result of prison reform efforts—sustained advocacy on behalf of women in prison, most of whom are parents to minor children and are separated from their kids upon their incarceration. In some cases, this advocacy has resulted in the reestablishment of prison nurseries that allow babies to stay with their mothers behind bars, essentially incarcerating more people (babies) for the sake of a humanitarian "alternative." Prison nursery programs are not new: they've been around since the nineteenth century, though nearly all disappeared during the 1970s and 1980s because of rising costs as well as concerns about security, management, and child welfare.[3] In the 1990s, as the female prison population ballooned, several states established new ones, albeit with stringent criteria and restrictions, to address the growing numbers of women who were separated from their newborns within seventy-two hours after giving birth.

What's newer are the community-based institutions, such as the one that Minson and her daughter entered. These are generally located within cities, not inside prisons, and the people locked within are sometimes granted limited "movement": restricted opportunities to venture beyond the building.

Interest in these types of community-based alternatives has grown as women's incarceration continues to skyrocket and the rising number of children affected by parental incarceration gains more attention. With this increase comes calls for reforms aimed specifically at mothers and children. These range from demands for more prison nurseries to proposals for non-prison alternatives, such as the center where Minson and her daughter live.[4] Advocates for "community-based" alternatives like Minson's center say they are serving as supportive services for mothers. But they're still characterized by confinement and control, expanding such control into the community. Many of their rules and restrictions match those found within the prisons to which they are presented as alternatives.

Lynne Haney, a sociologist at New York University, conducted an extensive study on these community-based facilities, which she dubbed "mother-child prisons." Haney examined one such facility, which, though located in the community, operated under prison-like rules. Residents had to adhere to strict schedules determined by staff. They were subject to regular pat-downs and searches. As in prison, lockdowns—in which mothers and children were not allowed to leave their rooms—were a regular occurrence.

Even the residents' parenting was subject to strict surveillance. Mothers were expected to follow the center's rules for how to relate to their children, when and where they were allowed to spend time together, and when (or if) they were allowed privacy away from the watchful eyes of guards and counselors.[5] Restrictions and rules intruded into even the minutiae of parenting, such as what snacks moms could give their kids and what TV shows they allowed them to watch.

Meanwhile, the actual issues that make parenting especially difficult for most women who end up incarcerated—namely, poverty and lack of access to resources—remained entirely unaddressed. Instead, the institution framed the problem as the mothers themselves, and the solution as tight monitoring, policing, and confinement.

This is a pattern that repeats itself throughout the realm of parenting-oriented reforms: problems that stem from socioeconomic injustice, such as substandard housing conditions or lack of childcare, are portrayed as the result of individual bad parenting. As such, the institutions that result, like family-based prison alternatives, often prioritize *controlling* mothers rather than helping them meet their basic needs, such as housing, income, childcare, and health care.

Rules for parents at these alternative institutions are strictly enforced, and the stakes for compliance are high. Failure to follow these rules can lead to the very separation that mothers had tried to avoid in the first place. For example, at the Miami-based Families in Transition program, one of the first such centers, most residents are already involved with child protective services and therefore at risk of losing custody of their children. Families in Transition, like the facility Haney describes and the center where Minson stays, promotes itself as a reunification program, allowing mothers and children to remain together. However, if residents do not maintain complete abstinence from substances, their Families in Transition therapist often recommends to a judge that their children be sent to foster care. A mental illness diagnosis can also prompt such a recommendation.[6]

As is the case with electronic monitoring, mandated psychiatric treatment, locked-down drug rehabilitation centers, and intensive probation programs, many mother-child institutions operate through prison logic: violate a certain set of norms and punishment comes quickly. Though the institutions are portrayed as rehabilitative alternatives, mothers often aren't offered key rehabilitation services, such as navigating regaining custody of other children, locating safe childcare options, or finding affordable long-term housing. People incarcerated in mother-child programs are still entirely subject to the dictates of the authorities that govern their daily lives. Control and punishment remain the go-to response to problems. When community alternatives look like prison, their expansion is actually a reinforcement of the prison industrial complex.

Meanwhile, for Minson, life at the center has not given her the chance to devote herself to parenting her infant daughter to the best of her ability. As a resident in the treatment center, she is required to attend recovery groups and parenting classes for several hours each day. During this time, her child is placed in the care of other residents—including residents who aren't ready or willing to be working in childcare but are mandated to work childcare shifts on a rotating schedule. Minson is frustrated by having to leave her child in the care of another person who is being forced to watch multiple kids while she is, separately, being "taught" how to parent, handed abstract information about parenting philosophies, and led through hypothetical discussions about disciplinary practices.

By the center's logic, it's a double whammy of helpfulness for mothers: mandatory treatment is taking place and, simultaneously, the residents who are assigned to childcare duties are doing community service—in other words, unpaid work. But Minson says caring for her own child would have been more helpful to developing her own agency and her recovery.

Some residents refer to alternatives like the center as "prison lite": these programs are still incarceration, but at least they're a little *nicer*. But Minson isn't so sure about that. "I was thrown into a toxic environment," she says of her transfer to the center. Previously, in the prison nursery, she and her newborn were sequestered in a program where all participants were prescreened and eager to remain in the program. In contrast, some of the center's residents are not enthusiastic about being in the program and have given Minson and others a hard time about their commitment to their own recovery, a toxicity she never encountered in the prison nursery. Minson also fears for her child's physical safety in the treatment center, which is even more poorly maintained than the prison. The center has windows that don't open, elevators that aren't maintained, and malfunctioning showers. For months, Minson and her toddler couldn't take hot showers. "There's no doubt in my mind that the prison was a safer environment for me and my child," she says.

Beyond comparisons of the prison nursery and the center, though, Minson wonders why it was assumed that she needed to be confined in the first place. Each of her arrests stemmed from her drug addiction, but she had never been offered an option that prioritized real treatment—cost-free, in the community, and with the freedom to parent all of her children—over confinement. Instead, she says, "anytime I've gotten into trouble legally, it's been resolved by being locked up. It's always, 'Okay, you're going to do time.'"

Indeed, few family reunification programs, from prison nurseries to community-based mother-child centers, challenge the notion that these mothers must be placed in a locked institution. Reforms aimed at keeping families together and keeping children safe are usually predicated on the assumption that the way to ensure safety for families and children is by controlling parents.

As Dorothy Roberts, law professor and author of *Shattered Bonds: The Color of Child Welfare,* puts it, the goal of such institutions is still to "regulate, monitor, and punish the parent. Underlying all of this is blame—blaming parents for the hardships their children face rather than deal with the structural inequality. . . . The state may be expanding who comes into the system and how long they're there, because now that you've got a less harsh-seeming punishment, it may be easier to bring more people into the system," she says.[7] It's the same danger that allowed for the expansion of the prison itself: make an institution look good enough—helpful enough—and it becomes acceptable to funnel more and more people through its doors. Mother-baby programs such as the center where Minson was sent become an excuse to normalize the logic of prisons in community and family life. And when the lines between helpful and harmful institutions are blurred, there are no limits to the ways in which people can be pulled into their clutches.

The "Child Kidnapping System" as the New Jane Crow

One doesn't need to be enmeshed in the criminal punishment system to be surveilled, confined, and policed as a mother or caregiver. Beyond the walls of prisons and prison-like institutions, extensions of the prison industrial complex specifically geared toward parenting abound—often cloaked in the guise of helping.

Mariame Kaba aptly terms foster care the "child kidnapping system"—a set of practices that break apart families and punish marginalized people, much like the prison system itself.[8] That's a term that rings true in the case of Angela Willard, a Pennsylvania mother of seven.[9] Willard is white, but she lives below the poverty line and has a serious medical condition, two strikes that have been used against her when she has sought help. In 2012, Willard married a man who was on the sex offender registry. Willard signed a "spousal agreement" vowing never to leave her children unsupervised with her husband. But despite her precautions, the calls to the Department of Human Services (DHS, Pennsylvania's child protective services agency) began. The calls were from neighbors who'd seen her husband's name and address on the sex offender registry and wanted him out of the community. Sometimes someone would call simply because they were upset with Willard's family for another reason. Disputes between neighbors became an opportunity for vindictive attempts to get Willard's children taken away from her. DHS visited Willard's house seven times over the next four years in response to these calls; it ruled every complaint "unfounded."

However, these visits meant that DHS caseworkers were familiar with Willard's home when they arrived for a different reason in April 2016. This time, they were responding to a call regarding Willard herself.

Willard's husband had turned abusive the previous year, beating her regularly and eventually pushing her thirteen-year-old son when he tried to intervene. So Willard called Women Against Abuse, a large Philadelphia nonprofit that provides services to domestic violence survivors.

The counselors at Women Against Abuse told Willard they could temporarily arrange for shelter for her and two of her four younger children. (By then, her three oldest children were adults and living elsewhere.) Willard had no one else to care for her other two children, so she decided to stay put with all of her children and plan an escape on her own. Eleven days later, DHS was at her door, threatening to take her children.

This is because Women Against Abuse is a mandated reporter, meaning that employees are required to notify DHS if they suspect a child is in an abusive situation. When Willard didn't leave her husband, the agency informed DHS about her disclosure of domestic violence. The agency that was supposed to help Willard instead surveilled her because it was mandated to do so. Now DHS had arrived to take away her children.

Child protective service agencies and the foster care system exert social control over hundreds of thousands of families across the United States, and these numbers are growing. A 2018 report by the Department of Health and Human Services found a 10 percent rise in children in foster care nationwide—from 397,600 in 2012 to 437,500 in 2016.[10] Meanwhile, the complete termination of parental rights has also risen precipitously, increasing by about 60 percent from 2010 to 2016.[11] This dramatic rise in both foster care and parental rights termination targets low-income parents of color, particularly Black and Native parents. Advocates have dubbed this phenomenon "the new Jane Crow" given that the criminalization of parenting falls largely upon mothers of color, particularly low-income Black mothers.[12]

Contrary to popular opinion, most of the time, when children are removed from the home, it's not because of abuse; the allegation is usually neglect. Neglect is an allegation that encompasses a range of problems—in addition to leaving a child alone for periods of time, it can refer to homelessness or substandard housing, a lack of weather-appropriate or clean clothing, and chronic latenesses or absences from school. Many of these problems stem from poverty and lack of adequate access to housing, food, and other resources rather than parental malice or indifference.[13]

The swelling of the foster care system is another case in which reforms are driving the expansion of surveillance and punishment. The net is widening—and more and more families are getting caught in it—in part because of a supposedly more compassionate approach to child welfare. Roberts, who has studied the issue for nearly twenty years, has noted this change in child welfare approaches. Children may come across the authorities' radar for a host of reasons, such as a neighbor calling the police to report the scent of marijuana in the hallway, school officials calling child protective services after noticing a student's continual absence, or a bystander calling in to report a child seemingly left alone in a playground. Not all complaints warrant removing a child from their family, but in response to increased scrutiny over their actions, child welfare officials are increasingly dividing children into "low-risk" and "high-risk" groups. "Low-risk" youth are not considered to be in immediate danger and are generally not removed from the home right away. Instead, their families are given requirements to fulfill and their actions are supervised by child services. In practice, this means that many "low-risk" families who previously would never have fallen under state surveillance are now swept into the net. Then, if the social workers surveilling their homes discover any infraction, their children are more likely to be placed in foster care.[14]

Although the words "foster" and "care" convey supportiveness and nurturing, in practice the system often doesn't fit these descriptors. Foster care shatters the lives of both adults and children: as reported by the National Coalition for Child Protection Reform, a coalition of child welfare professionals working to reform the child welfare system, people who have been in foster care have significantly higher rates of post-traumatic stress disorder than war veterans, and on average, even children who have been abused or neglected have fared better when they've remained in their homes than when they've been placed in foster care.[15] Meanwhile, parents are often left defenseless in the face of a system that penalizes them and their children for forces beyond their control, such as poverty, homelessness, and domestic violence.

This brings us back to Angela Willard, who called a social service agency for help—and ended up with DHS at her door. DHS insisted that Willard's children be removed from the home. Wanting to ensure their safety, Willard agreed to have the caseworkers take her four children to the home of her twenty-five-year-old daughter, who was living in another county. But the next day, caseworkers called Willard and told her she wouldn't get her children back until she "got safe." However, she says, "They didn't tell me where to get safe *at*. I had no place to go."

She waited a couple of days to make a move. One night, while her husband was sleeping, Willard grabbed some money, a backpack, and her children's computer and left the house, not knowing where she was headed.

For a while, the answer was nowhere. Willard became homeless, and has been ever since. She also became severely ill: born with hypertropic cardiomyopathy, a serious heart condition, Willard had health issues that were exacerbated by her devastating circumstances. Not long after leaving home, she had a heart attack and stroke and was admitted to the hospital. To add insult to injury, DHS added her health to its list of reasons Willard was unfit to care for her children.

Willard's poverty proved to be another strike against her. When her children were taken away, she was waiting to be approved for social security payments based on her disability. As she attempted to get her children back from DHS custody, she was told that her lack of income was an additional reason she was considered unfit. For her, the unfairness of the system was palpable: although those who care for others' children in foster care and kinship care are given state money to do so, no one ever offered her financial support to care for her own children.

In other words, child welfare officials were paying her daughter to care for Willard's four children while keeping them separated from Willard for being poor.

Willard tried hard to take DHS's mandate to "get safe" to heart. However, all forms of help came with mandates, surveillance, and control. Mirroring police tactics, DHS caseworkers tracked Willard's every parenting move and punished her for her poverty, poor health, and status as an abuse survivor. Rather than helping her find housing when she was sleeping on a bus, DHS gave her a long list of demands to meet in order to get her children back.

Desperate for reunification, Willard followed the agency's instructions to a T. She took a slew of required classes that filled her days. Even after a heart attack and a stroke, she never missed a class, committed to doing whatever it took to get her children back.

Willard was too ill to hold a job, which, she says, gave her one advantage: were she working, she never would be able to meet all of DHS's mandates. Eventually she began to receive disability checks due to her heart condition, giving her money to live on. But this reality doesn't bode well for most mothers and caregivers, who must work in order to survive and have any hope of reuniting with their kids.

Among the classes that DHS mandates to regain custody are domestic violence workshops, parenting classes, and anger management courses. Child protective services' parenting classes, as well as the other classes mandated on the path to reunification, tend to follow an assumption that people have lost their children because of individual failings, not because of poverty, racism, and victimization.

Willard put in the work and checked all the boxes to "learn" how to be a good parent—but without help securing basic needs like housing, she still didn't meet DHS's definition of "fit."

Willard now lives at a city homeless shelter. Despite her efforts, she still doesn't have custody of her children; instead, she is allowed only two hours a week of supervised visits. A judge has told her that even though she's met the requirements for reunification in terms of classes, visits and other steps, she must also pass a parent capacity test. Willard is worried about the test. She's had serious problems with her eyesight since her stroke, and the test's written portion consists of 564 questions on a computer screen. She asked DHS whether accommodations could be made for her vision issues—like arranging for someone to read the questions to her. The answer was no. The parent capacity test determines whether Willard will get her children back, but no one will help her see the computer.

"The system is so messed up," she says. "They set you up to fail."

Willard is tired. She has spent nearly two years jumping through the system's hoops, submitting to its surveillance, meeting its mandates. But all of the measures that were supposedly taken for her own good—or for the good of her children—have gotten her nowhere. She's worried about her health, scared that her time is running out. She fears that she could die any day—and is heartbroken that she's still only allowed two hours a week with her children.

Willard's life now is built around meeting DHS's requirements—as well as the requirements of the shelter, which has its own set of restrictions and surveillance mechanisms: she can't bring in food, she must be in bed by 10:00 p.m., she can't get out of bed before 7:00 a.m., she must do chores on Saturdays regardless of her health.

The only way to get her kids back is to have adequate housing, and to qualify for housing assistance, she needs to stay in the shelter. This means that Willard must remain semi-confined in the shelter, waiting for DHS's next move. She's going to keep trying: she'll take the capacity test, whether or not she's able to read the words on the screen. But she can't help wondering whether, after that, yet another barrier will be set in front of her. Everything in her life revolves around regaining custody. "I love my kids," she says, crying, "and I want them back."

Like an increasing number of mothers and caregivers—overwhelmingly mothers of color, mothers who are living in poverty or struggling with substance use, and disabled mothers—Willard has been trapped in a system that insists it is helping and supporting her and her children. The system is providing classes; its messengers and enforcers are called "caseworkers" and "social workers," not police; its requirements, and even the title of its department, are labeled "services." Yet foster care and child services are deeply entangled with the prison industrial complex and the punishment paradigm more broadly.

The children of incarcerated parents are provided with the "service" of being shunted into foster care when their parents are locked up. Eight to 10 percent of incarcerated mothers have children in foster care; this does not include children who are in kinship foster care arrangements, where the state places them with other family members.[16]

For children, foster care often plays out like punishment: not only are they torn from their own families, they're frequently placed in dangerous situations outside the home. A 2017 Senate Finance Committee investigation found that children in the care of the MENTOR Network, one of the United States' largest foster care agencies, were dying at high rates. "The very agencies charged with and paid to keep foster children safe too often failed to provide even the most basic protections, or to take steps to prevent the occurrence of tragedies," charged the committee.[17] The committee's conclusions pointed to the problems with private foster care agencies, but the issue is clearly broader than that. Research in numerous states over the past two decades has found that children in foster care experience much higher rates of sexual abuse and physical abuse than children who have not been taken from their homes.[18]

Foster care also serves as a pipeline to prison, particularly for Black children, who are targeted by both systems.[19] Foster youth grow up to become mired in the criminal punishment system in vastly disproportionate numbers. A University of Chicago study showed the majority of former foster youth (43 percent of women and 74 percent of men) surveyed had been incarcerated by age twenty-six.[20] In California, 14 percent of people in the state's prisons had spent time in foster care.[21] In Massachusetts, 72 percent of youth in the juvenile justice system had been involved with child protective services.[22] In other words, these structures not only are interlinked but also feed each other.

While police have many vocal critics, social workers are almost universally portrayed as a benevolent force in society. In reality, however, the child welfare system replicates the practices of policing and prisons. "The social workers who go and work for the child welfare system are themselves being turned into kinder, gentler cops," says Kaba. When DHS knocked on Willard's door without notice, took her children, tracked and surveilled her actions, and repeatedly penalized her poverty and disability without providing material support, it was meting out punishment in the name of safety. This is the logic that drives policing and prisons, and that has now expanded to social workers, too.

Punishment Instead of Support

Child welfare agencies and their caseworkers, who should be—and often want to be—offering support to parents and families, are instead tasked with controlling and even punishing them. Federal and state governments have dramatically slashed the social safety net over the past few decades, resulting in less and less support available for families living in poverty. Since the enactment of the 1996 federal welfare law—which imposed work mandates, time limits, and other restrictions on support for poor families—poverty has increased considerably among children and those living in women-headed households.[23] Between 1995 and 2011, the number of families with kids who lived on less than $2 per person per day more than doubled, from 636,000 to approximately 1.65 million.[24] In 2018, 41 percent of all U.S. children under 18 were low-income.[25] Meanwhile, the federal government spends nearly $7 billion annually on foster care and adoption; in comparison, it spends $546 million on child abuse prevention and family preservation.[26] This disintegration of supportive programs has paralleled both the rise of mass incarceration and the increase in foster care numbers. In all of these realms, we've seen a shift from somewhat supportive to largely punitive responses to poverty and victimization, in which social workers mete out consequences instead of providing access to resources.

The way that requirements are heaped onto parents is consistent with the current punitive model for social services, in which everything comes down to personal responsibility. Instead of addressing parents' lack of resources, for example, it's assumed that the problem lies with some "pathology" of the parent. Parents who are sucked into the child welfare system are almost always mandated to attend classes, even when the problem that led to their involvement was entirely driven by poverty. It is useful to consider how this relates to both psychiatric diagnoses—which can lead to punitively mandated treatment—and criminal charges, which can lead to incarceration. Instead of providing actual support, each of these systems enacts new forms of control and calls them support.

There's a clear correlation between increases in foster care placements and decreases in access to social welfare programs like food and housing aid. When more people receive Temporary Assistance for Needy Families benefits, child maltreatment cases decrease. When benefits are cut, cases increase. For example, states that restricted welfare benefits to less than sixty months experienced an increase in documented child maltreatment victims of 34.4 percent and in neglect victims of 37.3 percent. In states that implemented policies that took away people's welfare benefits if they didn't meet work requirements, foster care placements and documented abuse and neglect victims increased by 12 to 23 percent. As Republican politicians have made concerted efforts to cut welfare programs in states such as Kansas,

Georgia, and Arizona, foster care caseloads have swelled.[27] Yet the system remains fixated on the notion that meting out consequences for parents is the answer to reports of child maltreatment.

A Legacy of Slavery and Genocide

Like the prison industrial complex more broadly, foster care disproportionately impacts people of color, particularly Black people. Twenty-three percent of foster youth in 2015 were Black, although Black children make up only 14 percent of the population.[28] In some states, these numbers are more drastic: in California in 2013, Black children made up nearly a quarter of those in foster care, although they represented just 5.7 percent of the total child population of the state.[29] It's not merely a question of disproportion. Just as mass incarceration was built to target communities of color, particularly Black communities, the current foster care system was constructed to target Black and Indigenous families, especially mothers.

We can see how the child welfare system—like the prison system—evolved into a system of punishment as its recipients became less white. At least on paper, the prison system emphasized redemption and rehabilitation before the 1970s, when the majority of its inhabitants were white. Similarly, when white children were the primary ones in the child welfare system, the system—and its actors—placed more emphasis on supporting families in their current living situations. But as the child welfare system increasingly focused on Black families—a shift paralleling the mass incarceration of Black people—it became increasingly focused on shunting children out of their homes.[30]

At the same time, cultural assumptions about Black women—vestiges from the time of slavery—fuel and normalize the idea that taking Black children away from their mothers is in everyone's best interest. As Mariame Kaba and others have theorized, following the legacy of slavery, the state does not understand Black women as real, loving mothers, so the systems of child services and foster care can step in with claims of the need to provide children with "loving homes."

The legacy of Indigenous genocide also plays out through foster care. Throughout colonization, the U.S. government and white settlers aimed to assimilate Native youth as a strategy to eliminate Native communities. In the early nineteenth century, the federal government began funding initiatives to remove Native children from their communities and place them with white missionaries.[31] These placements grew into a large-scale network of residential schools (run first by missionaries and then by the government) in which Native children were separated from their families and cultures and forcibly taught behaviors, practices, trades, and lifestyles of the dominant culture. This violence was framed as a form of help—saving Native youth by "civilizing" them.

By the 1970s, 17 percent of Native children were being torn from their families to attend Bureau of Indian Affairs boarding schools.[32] Youth were removed from their homes on the grounds that their parents had proven themselves "unfit"—not because of physical abuse but because of "neglect." Beyond the issue of poverty (Native people remain the poorest population in the United States), authorities often pointed to the issue of Native parents leaving their children in the care of relatives for an extended period of time—a common practice in many Native communities that did not jibe with the nuclear-family-centric model of white U.S. culture.[33]

Thanks to the long-term efforts of Native activists, particularly Native women, the residential school system was eroded, and in 1978 parents finally won the right to refuse their children's placement in residential schools.[34] By that point, however, the foster care system had taken off, and Indigenous children were some of its prime targets. They continue to be: national statistics for Native children are even less available than for Black children, but we can glean some insight from state data. In South Dakota, where Native children made up only

15 percent of the state's children, nearly half of all children in foster care in 2015 were Native.[35] The majority of foster youth in Alaska are Native, even though Native children make up just 18 percent of children in the state.[36]

Mothers and caregivers with disabilities are also singled out for child services' help. Willard's medical condition was used against her in court, and she's certainly not alone. Two-thirds of state dependency statutes allow judges to declare a parent "unfit" simply based on their disability.[37] For parents with psychiatric disabilities, the rates are sky-high, with removal rates in child custody cases reaching 70 to 80 percent. Such parents are often grappling with other systems involving surveillance and control, such as mandated treatment, monitoring, or incarceration.

As the child welfare system grows, some white children (overwhelmingly poor ones, like Willard's kids) are also pulled into its clutches. Nowadays, white children make up 51 percent of the U.S. population and approximately 43 percent of children in foster care.[38] In Alabama alone, 479 women were charged with "pregnancy-related exposure to drugs" between 2006 and 2015; 75 percent of them were white.[39] Such prosecution was made possible by a punitive approach that was created during the 1980s and 1990s to target Black women who used crack. In other words, once built, the apparatus simply expands to sweep more families into its net.

Mandated Reporting
and the Surveillance of Motherhood

The criminal punishment, child welfare, and mandated "treatment" systems are not only interlinked; they are also overlapping. Those who are targeted by one system are much more likely to be targeted by others, perpetuating the cycle.

Willard's nightmare transpired for many reasons, but it began with a social service agency reporting her to DHS. The nonprofit organization that she called for help in the midst of rampant domestic violence was—like nearly all social service providers—a mandated reporter. This meant that if its employees suspect a child is being abused or neglected, they are required to alert DHS. Willard, in asking for help, disclosed that domestic violence was occurring in her home, triggering a social worker to ring the alarm bell.

In practice, mandated reporters make exceptions to their mandates on a regular basis. For example, white middle-class and wealthy people who share with their doctors or therapists that they use drugs or are experiencing domestic violence often need not worry that DHS will show up on their doorstep to take away their kids. But as Malcolm X pointed out half a century ago, people who receive public aid or seek support from service organizations are especially vulnerable: their lives are an open book for state scrutiny, particularly if they belong to another marginalized group.

Just as people who are mandated to psychiatric treatment often develop a deep distrust toward doctors and medical staff, mandatory reporting makes children less likely to seek help when they are abused. They worry about being thrust into a situation like that of Willard's children—flung into the foster care system and separated from loved ones. In a study of abuse survivors who identified as LGBTQ, nearly half of survivors under eighteen decided against seeking help because they were worried about the consequences of a mandated report. Of all survivors surveyed (comprising a range of ages, including adults), women, girls, and trans people were especially afraid of a report being filed if they sought help.[40]

At the same time, mandatory reporting laws also mean that people who fear they may be at risk of abusing children are also much less likely to seek treatment. At the Johns Hopkins Sexual Disorders Clinic, after mandatory reporting laws requiring staff to report disclosures to authorities went into effect in 1989, the number of people who voluntarily came to the center for treatment to avoid abusing children dropped to zero.[41]

The concept of mandated reporting was itself a reform developed in the wake of a sudden burst of attention to child abuse in the 1960s.[42] A group of medical doctors launched a push for laws that would require professionals who might come in contact with abused children to report suspicious situations. The idea caught fire: in 1963, the U.S. Children's Bureau drafted a law mandating that doctors report suspected abuse to authorities. Within a few years, every state had passed a similar mandate. From there, states began expanding the requirements, including additional professions and types of situations to be reported. In the early 1970s, a national law, the Child Abuse Prevention and Treatment Act, further codified mandatory reporting, making it a condition for federal dollars for many social service agencies.[43]

As mandatory reporting laws have expanded, turning an increasing number of professionals into police-like figures, the numbers of reports filed has multiplied, too. But most of those reports are not substantiated. In 2015, 4.1 million children were subjects of child maltreatment reports in the United States, but only 17.3 percent of these reports were substantiated.[44] But all of these families were subjected to the invasion of home life, the interrogations, and, often, the trauma that comes along with a child services investigation—including, sometimes, removal from the home—even though ultimately no abuse, neglect, or maltreatment was discovered. And of course, not all cases in which the state "substantiates" maltreatment can be trusted, given its tendency to punish poverty and marginalization.

Child services departments have become a type of police. In New York City, staffers of the Administration of Children's Services are now learning criminal investigation tactics at the police academy.[45] A New York *Daily News* article on the practice observes, "While child protective specialists do not have any arrest powers, they can be the first step in launching a child abuse investigation," and a social worker quoted in the piece notes, "Our ultimate goal is the same as the cops."[46]

Though they can't arrest people, child welfare workers can—and do—call in actual police, even for actions that are not illegal. That's what happened to Jazmine Headley in New York City. In December 2018, Headley, a Black mother of an eighteen-month-old, learned that her childcare voucher had been unexpectedly cut. She took the day off work to speak with a caseworker at the city's Human Resources Administration office. All of the chairs in the waiting room were occupied, so Headley and her toddler sat on the floor. An agency security guard told her to leave the area. When she refused, security guards called the police, who forcibly pulled her child from her arms, arrested Headley, and threatened to tase onlookers. Headley spent four days at Rikers Island. (Following public outcry, all charges against her were dropped.)[47]

What happened to Headley is shocking, but even in many more mundane cases, mandated reporting requires those in the helping professions to "turn in" their clients, thus subjecting them to state punishment. It represents an expansion of surveillance and social control while the resources that would actually support parenting—such as housing and food assistance—become more and more difficult to access.

It's not only social workers, doctors, daycare workers, teachers, and other child-related professionals who are being forcibly transformed into child services' police force. In some states, it's all of us: eighteen states currently have "universal reporting" requirements on the books, meaning that any resident who suspects child maltreatment or neglect is obligated to report it to child protective services.[48] (Almost all states make exceptions for defense attorneys.)[49] These types of expanded reporting requirements have been spreading across the country over the past few years, part of the ongoing widening of the child services surveillance net. The result is a burgeoning system bent on accusing and investigating people, in which the accusations and investigations become holes into which vast amounts of money are sunk.[50]

Like foster care, mandated reporting especially harms marginalized families who are already under surveillance, whether because they receive welfare benefits, because they are involved with the criminal punishment system, or simply because they are Black or Brown. According to a study by the Center for the Study of Social Policy and the Annie E. Casey Foundation, "persistent evidence" shows that people of color are more likely to be reported to child protective services.[51] We can see the contours of this picture through the limited state data available. In Washington State, for example, Native children are almost three times as likely to be reported as white children. In Texas, Washington, and California, Black children are nearly twice as likely—if not more—to be reported as white ones. Moreover, police are mandated reporters, and the fact that Black and Brown people are more likely to be targeted by police makes them more likely to be subsequently sucked into the orbit of child protective services.

Even some officials within the system recognize the dangers of expanding mandated reporting, and the unregulated, ubiquitous surveillance that accompanies it. Joette Katz, commissioner of the Connecticut Department of Children and Families, noted of the expansion laws, "I worry about the children, some of whom will be traumatized by being needlessly subjected to forensic interviews and invasive medical procedures—a form of child abuse in and of itself."[52]

It's a warped picture: the system that claims to be addressing and preventing child abuse is abusing children on a massive scale. And with the bounds of surveillance widening every year, reports—and, therefore, investigations—are multiplying to the extent that by the time they turn 18, 37.4 percent of children in the United States will experience a child protective services investigation. For Black children, it's 53 percent.[53]

The justification for heightened policing of parenthood is that it keeps families and children safe. But if all of us are expected to police our neighbors—in the name of the safety of children, the "helping" of mothers and caregivers, and the greater good—our communities and our individual relationships become saturated with state domination and control. Meanwhile, on a broader level, social welfare institutions are cooperating with the forces of state violence to hasten the prisonization of our homes, our neighborhoods, our families, our relationships and our lives.

Mother-baby programs were put forth as an alternative to family separation for incarcerated parents. Social welfare and child protection agencies were put forth as a protection against child abuse. But just as mother-baby programs have become "prison lite" in the community, child protective services and mandatory-reporting laws operate as punitive institutions of their own, targeting the most vulnerable families. They threaten parents with one of the worst punishments of all: separation from their children. And they are transforming more and more service providers into agents of control and punishment—essentially, police.

We must recognize this wave of parenting reforms for what it is: a dangerous expansion of the prison nation. Not all prisons have steel bars, not all police carry guns, and not all punishments are called punishments. Sometimes the police are called "social workers" and the punishment is called "care."

5

COMMUNITIES AS OPEN-AIR PRISONS

They're using the community to tell on the community.

—Josmar Trujillo, anti-policing activist and journalist

Police have been a presence in twenty-one-year-old K's life for as long as he can remember.[1] The officers assigned to Red Hook, a rapidly gentrifying part of Brooklyn where K grew up, see the same kids on the same blocks day in and day out. They're a part of New York City's neighborhood policing initiative, a reform officially created as an answer to "mistrust" and "strained police and community relations," ostensibly in response to the protests that have emerged over police violence and murders over the past several years.[2] Under neighborhood policing, "the same officers work in the same neighborhoods on the same shifts, increasing their familiarity with local residents and local problems," according to the New York City Police Department (NYPD).[3] In theory, this consistency enables them to build relationships with the people that they see every day, thus lessening the likelihood that police will resort to avoidable violence or other violations. Other cities use the term "community policing" to describe a similar practice. But regardless of its name, fostering familiarity with police officers doesn't always build a sense of trust or neighborliness, particularly in low-income communities of color.

For K, a young Black man, this became apparent one hot July night in 2018. He and a group of friends had gathered in a Brooklyn apartment for a candle-lighting ceremony for a friend who had been killed by police. After the friend's mother said a final prayer, they began filing out to the street, which they quickly noticed was filled with police officers of various types, including neighborhood police officers. The group of friends walked to a different block. Several unmarked vehicles pulled up and the number of police officers multiplied—and then they began to approach the group.

One of K's friends was arrested, allegedly for vandalizing a government vehicle. When the police grabbed the young man, K and his friends pulled out their phones and started filming. One officer then ordered K to step onto the sidewalk. He complied but continued recording. A plainclothes officer ordered him to back up. K complied but did not put his phone away. The officer began pushing him, and when K tried to record his badge number, he was thrown to the ground before being tightly handcuffed.

On the drive to the precinct, K told officers that his hands were numb, but they refused to loosen the handcuffs. Two weeks later, his wrists were still black and blue, with grayish white scrapes still showing, and he had a new round scar the size of a dollar coin on his shoulder.

K was charged with obstruction of justice, which means that despite attending college in upstate New York, he needs to travel the 250 miles back to Brooklyn regularly to attend court dates.

The stated mission of policing is "public safety." In theory, neighborhood policing is supposed to build public safety by allowing cops to get to know the neighborhood, develop relationships with residents, and build community. Billboards around New York City declare that neighborhood policing is about "bringing communities together." "We're all neighbors making up our communities," the signs proclaim.[4] In 2018, the NYPD announced its plans to extend neighborhood policing to every precinct in the city by 2019.[5]

K was born and raised in Red Hook, where craft breweries are popping up alongside bodegas, market-rate apartments renting for thousands are springing up across the street from housing projects, and white hipsters live on the same block as low-income Black residents.[6] Although the NYPD implemented neighborhood policing in 2016, K sees no difference between neighborhood police and regular local police.[7] In his area, there are also police service area officers, who focus on policing public housing; combined with neighborhood police, they create a constant saturation that feels akin to an open-air prison.

That constant presence is characteristic of neighborhood policing. In the NYPD's promotional video for its revamped neighborhood policing initiative, an officer explains, "A lot of people in the community develop a familiarity with us. They see us all the time."[8] The rationale is that by becoming familiar with individual police officers, residents and business owners are more likely to turn to the police for help—or be willing to cooperate with them.

But that doesn't translate into police being a positive force for everyone in the community. Instead of acting like Officer Friendly, neighborhood police make it less possible for K and other youth of color to simply live publicly in their community. The police are ever-present, and instead of actually preventing crime, solving crimes, or fostering safety along their neighborhood beats, their main role seems to be to corral K and his neighbors into and out of spaces.

Even before the attack at his friend's memorial, police would harass K and his friends while they were sitting outside, listening to music or hanging out on the stoop. Police harassment is a reality for many kids of color in New York City when they become old enough to leave their houses but are not yet old enough to spend their time (and money) in bars or other commercial establishments. When they sit on park benches or stoops or in other public places, they're often harassed and told to move by police officers, even when they've broken no law.

Neighborhood policing exemplifies how the prison nation does not always manifest as confinement in locked-down physical space. Police interactions are people's first engagement with the prison system. Police can be in any public setting. They're on the street. They're in hospitals, libraries, train stations. They're in our schools. They're in our workplaces. They enter our homes—sometimes when summoned, sometimes by force, with or without a warrant. As K's experience illustrates, police bring the threat, and often the reality, of harassment, surveillance, criminalization, arrest, and even death. Police even establish a visible presence in spaces of resistance. Patrolling protests—including protests against the police—is part of their job. Police ensure that, particularly for marginalized people, there's always a possible path from everyday life to prison.

In recent years, police haven't just provided a path to prison; they've also worked to build open-air prisons within communities, through the type of control and harassment K and many others experience on a daily basis.

The Trouble with Community Policing

Following the police murders of Eric Garner, who was choked to death in New York, and Michael Brown, who was shot to death in Ferguson, Missouri, anti-policing protests and organizing, including Black Lives Matter and the Movement for Black Lives, rolled across the nation. In response, some politicians and mainstream advocates have held up community policing as a compassionate and necessary reform. The image of the friendly cop-as-neighbor has graced TV ads, billboards, and neighborhood meetings in major cities, corresponding to liberal notions that police must strengthen their "relationships" with communities.

From Chicago to New York to Los Angeles and in smaller cities around the country, police departments have put forth community policing as the solution to police violence as well as a recipe for reducing prison populations.[9]

A 2016 report from the Brennan Center reflected the thinking of many reform advocates when it condemned mass incarceration—and proceeded to recommend that much of the money saved from decreasing incarceration should be invested in community policing as well as reentry programs and alternatives to prison.[10] Appropriating the language of activists, some scholars and reform advocates have even called the prospect of increasing numbers of police—particularly for community policing—a type of "harm reduction" that could decrease imprisonment.[11]

Former president Obama repeatedly positioned community policing as the antidote to police violence, and he claimed that the strategy would require bigger police budgets and more officers. He told a 2015 meeting of the International Association of Chiefs of Police:

> A lot of times it means more resources for police departments because it's more labor intensive. If you want that kind of community policing, then you got to have enough police to be able to do that because it takes time to do more than just respond to a call.[12]

Two years later, a different politician uttered a similar statement to the same association:

> Community policing builds trust and mutual respect between communities and law enforcement, and that helps

us reduce crime. . . . Under President Trump's strong leadership, this Department of Justice will continue to provide
law enforcement officers with the resources and tools they
need to make this country safe.[13]

That politician was Donald Trump's first attorney general, Jeff Sessions, notorious for being one of the most "tough-on-crime" federal
public officials in recent memory.

There's a reason for the mainstream bipartisan consensus around
community policing: it maintains and expands the status quo. As
advocates call for fewer police and less policing and criminalization,
community policing becomes a way to reshape the narrative to position police as friendly beat cops who know everyone's name. But community policing doesn't make policing more effective, less hostile, or
more accountable to the communities they serve in. Instead, it allows
police to further entrench their presence in neighborhoods, justify
increases in their numbers, and even mobilize community members
to participate in policing by surveilling their neighbors.

When asked how he'd respond to those who see neighborhood
policing as a "kinder, gentler force"—an integral and familiar part of
the community—K points out that though these police officers are dis-
patched to the same neighborhood each day, they're not actually a part
of the community. They don't understand the dynamics of the neighborhood or the relationships between people, and are always on the
defensive—always poised for violence, he says. For K, and many other
young Black and Brown people, recognizing a police officer's face from
seeing it every day simply means recognizing the person who is targeting, harassing, brutalizing, and arresting them.

Joe, another young Black man and a researcher at the youth empowerment organization Red Hook Initiative, similarly identifies the irony
of community policing.[14] At Unity in the Community, an annual basketball tournament organized by the NYPD's 76th Precinct, which

serves Red Hook, cops and local youth play basketball with each other, on the same teams.[15] In 2017, while waiting for the basketball game to begin, Joe participated in a pickup soccer game in which four cops, at least one of whom was a neighborhood police officer, also played.

But that familiarity didn't stop the same police officers from harassing Joe, his younger brother, and their friends on a regular basis. Once when the young men returned from shopping, police appeared and ordered them off the block. Again, it's a common coming-of-age story for Black and Brown kids, but this time, Joe's younger brother protested. The police arrested him, throwing him into their squad car headfirst; this incident, Joe recalls, "had me scared out of my life for three nights straight, not knowing if my brother's safe, not knowing if he's alive."[16]

His brother survived, but Joe has increasingly noticed the disconnect between the neighborhood policing rhetoric and its reality. He's seen a neighbor chased by police for tossing a paper plate on the floor. He's seen a large group of cops throw someone on his head and slam him down—for gambling. For Joe, it's often hard to tell who's a neighborhood officer and who's a regular cop, as the standard practices of racial profiling and abuse play out across the board.

Joe didn't participate in the Unity in the Community game the following year. He's done with the idea that police and community-building go hand in hand. He's tired of seeing officers be friendly while politicians are watching but then return to stalking and harassing neighborhood residents the next day.

The behavior of neighborhood police around the city underscores Joe's analysis. In August 2018, a neighborhood policing officer was caught on camera responding to a minor noise complaint by putting someone in the type of chokehold that killed Eric Garner (the Staten Island man whose death by police was filmed in 2014), which had already been banned by law for the past twenty years.[17] The victim had merely been listening to music outside and was preparing to leave.

When he turned around to fold up his chair, the officer put him in a chokehold before throwing him onto the ground and tasing him.

Joe says he's stopped, harassed, or stalked by the cops every day. So does K, who describes a climate of unrelenting targeting by police (including neighborhood police) that is reminiscent of prison. "This is nonstop," he says.

A Story of Expansion

Some key history led to the current expansion of police forces in the form of "community policing." Contemporary community policing, according to the City University of New York's Abolition Research Group, is a merging of two schools of policing that emerged in the 1980s: broken-windows policing and problem-oriented policing.[18] In 1982, criminologists James Q. Wilson and George Kelling coined the term "broken-windows policing." The philosophy is that low-level offenses such as turnstile-jumping, breaking windows, vandalism, and public drinking—things that are against the law but aren't hurting anyone—lead to more serious, sometimes violent offenses. Police subsequently began more aggressively targeting people for these smaller, less serious offenses—with the mandate of preventing more serious crimes. Yet this supposedly "preventative" innovation ended up simply increasing arrests for small offenses. The jump in arrests took an economic toll on communities, as people missed work while they lingered in jail.[19] Broken-windows policing also increased distrust of police and contributed to police violence, overwhelmingly against Black and Brown people.[20]

Three years earlier, in 1979, criminologist Herman Goldstein put forward the theory of "problem-oriented policing," which proposed that police should be working with communities to address underlying causes of crimes rather than simply responding to crimes. In practice, this widened the range of police duties, encouraging them to be the go-to entity to deal with issues such as education and mental health. Policing, even when its goal was to address real problems, still led to a greater investment in police.

From the start, community policing became an excuse for growing the size of the police force. For example, in the early 1990s, New York City mayor David Dinkins proposed adding six thousand officers to the force in the name of community policing. He said more cops were needed because each one would need to take time to work on cementing relationships with people in the community.[21] When Rudy Giuliani became mayor shortly thereafter, he ditched the community policing part . . . but kept the planned addition of six thousand cops.

The concept of community policing rose in popularity, and in 1994, a federal office expressly for that purpose was established. The Office of Community Oriented Policing Services (COPS), which lives on today, began doling out grants to police departments—growing police budgets so that more community policing officers could be hired and trained. The *New York Times* called community policing "the most promising trend in law enforcement."[22] In 1996, the *American Prospect* called community policing "ubiquitous," noting, "Like welfare reform, everybody's got to have it, even if no one knows exactly what it is."[23]

Two decades later, in response to Black Lives Matter and other grassroots organizations such as INCITE! Women, Gender Non-Conforming and Trans People of Color Against Violence, Black Youth Project 100, and Critical Resistance calling for an end to police violence, the same community policing model was trotted out yet again. In 2015, the New York City Council's solution to police violence was a proposal to add one thousand cops specifically to focus on community policing.[24] Between January 2017 and April 2018, efforts to add around one thousand officers to Chicago's police department led to fourteen hundred new recruits being hired. The city's police superintendent said that these new recruits would be "tasked with personifying our community policing policy," and Mayor Rahm Emanuel used "our belief in community policing" as a justification for a plan to build a $95 million police academy in a poor, majority-Black neighborhood.[25] Chicago recently added a new Office of Community Policing as part of an effort to "rebuild trust" in the wake of a 2017 Department of Justice report condemning police violence and racial oppression perpetrated by the Chicago Police Department.[26] One of the report's main recommendations was community policing.

Beyond its role in expanding police budgets and departments, community policing promotes the idea that police are the solution to problems within a community, ignoring the fact that police are actually part of the violence against and fracturing of communities. Like so many other "alternatives," community policing expands and extends the prison industrial complex. Having more police can simply create more opportunity for them to surveil, target, and arrest more people.

Your Neighbor Is Your Jailer

"More police" doesn't always refer to patrolling officers. The trend toward community policing also mobilizes community members to do the work of the police. It encourages neighbors to watch and report on each other's activities. This facet of community policing isn't new. In fact, it's as old as the United States itself.

American policing emerged from the nation's history of civilian-based efforts to control and harm certain groups of people, particularly Black and Native people as well as those considered dissidents. Many southern police departments started as slave patrols during the antebellum years: volunteers served on these patrols to capture enslaved people who had escaped or were perceived as trying to flee.[27] In the American North, community members were often expected to serve on "night watches," other early forerunners of what would become American police. The first formal night watch was formed in 1636 in Boston, primarily to patrol the streets and watch for residents involved in sex work or other behaviors deemed deviant. Men over eighteen were expected to serve.[28] Volunteer police helpers also have a long history in the United States of facilitating Indigenous genocide. In the nineteenth and early twentieth centuries, for example, the Texas Rangers chased down and killed Native people rumored to have attacked colonizers, and they lynched Tejanos, or Texans of Mexican descent.[29] But the Texas Rangers were not actual police, military, or even militia forces; instead, these volunteer vigilantes were essentially "community members" playing a collaborating role in policing and protecting newly arriving white colonizers.

The role of community member involvement in policing, including the night watch, never went away. The idea of a neighborhood watch—with police rallying residents to come together to look for suspicious behavior—gained popularity in the 1960s. In the early 1970s, the National Sheriffs' Association established the National Neighborhood Watch Program.[30] Official accounts say that the trend was a response to a surge in crime in the late 1960s.[31] But the 1960s, like today, were a time in which large numbers of people were calling attention to and challenging the ways that police were attacking their communities. The civil rights movement and the repression of leftist movements, such as the Black liberation movement, brought wider attention to police violence, particularly against people of color and dissidents. In response, the idea of neighborhood watch was revived and branded as community policing, reaffirming the overall legitimacy of the police. We can see a similar dynamic at work today as cities respond to a renewed spotlight on police violence with a renewed emphasis on community policing.

Why is community policing such a time-honored tactic for repairing police legitimacy? Some of it is certainly a public relations stunt—the word "community" evokes images of friendly relationships rather than hostile encounters that result in violence and arrest. It's also a strategy that easily rakes in extra dollars from city budgets to put more

cops on the street while diverting calls for real changes and accountability. But it's also a more sinister game: when the legitimacy of the
police is questioned by community members, what better way to rein-
state it than by turning (some) community members themselves into
police?

As K, Joe, and other Black and Brown residents continue to face
police harassment on a daily basis in New York, the city's neighborhood policing campaign Build the Block is being heavily promoted
on subway billboards, in local TV commercials, and on top-40 radio
stations in an attempt to draw people to neighborhood policing meetings.[32] "Cops are hosting meetings in local neighborhoods to find out
what's it gonna take to make us all feel safe. They want to know what we
think, so why not tell them?" one Build the Block promotional video
asks. The video ads always conclude with the words, "Your Safety. Your
Neighborhood. Your Voice."[33] But collaboration between police and
communities often has an ominous effect, turning neighborhoods into
highly surveilled zones in which certain residents are always under
watch, punishable at a moment's notice. In effect, neighbors are being
asked to spy on each other.

"Community policing is always about intelligence gathering," says
Alex Vitale, the coordinator of Brooklyn College's Policing and Social
Justice Project.[34] He points to public meetings in which community
members are encouraged to come and discuss safety issues, and are
then asked to provide information about their neighbors. "Police rely
on these meetings to identify the 'bad guys,' where they are, what they
are up to. That information is then used to populate gang databases,
identify hot spots, and target people." And, Vitale notes, just because
this "intel" comes in via community policing doesn't mean there's a
warmer, fuzzier, community-oriented response; "it just feeds primarily back into traditional law enforcement practices."

As community policing has picked up steam in the twenty-first
century, its extended reach has played out in neighborhoods around

the country. Take the Onset neighborhood in the town of Wareham, Massachusetts, where "armed with two-way radios and a hefty dose of community pride, Onset Community Crime Watch volunteers patrolled the streets in marked cruisers, looking out for graffiti vandals, suspected drug dealers, and people loitering and drinking on the sidewalks." It's similar to Project ROSE in Phoenix, where social workers patrolled with police to pick up anyone suspected of sex work. But Crime Watch participants don't have the power to make arrests on their own. Instead, as its volunteer captain explains, "We're basically the eyes and ears for the Police Department."[35] In other words, community policing involves not only cultivating relationships with (certain) members of the community but also turning these members into the eyes and ears of the police.

As New York City anti-policing organizer and scholar Josmar Trujillo puts it, "They're using the community to tell on the community."[36] The NYPD encourages a high volume of complaints to obtain information on who community members suspect to be gang members or terrorists, regardless of the fact that such suspicions are often driven by racism and Islamophobia. The same holds true in other cities, such as Chicago and Seattle.[37] Community policing even turns family members into informants. Trujillo has attended events in which neighborhood policing officers instruct parents on how to spot whether their kid is a gang member—assessing small changes like the colors they're wearing. Trujillo compares these tactics to counterinsurgency measures in Afghanistan, in which rewards are offered to people who turned in their neighbors.[38] "Neighbor"-led community watch efforts can have dangerous results. When neighbors see their role as the "eyes and ears of the police"—whether because of community policing initiatives or less structured neighborhood watch attempts—vigilante violence can result. In 2012, seventeen-year-old Trayvon Martin was shot to death by George Zimmerman, who played a prominent role in his neighborhood watch program facilitated by the local police department.[39] When called to the stand during Zimmerman's trial, the coordinator of neighborhood watch programs insisted she hadn't encouraged people to play vigilante. She'd simply asked them to be the "eyes and ears" of the police.[40]

In the age of social media, the "eyes and ears" mentality encouraged by community policing is intensified by neighborhood Facebook groups, where residents communicate about alleged threats and dangers, cultivating a culture of fear. Community policing initiatives are driven by fearmongering: at a time when New York is seeing record lows in crime, including gang violence, the NYPD has labeled gangs a "growing problem."[41] At the same time, a study published in the *Journal of Experimental Criminology* found "no evidence that community policing decreases citizens' fear of crime."[42] In other words, community policing does not actually deter crime, nor does it decrease fears of crime and violence. It simply reinforces the refrain that policing is the only mechanism available to keep society safe, a refrain that has been used to justify expanding police forces while quieting demands for real change and real safety.

Dividing the Community

Rising calls for community policing should prompt a question: What and who is the community? In the context of probation and electronic monitoring, "community" supervision means being confined outside of prison walls. In the context of mandatory outpatient treatments, living in the "community" means staying outside an institution but still being bound to strict rules governing one's body and mind. Similarly, in a policing context, "community" also refers to an expansion of the prison nation—multiplying the number of eyes and ears geared toward surveillance.

Police tend to identify the community as the members of a neighborhood that they are *not* targeting. Often these are the people with more money; in a mixed-race neighborhood, often these are white people. This makes it possible to pit residents against each other, stoking pre-existing biases in order to encourage people to surveil their neighbors.

The NYPD billboards that adorn the city's subways read, "We're all neighbors making up our communities—straphangers, business owners, teachers, retirees and cops—so let's reach out, speak out, and look out for each other." It's worth noting that aside from "straphangers" (simply a word for people who ride public transit), the people mentioned in conjunction with cops are predominantly middle-class, including older people who are able to retire.

For Malik, a Black twenty-five-year-old community organizer born and raised in East New York, an almost entirely Black and Latinx neighborhood in Brooklyn, the police definition of "community" doesn't include people like him.[43] The police make an effort to pull older residents, not people his age, into their neighborhood meetings. The police stoke older residents' fears about gangs, violence, and crime, worsening the neighborhood's generation gap and pushing them to align with the cops. At the same time, despite increasing media coverage of racial profiling and police violence, many people believe that if police are harassing a person, it's because that person is doing something illegal. "When you keep telling people the same thing, they start believing it after a while," Malik says.

In a community policing model, the police always decide which members constitute the "community." In Los Angeles, says Vitale, police determine which community members are chosen as the community leaders that the department interacts with when developing its community policing plans. These leaders are nearly always people who tend to be sympathetic to police—such as homeowners, religious leaders, and business owners—while homeless people, youth, and formerly incarcerated people are nowhere to be found.[44] Similar police selection of community participants takes place in cities throughout the country. In 2015, following the rise of the Black Lives Matter movement,

Chicago police conducted a "listening tour," with the stated intention of reconnecting with communities and repairing distrust. However, the meetings were only open to invited guests and the meeting results were not publicized.[45]

The "listening tour" was not atypical of Chicago's community policing efforts. Meetings organized by the city's community policing program, Chicago Alternative Policing Strategy (CAPS), are "places where a self-selecting group of residents are mobilized by police to surveil their communities, report information to CPD . . . and volunteer their time to 'take back the streets' in CPD-organized 'positive loitering events,'" according to a report by We Charge Genocide, a Chicago grassroots organization focused on ending police violence. These meetings don't strengthen communities; they often harm them. By selecting certain residents to surveil and report on their neighborhoods under the banner of safety, the police department is turning communities into surveillance states. We Charge Genocide calls these initiatives "anticommunity policing," noting that in reality, "these initiatives sharpen divisions within communities along lines of race and class and fracture social bonds."[46]

The dynamics of gentrification also play a role in defining who is part of "the community"—and who isn't. Chicago anti-displacement organizer Lynda Lopez has seen complaints in local Facebook groups about her own neighborhood, Hermosa, a working-class, mostly Latinx community that is quickly gentrifying. Often, when someone posts a notification about a dangerous presence who warrants police attention, "dangerous" equals "young, Latino males."[47]

It goes beyond social media threats. Chicago's "Albany Park Neighbors" group, located in one of the most ethnically diverse neighborhoods in the United States, often focuses on businesses that are accused of bringing in "outsiders," particularly people of color, homeless people, and people who appear to have substance addictions.[48] For example, the group has targeted the local blood bank, saying that the people gathering around the building, many of them low-income and Black, were endangering the neighborhood's safety. The group also singled out a small, family-owned convenience store, where residents said people exhibiting "drunken behavior" were gathering. After pressure from the group, the store committed to restricting its sales of alcohol and to hiring security guards (both steps that could exact a financial toll from this local business). The group encouraged people to call the police and the local alderman's office if they observed "drunken behavior."[49] These residents frame their complaints as a problem of outsiders infiltrating the neighborhood, even when the targets are actually longtime residents who, sometimes, are in the process of being pushed out by gentrification.

Jennifer Viets, a Chicago-based restorative justice practitioner, lives in the diverse West Ridge neighborhood, which includes substantial populations of Asian, Latinx, and Black residents as well as white immigrant groups.[50] Yet she has noticed that the people engaged in community policing—the ones who show up at CAPS meetings and participate in neighborhood watch—are generally white homeowners.

Viets attended a CAPS meeting in West Ridge at which the alderperson, police, and some residents urged people to sign up for the neighborhood watch program. Participants would wear yellow jackets, walk the streets at night looking for "suspicious activities," and call 911 about any suspicions.[51] The meeting's organizers joked, "You can bring your dog, but don't carry any weapons," and spoke of the program as an effort to keep outsiders away from the neighborhood. At the second meeting, Viets was struck by the emphasis on controlling who "belonged" in the area.[52]

At a certain point, Viets had had enough. "I stood up and said, 'This is ridiculous. This is racial profiling.'" Other activists who'd come with Viets, including youth of color, also stood up and objected. When supporters of the neighborhood watch shouted, "This isn't your neighborhood!" the activists replied, "No, we do live in this neighborhood. Why are you assuming we don't live in this neighborhood?"

The lines had been drawn: the police had defined white homeowners as "the community," and police-allied attendees of the CAPS meeting had taken the bait. To them, the neighborhood didn't belong to the Black and Brown youth attending the meeting and challenging police practices.

K, the young man born and raised in Red Hook, Brooklyn, says that the constant police presence and targeting of Black youth make him feel like an outsider in his home. K's concern comes at a time when gentrification runs thick in Red Hook as more *actual* outsiders are moving in.[53] "We have IDs that show our address. It's obvious we live here," he says. "It's like they're trying to kick us off of where we grew up at."

Community policing takes advantage of the fact that many white people already assume the "eyes and ears of the police" role in society, calling the police on perceived—usually Black or Brown—"outsiders." This dynamic is evident in well-publicized events, such as white people calling police on Harvard professor Henry Louis Gates Jr. for breaking into his own house and police swarming musician Bob Marley's granddaughter as she exited an Airbnb, and in the less-publicized moment-to-moment experiences of many millions of people in this country every day.

Meanwhile, some groups are simply left out of the definition of "community member" in the context of community policing. One case in point: suspected gang members. "What they're trying to do . . . is to leave people who are gang members out and to tell communities, 'This is not you. This is the bad element. We want to talk to *you*,'" notes Trujillo. "The police want you to cut [gang members] off, like an arm that has gangrene." In other words, gang members are made to seem like a group *outside* of community—a group that is disposable. This is the kind of logic that encourages K's older neighbors to fear the children on their block as they grow into young adulthood. It's the logic that allows police to harass, intimidate, arrest, and brutalize people with impunity in their own neighborhoods. It's also the logic that overlooks the reasons that gangs tend to exist in underresourced, marginalized communities in the first place.

Trujillo agrees, noting that "[police] don't have the conversation about poverty, and lack of resources, that actually drive violence. If you were really genuine about having a conversation about the community, you would have the conversation about why people end up in gangs, what gangs have politically meant. . . . This is a place where people organize, this is a place where people find community."

In the housing projects near his home, members of different gangs come together for basketball tournaments. Trujillo does not deny that some gang members engage in violence, but points out that they also organize community events and strengthen community ties in neighborhoods with few resources and even fewer support structures, areas that the city government has largely abandoned.

"Some people are convinced by what the newspaper headlines say or what the police say, but people also understand that this is part of our community," notes Trujillo. "These are the people who are doing basketball tournaments, who try to do something for themselves."

In sum, Trujillo says, the police are "breaking up communities even as they're talking about community." They're interrupting *actual* community-building efforts in an attempt to be in charge of what's happening.

Community policing normalizes the idea that police should be "in charge" of programs that might ordinarily be outside their wheelhouse. Placing cops in charge of other programs and services, such as mental health or homeless services, means that departments can justify the placement of police pretty much anywhere.

In a wide-ranging study of community policing in Seattle, political science professor William Thomas Lyons notes, "Community policing colonized community life."[54] At the same time, he writes, the infiltration of the community by the police made it possible for the police department to "shield itself from critical public scrutiny," because so much of its work was done in partnership with community groups.[55] The "community" end of the partnership becomes simply a "docile and dependent client," and community policing ends up "replacing more critical forms of public scrutiny with citizen surveillance plugged directly into state information systems." In other words, community policing became a brilliant public relations move that bolsters both popular support and additional resources for the police without demanding real change or safety. Not only does it increase the amount of surveillance in play and stoke the fires of existing power dynamics in the community, but it also masks the actual role of police on the ground. Trujillo reminds us that regardless of rhetoric, "policing is still happening, so you still feel like you're in an open-air prison."

He challenges the idea that "building trust" with the police—a phrase that pops up again and again in reformers' arguments for community policing—is ever a good thing. "When you trust someone, you let your guard down, you let things bypass, you give cops the benefit of the doubt," he says. "We know what the relationship with the police is, and it's been repeated to us generation after generation; it's clear. We're not supposed to mend bridges with an abuser. We're supposed to hold that abuser to account."

The NYPD has been experimenting with various forms of community policing for decades—including at the height of its own violence. High-profile police-perpetrated murders have occurred in several other cities—from Cleveland to Charleston to Baltimore—that received significant federal COPS funds for community policing. COPS grants are supposed to make communities safer, but instead, we've seen the opposite. For instance, Timothy Loehmann, the Ohio police officer who fatally shot Tamir Rice, a twelve-year-old playing with a toy gun in a city park, was hired as a result of a COPS grant.[56]

In other words, the problem with policing is not that relations simply need to be improved between the police and the community. Patrick Reilly, a researcher at the University of Illinois at Chicago who has studied the history behind CAPS, notes that the community policing program was preceded by more than a decade of advocacy around making communities "equal partners in crime-fighting," through an organization called Chicago Alliance for Neighborhood Safety (CANS), which was founded in the early 1980s. However, a few years after CANS succeeded in winning the adoption of CAPS in the 1990s, it released its own study showing that widespread police discrimination persisted against youth of color. This exposes that some problems attributed to "mistrust" are actually ingrained in the practice of policing.[57]

History shows us that it's time to move beyond reforms that simply put a friendly face on status-quo policing. The problems with policing are symptomatic of the larger violence of the prison nation, which thrives on surveilling, capturing, and confining millions of people. The promotion of community policing attempts to erase that larger violence.

Predictive Policing, Precision Policing, Gang Policing: Big Data as "Alternative"

Community policing isn't the only police reform that has been proffered in the past few years, as mass incarceration and police violence have come under more scrutiny. Other reforms have revolved around the idea of making policing "smarter," often through technology and data-driven means of "predicting" where crime will happen and who will be behind it.

Mainstream academics, experts, and media outlets have promoted the idea that data is key to changing the way policing is done. A 2016 *Harvard Law Review* article argues that "preventive strategies"—like intensifying police presence in areas deemed "crime hot spots"—can decrease racist arrests and therefore "diminish the harms associated with mass incarceration in these vulnerable communities."[58] According to this logic, increasing police in a certain area will actually decrease imprisonment. Similarly, in a *New York Times* op-ed, Yale sociologist Andrew Papachristos observes, "In this era of mass incarceration and hyper-surveillance of our most vulnerable communities, algorithms might help narrow the focus and reach of the justice system, leading to fewer and fairer contacts with citizens."[59] Technology becomes a magical solution: a way to tackle the problem of mass incarceration not by shrinking the size of the prison nation but by making it more "intelligent." Lawmakers, experts, and police officials promote new high-tech practices as ways to get policing *right*.

As a report by Upturn, a Washington, DC–based policy analysis team, explains, "Predictive policing is a marketing term—popularized by vendors in the public safety industry—for computer systems that use data to automatically forecast where crime will happen or who will be involved."[60] Upturn points out that the practice of determining "hot spots" where crime occurs frequently has already been in play for a number of years. Predictive policing takes that a step further, aiming to use that data as "place-based tools" to predict locations and times where future crime will take place. There are also "person-based" predictive policing tools, such as Chicago's Strategic Subject List, initiated in 2013, which specifies which people are supposedly likeliest to become involved in gun violence.[61]

Data-driven policing has been held up as a solution to racial bias in policing, with the justification that data, unlike individual police officers, is a race-neutral determiner of where and whom to target.[62] However, the reality is that crime data itself is biased: it's based on who has been arrested in the past. Police are more likely to have targeted and arrested Black and Brown people in low-income neighborhoods, so data that relies on previous patterns retargets and recriminalizes the same people, largely people of color.

Similarly, the practice of "precision policing" has gained popularity. In a 2018 interview, former New York police commissioner William Bratton, who coined the phrase, describes precision policing as a combination of data-driven predictive policing, broken-windows practices, and community policing that will usher in a "new era of public safety."[63] The concept mixes predictive policing with community policing, ensuring that low-income communities of color are targeted with multiple kinds of enhanced surveillance: the data-based kind and the neighbors-policing-neighbors kind. Precision policing is especially popular in New York, championed by Bratton and liberal mayor Bill de Blasio.[64] In a 2018 *Christian Science Monitor* article, former police officer Peter Moskos admits, "In some ways, [precision policing] is a way to rationalize racially disparate policing."[65] In Moskos's uncritical view, there will always be racial disparities in policing, and so it is necessary to find justifications for why police are targeting people of color. This sleek new buzzword is as good as any.

Even in cases where specific high-tech measures are not used, the practice of gang policing, in which police use insidious tactics to identify possible gang members and locations, is also a practice of "prediction"—labeling certain people as future threats. PredPol itself is now entering the arena of gang policing, creating an algorithm for predicting which crimes are gang-related by using previous data on which crimes police have decided were gang-related—which, of course, are racially influenced determinations.[66]

Gang policing increased in New York after the city's stop-and-frisk practices came under scrutiny and were declared unconstitutional.[67] Under the stop-and-frisk initiative, police were free to stop people on the street and interrogate them at will; they overwhelmingly targeted Black and Brown New Yorkers. The city officially ended stop-and-frisk in 2013, when a judge ruled that New York police were implementing it in a racially biased way that violated the Constitution. Yet stop-and-frisk and gang policing have a lot in common.[68] If someone is labeled a gang member by the police, or lives on a block marked as "gang-ridden," they're more likely to be seen as a person who'd commit a crime and more likely to be arrested, potentially as part of a gang raid.

Malik knows something about the intensity and scope of gang policing. He has no criminal record—yet he's been stopped by police repeatedly since he was thirteen years old, when he was snatched up in a case of mistaken identity. Malik, who now works with the grass-roots group VOCAL-NY, is from the majority-Black neighborhood of East New York, which is an ongoing target of prediction-type polic-ing (parts of the neighborhood have long been considered "hot spots" by NYPD), particularly policing focused on gangs.[69] It's flagged in the police department's location data as a neighborhood with a high con-centration of gang activity, which means it's heavily surveilled, and those suspected of being in gangs are, in effect, stalked.[70] "Mistaken identity" cases aren't uncommon: often it's assumed that if you're a young Black person living in the neighborhood, you may well be in a gang, and if you're in a gang, you're involved in violence.

Malik was once in a gang, but hasn't been for years, and is not sure if he's personally on the gang database. As with the national no-fly list, no one tells you when you're entered into the system.[71] But since Malik's area is highlighted by NYPD as a gang-filled place, and he's young and Black, he's subject to similar types of policing whether or not his name is on the list.

Like surveillance practices in prisons, the tactics Malik has experi-enced presumed guilt instead of innocence. When Malik was eighteen years old, he was walking home with friends the night before Thanks-giving when a couple of undercover officers jumped out of a vehicle and handcuffed him and several others. They threw him in the back of their car and drove away.

The police told Malik they'd seen him "toss the gun." He had no idea what they were talking about. Then they threw him into a holding cell, warning him that they were going to find "the gun" and that it "would probably have your fingerprints on it."

Not long after, however, they let him go—an admission that not only did they have the wrong person, but they couldn't build a case against Malik, a college student with no criminal record. One's record often seems to matter more than whether a person has committed the crime in question. "Precision policing" largely means targeting specific people and places, and so a young Black person with a criminal record in East New York is *predicted* to be a person who needs to be arrested. The gang database, the logic of place-based "crime hot spots," and predictive policing techniques that target people with previous convictions all combine to make the repeated arrest (and, often, incarceration) of certain marginalized people all but inevitable.

Malik didn't have a record and was released. His brother, however, did have one, and when he was targeted by the police through some of the newer gang policing tactics, he experienced a very different fate. His arrest happened during the 2012 gang indictment Operation Tidal Wave, during which police rounded up more than forty young people between the ages of fifteen and twenty-one whom they suspected of being gang members.

"The detectives, they would drive around and take pictures of us on the corners and parks and anywhere that we'd be congregated. They constantly did this," Malik says. "On their phones, on regular cameras, they would take pictures out of nowhere. When they would harass us, instead of being aggressive with it, they'd try to be like, 'You know you can't be in this area, so we're going to take your name down but not arrest you.'"

The police wrote down Malik's name and the names of his friends, again and again. He watched as the police drove by snapping photos and taking pictures at basketball courts. The officers didn't tell Malik and his friends why they were following them. Some activists and academics arguing against such policing practices have compared them to the slave codes and the Black codes that came after slavery, in which it became a crime for Black people to simply congregate in groups.[72] As long as Malik and his friends were spending time together outside, the police were around.

This type of seemingly "kinder, gentler" surveillance has also made its way online over the past decade. NYPD has doubled down on efforts to track youth whom they suspect of gang membership on social media, following statements made on Facebook, Twitter, and Instagram. NYPD's Housing Bureau chief said in 2013 of its efforts to track youth suspected of robberies, "We are coming to find you and monitor every step you take. . . . And we are going to learn about every bad friend you have."[73]

In Operation Tidal Wave, "the officers who made this case became experts in the lexicon as they followed gang members on Twitter, on Facebook and on YouTube," according to Police Commissioner Raymond Kelly.[74] The surveillance was promoted as a slick innovation by NYPD. In the end, forty-three youth were indicted as a result of Operation Tidal Wave on gang-related charges, including murder, attempted murder, and conspiracy.[75]

In effect, bragging and threatening on Facebook got a number of people thrown in jail—including Malik's brother, who was charged with first-degree conspiracy. His charges were based on statements he made on Facebook, but they never discovered any physical evidence to support the claims against him.

Malik's brother took a plea deal: one year at Rikers Island, the city's notoriously violent jail complex. Although he'd never been convicted of a crime at that point, he'd been arrested twenty-two times before, a fact that was used against him. This is an enduring fact of predictive policing: if one's guilt is predicted based on previous arrests, then young Black men who are constantly targeted by police are viewed as guilty from the start.

As Andrew Guthrie Ferguson writes in *The Rise of Big Data Policing,* "With enough personal info about a person, police can create all sorts of suspicious links. Take a predicted area of crime, add a friendship with someone in a gang, and include a few prior police contacts in a heavily policed community, and suddenly a very ordinary young man walking home could be subjected to a stop on the basis of the confluence that he was in a high-crime area, was a known associate with a gang member, and had prior run-ins with the police. . . . Fourth Amendment protections fade in the darkness of the data."[76]

Ferguson refers to this kind of data as "black data" due to both its secrecy and its racialization—any statistics on previous police contact are marred by the fact that police overwhelmingly target Black and Brown people.[77] A 2018 ProPublica investigation of Chicago's growing gang database, for example, found that 95 percent of people listed were Black or Latinx.[78]

This kind of "black data" doesn't work to protect anyone's safety. A 2016 study by the RAND Corporation in Chicago found that the Strategic Suspects List was inaccurate in forecasting acts of violence and had "no effect on the city's homicide trend."[79] The list was supposed to predict who would be most likely to become a victim of gun violence, but, according to the RAND study, it completely failed at that goal. Meanwhile, people on the list, mostly Black and Brown men, were more likely to be arrested in connection with gun violence, but the study indicated that this was simply because police were more likely to target people on the list. The Strategic Suspects List didn't decrease violence, but it did increase surveillance of marginalized communities. In New York City, "black data" tactics are growing even at a time when violence rates are low and the violence that is happening is mostly unrelated to gangs.[80] But the reality doesn't matter when the city's police department can use fear to grow its budgets and its technologies.

What about predictive policing's potential as an "alternative"—preventing more arrests and incarceration by stopping crime in its tracks before it happens? Not likely, it seems. The Upturn report found that prediction tools haven't prompted police to develop new strategies for avoiding arrests. Instead, police are just using these tools in the service of the same old practices—making arrests and issuing citations.[81] The RAND study also cited an increase in arrests as police focused on targeting those on the "heat list."

People who are listed in police's gang databases are generally not told if they're included, and practically no one succeeds in getting their name removed, even if their place in the database is preposterous. The ProPublica investigation found that 163 people in their seventies and eighties (an age demographic for which violent crime is nearly nonexistent) were included in Chicago's database. Two of the people in the database were labeled as Black Panthers: their "gang" was a Black power organization.[82] One of the Black Panther members was sixty-four years old and had not been arrested since 1987.

Although the rationale for gang designations is secretive and often unclear, these designations have serious consequences. If someone is included in a gang database, they may be subject to a harsher punishment, such as prison time when they otherwise might've been sentenced to probation, or longer prison sentences.[83] Thus gang databases, and gang policing in general, have the potential to increase incarceration for targeted groups. Ferguson describes a "focused deterrence" program in Kansas City, Missouri, in which police compiled lists of suspects for violent crimes along with anyone ever arrested with them, and anyone ever arrested with anyone who'd ever been arrested with the suspects. These people were invited to attend a gathering—"part threat, part intervention, part 'scared-straight' lecture"—where police warned them not to commit crimes in the future. This "prevention" effort, however, also involved enhanced punishments for people who'd been warned through the program. For instance, one man who attended the "scared-straight" meeting was later convicted of a robbery. The state pursued the maximum possible prison sentence, citing his attendance at the meeting as a rationale.[84]

Programs similar to the Kansas City one—combining relationship mapping with "warning meetings" and harsh punishments for those who don't heed the warnings—have emerged in a number of places.[85] They feed the type of gang indictments to which Malik's brother was subject. Hanging out with someone (or even hanging out with someone who hangs out with someone) whom police have deemed suspicious can sweep you into a surveillance trap that is incredibly hard to escape. As a 2018 article in *The Nation* puts it, these types of programs create "entire criminal networks out of preexisting communities" and are "incarcerating entire social networks of young people" in the name of moving past dragnet styles of policing like stop-and-frisk.[86] Behind the language of smart policing and data advancements, these practices are leading to more youth of color being labeled "criminals," sucked into a net of never-ending surveillance. Ferguson argues that predictive policing could even increase the risk of police violence, noting that "because the areas have been designated as more dangerous, police may also respond in a more aggressively protective posture."[87]

While terms like "precision policing" are tossed around, the reality is that for marginalized people who live in areas marked as hot spots—or for people listed on a database—surveillance and policing are the opposite of precise. This policing is constant, overwhelming, and punishing, Malik, K, and Joe all say—even when little violence is occurring. Crime levels continue to reach record lows in New York.[88]

Still, NYPD's predictive methods of targeting young Black and Brown people continue to intensify. In 2009 the database contained 21,537 names; by 2018, its size had doubled, reaching 42,334 in just under ten years.[89] Of those added to the database in the four years prior to 2018, 99 percent were people of color.[90]

Gang databases and predictive databases, and their attendant racist biases, have grown in other cities as well. Chicago's Strategic Subjects List, which began in 2013, has already grown to 400,000 names. An analysis by the Policing in Chicago Research Group at the University of Illinois at Chicago found that the vast majority of people listed on the database are Black and Brown.[91]

Upturn surveyed the country's fifty biggest police departments and determined that as of 2016, "at least 20 of them have used a predictive policing system, with at least an additional 11 actively exploring options to do so. Yet some sources indicate that 150 or more departments may be moving toward these systems with pilots, tests, or new deployments."[92]

Signs point to further growth for systems aimed at prediction. For instance, Donald Trump has frequently hyped his plans to collect more crime data regarding immigrants.[93] This is an especially ominous development, given that some data-driven policing methods, like the gang database, harm immigrants in particular ways. For instance, ICE uses the gang databases as tools to apprehend and deport people.[94] Even in so-called sanctuary cities such as Chicago, a presence on the database can disqualify someone from being granted sanctuary, and their information could end up in the hands of ICE.[95]

Predictive practices, from crime "hot spots" to gang databases and beyond, are not new-and-improved policing. Instead, beneath their flashy exterior, they are simply developing new ways to surveil, target, and arrest marginalized people.

Meet the New Police, Same as the Old Police

Police departments, as well as local, state, and federal governments, present community policing and predictive policing as solutions to mass incarceration, police violence, and community "distrust" of policing. But the only problem they're really addressing is the *image* of the police. Whether it's a flashy algorithm or the elusive idea of "trust-building," these so-called new practices are peddling the idea of a change, not an actual change.

These reforms are working in tandem, in ways that overlap and connect, to divide communities further and throw more marginalized people under the bus.

In Chicago, activist Rebecca Harris has worked with Jennifer Viets and another organizer, Rachel Hoffman, to facilitate educational programs about community policing. She and Hoffman attended a community policing meeting at which police described their new "prediction" technologies, including computer programs that sort through previously collected police data to predict which areas would be crime hot spots. Police are then deployed to those "hot spots" to address the crime that they *think* is going to happen there. The technologies were presented in a way meant to impress residents, lend legitimacy to the police, and freshen the department's image.

"There's this element of showmanship . . . with how this technology is being rolled out and presented," Harris says. "They made it sound like a video game for the police."[96]

Residents are invited to participate in the game by contributing their own surveillance. This so-called community element deepens the inherent bias of the predictions, with "racism baked in" to the data.

The simultaneous deployment of community policing and predictive policing strategies not only has the potential to dangerously intensify racist policing but also puts a friendly, reform-oriented face on that intensification. By focusing on people who police deem inherently dangerous, predictive policing can actually justify more aggressive policing tactics, at the same time as "community policing" promises some members of the community that the police are "on their side." It's a pernicious combination.

In all of its incarnations, the professed mission of policing is "public safety." But safety cannot truly happen in the context of an institution that regularly perpetrates violence, including the violence that is part and parcel of the system, such as arrest and incarceration. Community policing and predictive policing extend that violence while hardening the divide between those who are seen as "protected" and those who must be "protected from." The idea of policing that serves the whole community proves to be an illusion.

"I feel safe in my community," K says. "I'm only scared of the police."

6

YOUR SCHOOL IS YOUR PRISON

It feels like being punished. . . . It feels like jail, being checked every time we go to school.

—Isabelle Robinson, Marjory Stoneman Douglas
High School student

White kids get the opportunity to be kids. Black kids are not given that opportunity. The mistakes that land their peers in detention or less can land a Black kid in jail or, God forbid, the grave.

—Gregory McKelvey, Portland activist

ON VALENTINE'S DAY, 2018, A NINETEEN-YEAR-OLD FORMER STUDENT shot thirty-four people at Marjory Stoneman Douglas High School in Parkland, Florida. Seventeen of them died. The impact of this horrific tragedy ricocheted across the country. High school and middle school students organized walkouts against gun violence and the policies that exacerbate it. For some students, that meant advocating for gun control. For others, it meant calling for more school security officers.[1] For still others, the call was broader and meant drawing attention to the underresourcing of education, mental health care, and other needs in marginalized communities.[2] The Parkland shooting took place at a majority-white, largely middle-class school, but leading student activists pointed out that in many Black and Brown communities, violence happens regularly with much less national attention, and is driven by structural racism and poverty.

As the voices of student protesters rose, the voices of adult authority figures grew louder, too. While some echoed student activists' demands for more resources and services in underserved communities, other adults were shouting an old, familiar refrain. In the name of improving student safety and reducing violence, many authority figures called for a buildup of policing and surveillance in schools.

Expansions of the prison industrial complex tend to flare in the wake of devastating, highly publicized acts of violence, no matter who is primarily affected. Sex offense laws become more stringent in the wake of headline-grabbing occurrences of sexual violence against women and children. In the realm of child protective services, stricter mandatory reporting laws pass in the aftermath of highly publicized instances of child abuse. In the wake of a school shooting, politicians and pundits call for ramped-up school "security." But in a prison nation, security becomes another form of violence, often enacted against the very people it supposedly intends to protect—in this case, students.

In the months after the Parkland shooting, sheriffs reminded their officers that in order to continue to uphold their oaths to "serve and protect," they had to be willing to use deadly force.[3] Suddenly, the idea that police officers in schools were not willing *enough* to use deadly force broke onto the political scene with vigor.[4] Attorney General

Jeff Sessions called for more police in schools.[5] Governors funneled millions of dollars toward that end—sometimes shifting money away from core educational needs to bulk up security.[6]

The state of Texas pumped new resources into an existing armed marshal program, which permitted school employees to carry concealed weapons, ostensibly in order to defend against potential shooters. (At the time, eight states permitted teachers to carry firearms; three of them passed such laws after the Parkland shooting.)[7] In Maryland, Republican and Democratic legislators alike rushed to pass a bill requiring an officer (or else "coverage" by area police) in every school in the state.[8] Not a single senator voted against it.

As politicians flocked toward police-based reforms, many students—including some in Parkland—balked at these efforts to protect them. A month and a half after the shooting, Sarah Chadwick, a sixteen-year-old Marjory Stoneman Douglas High School student, tweeted, "Tomorrow we will have to go through security check points and be given clear backpacks, my school is starting to feel like a prison." Her classmate Isabelle Robinson commented to CNN, "It feels like being punished. . . . It feels like jail, being checked every time we go to school."[9] Their classmate David Hogg (who went on to become a national activist against gun violence) noted, "We have hundreds of police officers around our school now. . . . What I'm really worried is going to happen is that we're going to increase the school-to-prison pipeline which disproportionately affects people of color and lower socioeconomic status. . . . What we should have is more policies that have students feeling safe and secure in their schools, and not being fought against like it's a prison."[10]

Hogg's mention of the school-to-prison pipeline echoes the longtime advocacy efforts of Black and Brown students to call attention to the ways that their schools can be hostile to them—places where arrests and police violence are commonplace and where disciplinary measures regularly drive them into the criminal punishment system.[11] When officials, lawmakers, and media figures began vigorously promoting school security in early 2018, it was already a familiar tune for many. In the name of safety, Black, Brown, disabled, trans, and other marginalized students have long been heavily policed and surveilled within their schools. Students' movements and actions are severely restricted and intrusively monitored by school safety officers or actual police officers in many schools in communities of color. Police hover around every turn: 42 percent of U.S. public schools already have at least one school resource officer (SRO), a law enforcement officer dedicated to crime prevention in that school.[12] The threat of consequences—including imprisonment—becomes vividly ingrained in student consciousness.

For many Black and Brown students, the intensification of school policing in the wake of school shootings has made their school experiences more dangerous. When lawmakers and school officials ramp up school security measures, they say they're taking these actions in pursuit of "safety," particularly in the aftermath of a school shooting. But in the name of safety and security, students of color find themselves far less safe than they were previously, as they are violently policed, arrested, pushed out, and shoved onto a path toward prison.

An Armed Occupation

As Gregory McKelvey, a Black Lives Matter activist living in Portland, Oregon, who is now in his twenties, puts it, "My school was never a location of a shooting, so why should I have to pay for the sins of white kids in other locations?"[13]

McKelvey's high school may not have been the location of a shooting, but that doesn't mean he felt safe there. He grew up in Beaverton, Oregon, where Black students made up less than 5 percent of his school; most kids were white or Latinx. His neighborhood's demographics were similar, and in high school, he and other Black students grew accustomed to being stopped by police while doing nothing illegal. Sometimes they knew that their own neighbors had called the cops. "It is really impactful to know that just your existence in a neighborhood is looked at as suspicious and as we see from events such as the murder of Trayvon Martin, these perceptions can become deadly," McKelvey says.

The police maintained a visible presence at the school. Students had to pass a squad car to enter each morning. The school resource officer had an office with windows looking out into the middle of the school, an office that students had to pass to go from class to class. The officer walked the halls and monitored the cafeteria at lunchtime. In other words, the presence of the police was inescapable.

After a string of calculator thefts at McKelvey's school, school administrators and the SRO began questioning Black students about the thefts, zeroing in on McKelvey, whom they saw as a leader among his peers. The teenager told them he knew nothing, but they were not satisfied. One afternoon during McKelvey's junior year of high school, the school resource officer, armed with a warrant, came to his home with eight other officers, all dressed in riot gear. They kicked down his door, drawing guns on McKelvey and his grandmother, who lived with him and his parents. (His parents were at work at the time.) The warrant allowed the officers to take McKelvey's electronics—and even those of his family. They did so, throwing his bedroom into disarray as an officer, gun drawn, kept him and his grandmother sequestered in the kitchen. This is not unusual; across the country, police enter homes regularly, tear apart people's personal belongings, and cart away items under the guise of an investigation.

The next day, McKelvey had to go to school and face the same cop who had made him fear for his life in his own home. He was traumatized and terrified—but the questioning didn't stop. The officer continued to interrogate McKelvey repeatedly over the following year, sometimes pulling him out of class. Eventually the officer showed up at McKelvey's track practice, handcuffed him in front of everyone, and hauled him into the county jail. He remained incarcerated for hours, although he was not under arrest—the officer told him he was simply there to learn a lesson.

Simply being in the school building became terrifying. McKelvey spent his days fearing he'd get arrested even though he'd stolen nothing. Meanwhile, since the police had taken his electronics, he didn't have a computer and fell behind on his schoolwork, which impacted his prospects for college.

"I have never trusted police since then," he says. "For me and all of my friends it felt like police were in schools to make sure that the white kids were safe from Black kids, which has a huge impact on your idea of self-worth as a child. It's this idea that you are instantly a liability or a threat when you know you have done nothing wrong."

By the time he was targeted by the school police in high school, McKelvey had already experienced years of being seen as a threat in his white neighborhood, stopped by police for "suspicious activity" such as walking his dog, having a water bottle, or carrying a heavy backpack. When he was fourteen, he was walking with a friend who had recently been raped. She saw the person who had assaulted her and against whom she had a restraining order. But when she called 911, the police handcuffed McKelvey instead.

"This is just the life of a Black kid," he reflects, echoing the experiences of Malik, K, Joe, and countless other Black youth across the country. "It was the life of all my friends. We thought that was just life. We knew it didn't happen to our white peers but we just thought it's how it was."

The extension of the prison industrial complex into schools, via school-based policing, is a given in many predominantly Black and Brown neighborhoods. Like so many extensions of the prison industrial complex, it often happens under the guise of help.

Just one example: In Riverside County, California, the Youth Accountability Team program is a joint project of local police, the probation department, social work agencies, the district attorney's office, and some of the county's schools. The program declares that its mission is to "provide a collaborative and integrated multi-agency approach to rapid and effective intervention with at-risk youth and less serious juvenile offenders by providing necessary services to youth and their families."[14] However, according to a 2018 lawsuit filed by the ACLU of Southern California, the program is used by police, teachers, and administrators to punish students and send them into the criminal legal system. Students are often sentenced to probation for breaking an ambiguous California law targeting students who "persistent[ly] or habitual[ly] refus[e] to obey the reasonable and proper orders or directions of school authorities." Probation means rampant surveillance and strict requirements, including measures like weekly check-ins, drug testing, home searches, reports to law enforcement of late arrivals at school, and a mandate to "tour" a jail.[15]

The children targeted by the Youth Accountability Team program are between the ages of twelve and seventeen and are said to be displaying "pre-delinquent" or "delinquent" behavior at school. What these labels encompass is left to individual interpretation, and those interpretations are inevitably driven by racism, classism, and ableism. One eleven-year-old, for instance, was referred to the program for "pulling the race card" when interacting with the school staff, which indicates that challenging racial discrimination by school staff can result in severe punishment.

As the lawsuit charges, "This effectively brings more children, not fewer, into the juvenile justice system, relying on probation supervision to take the place of school-based interventions." It's a reform that expands the prison industrial complex—placing teachers and administrators in a position of carrying out the work of that system and enacting its racial violence.

In the vast majority of states, Black students are drastically more likely to be arrested in school; Latinx and Native students also experience disproportionate numbers of arrests.[16] In Chicago, a 2013 study by Project NIA and Loyola University revealed that more than 75 percent of arrests that took place in schools were of Black students.[17] In New York, Black and Latinx students together made up 90 percent of those arrested.[18]

Oumou Kaba (no relation to Mariame Kaba), a junior at a New York public school where most students are Black and Latinx, describes school as a series of different forms of control and policing, from harsh dress code enforcement to hallway patrolling to police violence. She doesn't know why the police have multiplied over the past year and a half, but that multiplication has left her feeling even less safe. In a familiar refrain, she describes, "It feels like jail. They're always patrolling; they always target us. They always want to get us in trouble."[19]

Far from being of help, the police seem to simply be waiting for students to do something wrong so they can intervene, Kaba says. Often, intervening means making conflicts worse by using physical force.

"I feel like they don't know what boundaries are," Kaba says. "When a fight happens, they tackle you and do unnecessary things when they could just handle the situation differently. . . . [T]hey're waiting for something to happen so they could bust [out] the handcuffs."

Even when they're not tackling or arresting students, the pervasive presence of police creates a prison-like atmosphere of constant surveillance. Kaba remains apprehensive about how she's moving, what she's saying, and what she's doing, just hoping they won't approach her.

Moreover, it's not only the actual police doing the watching and the threatening. The culture of violent surveillance also extends to the school administration. In March, when Kaba got into a fight with another student, the assistant principal tackled her. Then, she says, she was forced into writing a statement about what she did, and was subsequently suspended. By the time Kaba was allowed to return to school, it was May.

Keeping Girls "Safe"

Though discussions about the school-to-prison pipeline tend to revolve around the way that boys of color are targeted, girls of color, such as Kaba, are also targeted disproportionately. The policing of girls in schools is frequently framed as a practice intended to keep them "safe," even as they are—particularly if they're Black or Brown—simultaneously depicted as a threat.

For instance, six-year-old Salecia Johnson was arrested on battery charges for a "temper tantrum"—throwing toys, wall hangings, and books—at her Georgia kindergarten in 2012. Police essentially treated the six-year-old, who is Black, as an adult, handcuffing her and placing her in police custody. The town's police chief said Johnson was handcuffed "for her safety."[20]

The arrest of a six-year-old may seem egregious, but young Black and Brown girls are regularly targeted with harsh school discipline from preschool onward. A study by the National Women's Law Center found that "disproportionate discipline starts as early as preschool, with black girls making up 20 percent of girls enrolled, but 54 percent of girls suspended from preschool."[21]

Black girls are often singled out in uniquely gendered ways, for not conforming to dress codes or gender expectations, as Monique W. Morris, co-founder of the National Black Women's Justice Institute, exposes in her 2018 book *Pushout: The Criminalization of Black Girls in Schools*.[22]

MG, a Black high school junior in Brooklyn, has experienced the ways that school authorities assume Black girls are "looking for" sexual attention, and so increased surveillance and restrictions must be imposed.[23] Of course, this route to supposed safety is littered with blame-the-victim assumptions.

"Black young women are just more closely watched," MG says. "Let's say someone gets attacked—they believe it's the young woman's fault because of what she's wearing."

School authority figures often perceive Black girls as more adult than their peers, and that perception translates into attempts at control and harsh discipline.[24] MG knows this firsthand, having been given detention for wearing a spaghetti strap shirt and ripped jeans. "They said that I was having my arms out too much, having too much cleavage," MG says. She recalls teachers asking her, "'What are you looking for? What are your intentions?' I was like, 'It's just clothing.'" Meanwhile, MG has noticed that her male classmates are allowed to wear clothes—such as ripped jeans, shorts, or colorful socks—that she and her female peers cannot.

Stereotypes about race and gender collide to target Black and Brown girls, who are often viewed as more sexualized than their white or Asian counterparts. One day, MG's teacher decided that her friend's shorts were too short and sent her home for the day. The teacher said nothing to another girl whose shorts were even shorter. MG's friend is Black; the other girl is Romanian.

A 2016 study in the bimonthly academic journal *Urban Education* notes, "Black girls were more likely to experience exclusionary discipline outcomes for subjective reasons, such as disobedience/defiance, detrimental behavior, and third-degree assault, which depend on the judgment of school personnel."[25]

Sometimes this even means being disciplined more than boys. Nationally, Morris notes, "In ten southern states, Black girls were the most suspended among all students—an unusual and noteworthy problem."[26] In fact, nationwide, "Black girls are suspended at higher rates than . . . most boys," according to the U.S. Department of Education Office for Civil Rights.[27] This strenuous discipline comes down especially hard on LGBTQ Black girls (as well as other LGBTQ girls of color and gender-nonconforming girls of all races).[28]

Criminalization isn't only about handcuffs and jail—it's also about the ways that students are "disciplined" by being pushed out of school. The prison nation courses through these "normal" school discipline practices, carried out by deans and teachers. The actions of school personnel melt into policing: students who are suspended or expelled from school are more likely to become involved with the criminal punishment system.[29] Black students are most likely to be severely disciplined, including suspensions and expulsions.[30] Students with disabilities are also overwhelmingly targeted. Those disparities are growing and driving criminalization in a devastating cycle.[31]

Beyond suspensions, Black, Native American, Native Hawaiian, and Pacific Islander girls are disproportionately likely to be subject to a "school-related arrest."[32] In addition to students of color being disproportionately targeted on an individual level, schools filled with students of color are more likely to be filled with police—and issues that might have been addressed in another manner often result in arrest when police are present.

Preparing Students for Prison

The intensification of school policing that McKelvey, Kaba, and MG have experienced plagues millions of students around the country. Thanks in part to increased funding from the Department of Justice, the number of police in schools rose drastically in the first decade of the twenty-first century, thus increasing school-based arrests and heightening the involvement of the criminal punishment system in students' lives at young ages.[33]

A regular police presence in schools also paves the ground for police violence beyond arrests. In-school police have tased students, shot them with stun guns, body-slammed them, pepper-sprayed them, and choked them.[34] Moreover, Crystal Laura, a professor at Chicago State University and author of *Being Bad: My Baby Brother and the School-to-Prison Pipeline*, says a quieter type of violence is at work. By turning schools into sites of policing and surveillance, at least in relation to Black, Brown, disabled, and otherwise marginalized students, we are teaching students to operate in a prison-like environment: their education is an entry into the prison nation.

"We're not only reflecting prisons, but we're preparing young people to function in them," says Laura, whose book chronicles how her younger brother was funneled from school to prison. "If you think for a moment of the characteristics that really strike you as so prison-like—uniforms and IDs and security apparatuses and the actual physical structure, concrete, chain-link fences, terrible food, all these things—literally, I could play back that same list and instead of saying, 'I'm going to describe the characteristics that are prison-like,' I could say, 'These are the characteristics that are school-like.'"[35]

This isn't to say that schools *are* prisons, or that schools cannot serve as sites of growth and even resistance to injustice. Schools and universities have, thanks to the courageous efforts of students and teachers, become fertile grounds for a wide range of protest movements. However, this country's schools are not immune to the legacies of injustice coursing through all large U.S. institutions. The school has never entirely been separate from the forces of policing and surveillance, as activists and scholars (notably David Stovall at the University of Illinois, Chicago) have documented. The prison system didn't *do* this to schools; the prison system and the schooling system grew up alongside each other.[36]

Throughout American history, schools have served the purpose of "sorting" children into who will go where in a capitalist society—who will be managers and leaders, and who will be taking the orders. Education scholar Pedro Noguera notes that certain schools, those primarily populated by Black, Brown, and low-income students, "are generally regarded as educational wastelands and schools of last resort, and placement in these schools constitutes the ultimate sorting and socializing on the path to nowhere."[37] Many disabled students have also long been sorted into the "path to nowhere" pile by schools.

In the context of school policing, the path to nowhere is a path to arrest, expulsion, probation, and prison. Of course, it's not presented that way. Reforms, like the ones pushed in the wake of Parkland, aren't just deepening the prisonization of schools; they're also entrenching the notion that prison-like practices are what keep students (and faculty, staff, and administrators) safe.

The language used to describe policing in schools is draped in euphemisms. A police officer with a gun is a "school resource officer." The National Association of School Resource Officers explains, "In addition to improving security, SROs bridge gaps between youth and law enforcement, mentor students and serve as guest lecturers in classrooms."[38] When former attorney general Jeff Sessions announced the Justice Department's post-Parkland push for more police in schools, he invoked the safety of children, commenting, "No child should have to fear going to school or walking the streets of their neighborhood."[39] But many Black, Brown, and otherwise marginalized children fear going to school and walking the streets *because of* policing and surveillance.

McKelvey says that when it comes to discussing "school resource officers" versus police on the street, it can be unhelpful to even differentiate them. SROs aren't about "resources" or education. It's time to peel off the euphemisms. "They are the same people doing the same things," McKelvey says.

Policing-in-school tactics that are designed to be less punitive aren't the answer, either. For example, in New York City at the beginning of the fall 2018 school year, school police were provided with a new option: when a child was charged with a low-level offense, they could issue a warning card instead of a criminal summons. However, a pilot program in seventy-one of the city's four hundred schools the previous year showed that police usually didn't choose the warning card option. Instead, criminal summonses in New York schools increased that year.[40]

Why are police dealing with small problems in schools, anyway? Why don't counselors assume the role of handling these issues? For millions of youth in the United States, this isn't a possibility because their schools have no counselors, social workers, or even nurses—only police.[41] In New York, there are nearly twice as many cops as counselors in schools.[42] Counselors and social workers serve a number of purposes in schools, from helping students deal with trauma in their lives to supporting them in planning their next steps after high school. Studies have shown that the presence of counselors improves students' academic achievement, graduation rates, and attendance and lowers disciplinary incidents. In fact, counselors—unlike police—have been shown to make schools safer.[43] Activists working against the school-to-prison pipeline have long argued that resources should be shifted away from school policing and toward hiring counselors and other supportive staff. For instance, in 2016, Dignity in Schools, a national coalition committed to dismantling the school-to-prison pipeline, launched the Counselors Not Cops campaign to demand an end to police in schools and an investment in supportive services for students.[44]

In the early months of 2018, as students around the country protested against gun violence in schools, some students simultaneously rallied against another fundamental threat to their education and their lives: the prisonization of their schools.[45] They called for more guidance counselors and fewer cops.[46] They challenged the use of metal detectors.[47] They demanded the removal of school resource officers.[48] Just as adult authorities were summoning the forces of "security" and violently enforced "safety," throngs of young people were saying no to policing as a false solution to violence in schools and beyond. In fact, they pointed to the increase in SROs as a step *away* from safety.

When asked about the presence of police in her high school, one Portland, Oregon, student activist told KATU News, a local ABC news affiliate, "Students just really, really want to be able to go to school and be safe and learn. Having a gun on campus just seems really unsafe and unnecessary."[49]

Policing Restorative Justice

Even as SROs multiply and metal detectors proliferate, even as calls to arms rise in response to school shootings, discussions about the school-to-prison pipeline are expanding, too. More people are challenging the injustices that the criminal system perpetrates against youth. And even as they send more police into schools, authority figures are feeling the pressure to respond to the accusation that they are shuttling their most marginalized students on a fast track to prison.

Some schools—and even police departments—have offered restorative justice (RJ) programs as an alternative route for young people. In many ways, the broader use of restorative justice—a practice that, when done authentically, is fundamentally different than "discipline"—is exciting. According to longtime RJ theorist and practitioner Howard Zehr, "Restorative justice is a process to involve, to the extent possible, those who have a stake in a specific offense and to collectively identify and address harms, needs and obligations, in order to heal and put things right as possible."[50] Often, this means victims come together with those who have caused harm and others in the community who have been affected. Frequently, this happens by way of a facilitated "peace circle," in which each person shares their story about the incident in question. Connections are drawn, hard questions are asked, new relationships spring up, and old relationships may be strengthened. Instead of a punishment being doled out from on high—a state system sentencing a perpetrator—participants move toward an agreement for how to address the situation. How will the victim be supported in their healing? How will the perpetrator be held accountable?

How will the community move forward so that this harm is less likely to happen again?

These questions, and this framework, are not new. Restorative justice is a model that emerged from Indigenous practices that have been used, in different forms, around the world for thousands of years. For decades, restorative justice has been used more broadly by grassroots organizations, communities, and individuals to address problems and heal harm. It's not simply a program to be enacted within the current criminal legal system, but a whole different way of doing justice—actual justice.

Teiahsha Bankhead, co-executive director of Restorative Justice for Oakland Youth, defines restorative justice as "a humanizing approach where people see each other as equals and not as wrongdoers or as victims, because every human is capable of being either one."[51]

However, as restorative justice practices have gained popularity and innovative and useful programs are being implemented in schools and communities, a strange and disturbing thing has happened. Across the country, police departments, both inside and outside schools, are implementing their own versions of restorative justice, particularly for youth. The majority of states now include some form of restorative justice language in their official statutes and codes regarding juvenile justice, and many cities in states with no such codes still include "restorative justice" as part of their youth criminal legal system.[52] But the versions of restorative justice employed by police departments differ tremendously from the actual intents and purposes of RJ: children are arrested—an act of violence in itself—and *then* diverted to supposedly kinder, gentler "restorative justice courts." Police are included in peace circles, a practice that ignores their role as authority figures with nearly complete power over youths' futures.

As police departments increasingly set up shop in schools, officers frequently clash with those attempting to facilitate true restorative justice processes—practices that, in their true form, are antithetical to the punishment-oriented approach of policing. When those clashes come to a head, it's usually not the police who lose.

For Jesse, a school restorative justice practitioner in his late twenties, the presence of police in Chicago's public schools directly interfered with his ability to do his job.[53] Jesse works for an agency that places practitioners in schools for several weeks or months. The practitioners lead circles and develop a restorative justice infrastructure within the school, enabling the school to move forward with a program for building community and addressing conflicts even after the practitioners leave.

Jesse approaches his RJ work from a social justice standpoint. "It's actually about creating a healthy culture and a healthy community for young people to feel safe, for everyone really to feel safe—and for their voices to be amplified," he says. He also sees this as a spiritual practice: "For me restorative justice is not just about restoring our relationships to each other but it's also about restoring our relationships to nature, restoring our relationships to the land and restoring our relationship to our ancestors."

The biggest determining factor in whether a school ends up implementing a real restorative justice program is whether the administration is on board—or whether it is still set on a model of punishment. In some schools, the administration is open to real transformation in the way the school deals with harm and conflict. But in many schools, "restorative justice" becomes a moniker slapped on a program that still has punishment at its core. In this sense, restorative justice is sometimes seen by administrations as simply a milder alternative to sending kids to the police. It's presented to schools as a different way to deal with conflict rather than as a culture change that moves away from punishment and toward community-building and connection.

"Restorative justice was rolled out . . . to reduce suspensions, detentions, and arrests. It's coming from a reductionist framework," Jesse says. "They think . . . it's only focusing on when people are in conflict."

After working to build the restorative justice program for a year and a half at one high school, Jesse had developed close relationships with students, faculty, and staff. He'd even become friendly with the police who worked in the school; they chatted and shared pictures of their families. His relationships with the police weren't stainless, though. On a couple of occasions when he was in the midst of trying to do a restorative intervention, police sent him out of the room in order to deal with things their own way. Plus, Jesse was in the process of documenting violations by officers—situations in which he'd seen them grabbing students, throwing them against walls, and shouting "Fuck you!" at them. He describes an instance where his colleague observed an officer take a student who'd been involved in a fight into the bathroom. The student emerged with a bloody face and was taken away in an ambulance.

The dean publicized the fact that since she'd come to the school, arrests had significantly decreased. Jesse notes that her data documented arrests but not instances of brutality or threats. For example, he saw police put handcuffs on students in response to minor conflicts, telling them they'd lock them up, even if they weren't actually planning to arrest them. Arrests also happened, and sometimes for acts that might not be considered crimes: once, Jesse says, a student was arrested for throwing oranges. Given that his position was ostensibly arranged for this purpose, Jesse attempted to de-escalate situations whenever possible. At times this put him in conflict with the school officers—and eventually this led to his ouster.

One day, after lunch, as students were filing out of the cafeteria, Jesse heard an officer yell at them, "Get your asses back in the lunchroom!"

Jesse intervened, asking her to stop yelling.

The officer told him he was out of line. "If I want to yell, I'll yell," she said. She went on to say that her partner had had issues with Jesse challenging the officers' practices—and that it was time to "get this settled." She said she'd call her supervisor, a Chicago police sergeant, and Jesse should call his supervisor from his agency.

Jesse pleaded with her, saying he thought there was a misunderstanding. He didn't understand why the situation had escalated so quickly. But she called in her sergeant, who arrived before Jesse was able to get in touch with his supervisor. The sergeant told Jesse that he was going to charge him with obstruction of justice. Furthermore, he was giving his officers permission to arrest anyone in the school who challenged their authority. The principal backed the sergeant, saying that Jesse did not respect the school's existing systems and structures—structures based around discipline and police authority.

Finally, Jesse was able to get his supervisor on the phone. His supervisor wanted to talk to Jesse privately, but the principal grabbed the phone out of Jesse's hands and ordered the supervisor to come to the school right away.

Later that afternoon, there was a group meeting. "It was a big setup," Jesse says. During the meeting, the administrators and police insisted that they "loved restorative justice." However, any challenge to their authority was unacceptable. Jesse was told to gather his things and get out of the school immediately.

In Jesse's school, authority figures didn't just want a well-contained alternative that would operate quietly alongside the police. They wanted their RJ alternative to be *subject* to the police. And, like so many other structures in our society, it was.

Jennifer Viets has facilitated restorative justice circles in her community for several years and is now a practitioner of restorative justice—or "restorative practices" (RP), as it's often called within the school system—in Chicago schools. She points out that even when the school resource officers appear to be on board with a restorative approach, their place in the school is still grounded in their ability to impose severe punishment.

"Even though some of them might be super-nice or might be a mentor to some people, when push comes to shove, they're making school-based arrests," she says. In one school she was placed in, there were two police officers in uniform, plus four deans and a security team—all of whom were supposed to engage in RP. But the power structure means that even if everyone is physically sitting in a circle, the cops will always be at the front of the line.

"Everyone is always going to defer to the police," Viets says.

There's now an alternative youth court—a restorative justice court—on the west side of Chicago. The court launched in 2017 in Chicago's North Lawndale neighborhood, which is 89 percent Black, with a median household income of $22,383.[54] The restorative justice court is physically structured as a circle: the judge sits on the same level as the participants.[55] However, some RJ practitioners are wary of the fact that a judge is still present, and the "alternative" only goes so far. Fred Cooper, a peace circle facilitator in the community, told the *Chicago Defender* that he doesn't think RJ can have a true home inside the criminal legal system; being mandated to attend a peace circle doesn't make sense. Under an RJ framework, all participants are supposed to *choose* to be there—but if someone's only other option is incarceration, deciding to participate in RJ court doesn't seem like an actual choice. "Honestly, I just think we're not all on the same page here," Cooper told the *Defender*. "[Restorative justice] means too much to me."[56]

Similarly, in some school settings, students are being told that participation in these types of processes is mandatory. That was Oumou Kaba's experience after a school fight with another girl:

> It will be me, the other girl, the principal or the mediation counselor. We'll sit down and talk. But it's like you can't put two girls in a room who just had an altercation or fight. It's not going to work out. . . . And they will tell us to probably shake hands on it, or hug, and it's just like, I'm not about to hug somebody I just fought. I'm not doing that. . . . They did what they wanted to do. And it's like your voice don't really matter, because it's like, who are

you? You're a child compared to the students and teachers.
Not going to listen to you . . . Mediations don't do nothing.
And I still got suspended.

When a student is told that they are required to engage in a restorative process, or else they will be punished, it undermines the logic of restorative practices. The establishment of programs that label themselves "restorative justice" but carry out practices of control and punishment is a prime example of a reform that extends the reach of the prison nation.

However, RJ practitioners and advocates emphasize that the solution is *not* to give up restorative justice—an essential practice for dealing with harm in some situations—just because police are misusing the term to justify their own ends.

Mariame Kaba points out that while police may be throwing the term around for their own uses, restorative justice has not been co-opted—because the state isn't actually doing restorative justice. The goal, she says, should be to actually practice community-based restorative justice on a wider scale.

"Restorative justice hasn't permeated the culture enough yet for us to be talking about its cooption," Kaba says. "The state is always going to colonize ideas that it finds threatening to itself. If enough people were implementing restorative practices in their lives and in their communities, then we would have less to worry about with police having 'restorative circles.' For me, the question is how many people can we get outside that system, using the tools of restoration, and the practices of restoration, to drown out the fake stuff that the state tries to do. . . . The state is doing its work and we need to do ours."[57] A quest to get police to stop saying "restorative justice" is not going to succeed. Instead, it's vital to focus on expanding community-based restorative justice efforts, and supporting the activists and organizations who are doing this work already.

In addition to a serious community commitment to real RJ, communities and schools need resources to shore up this work. Cities and states have divested from marginalized communities as resources are shunted toward the police—and part of the problem with how restorative practices play out in schools is a lack of resources. Not only are there too many police, but there are too few Jesses, too few Jennifer Vietses.

There's also still too little understanding—among many administrators, staff, and educators—of the rationale behind the practice. Viets says she has received mixed reactions to RP in schools. Some teachers are all in, really excited to be chosen for RP participation. Others are much less enthusiastic. "There are teachers who are like, 'Oh hell no. I'm gonna quit this job before you make me do this.' And they do," she says.

She has also encountered naysayers who don't believe RJ can be effective, and their pessimism becomes a self-fulfilling prophecy. "There are people who do not implement it with fidelity and then say, 'We tried and it didn't work!'"

Even with these obstructions, Viets still feels good about the work she does in schools. She's working to reduce the system's harm, intervene when adults are hurting children, sometimes prevent situations in which the police might be called, and—when the police *are* called—help people deal with trauma in the aftermath of a police encounter. What's needed, she says, is *more:* a long-term, full-on investment in restorative justice, giving practitioners time and space to work on supporting people to shift the culture.

There's no doubt that restorative practices can help ameliorate conditions in schools. However, there's a limit to what RJ can do when simply inserted into a system grounded in punishment. Jesse's story doesn't tell us that restorative justice has been co-opted to a point that it no longer works. Instead, it shows how RJ can't simply be about changing one tiny corner of a school. It cannot happen in isolation. It can't be established as a "kinder" component of the punishment system. There must be a wider willingness to engage with a practice that is wholly contrary to "discipline."

In fact, engaging with real RJ—as opposed to a police-facilitated "alternative"—may well inspire participants to question the presence of police and other practices of control and discipline, Jesse says. When problems are approached honestly and all parties are allowed to speak, he says, students often draw connections between the policing of schools and the policing of society.

What these students are accessing is a central truth: the problem of policing in schools is part of the much broader problem of policing itself. Examining the ways in which policing and mainstream educational disciplinary practices intertwine demonstrates how both are functioning to maintain a status quo of social and racial control, in the name of "safety." Dismantling the school-to-prison pipeline will require rethinking and reframing not just school policing or school discipline but also ideas about safety in general. As new reforms pave the way for more cops in schools, it is time to challenge the notion that surveillance and policing are the answers to school-based violence. School safety does not come in the form of a uniform, a badge, and a gun.

7
BEYOND ALTERNATIVES

We have what we need to solve our problems.

—Mariame Kaba

WHEN WE CHALLENGE THE WAYS THE PRISON INDUSTRIAL COMPLEX has expanded beyond prison walls, people often ask: "If not this, then what?" Given how so many essential resources like social services, health care, and education are linked to the prison nation, it's easy to wonder whether it's possible to truly move beyond the prison.

The good news is that for as long as there have been prisons and prison-like institutions, there have been people imagining, and creating, a world without them. Prisons didn't exist for most of human history, and even today, plenty of truly non-prison strategies are already in practice regularly, all around us.

So the question is not "*Can* prisons go away?" The question is *how* do we make them go away? And how do we do so in a way that doesn't generate new oppressive institutions? How do we pursue the abolition of prison in all of its manifestations?

Many of today's prison abolitionists focus not only on tearing down the buildings formally known as prisons and jails but also on challenging, and ultimately ending, institutions of confinement, policing, and control wherever they may emerge, from psychiatric institutionalization to house arrest, from the sex offender registry to the school-to-prison pipeline. Unlike efforts to replace the institution of mass incarceration with a similarly shaped "alternative," abolitionists don't hold one uniform vision. Instead, they champion a range of approaches to work toward a liberated future.

The prospect of such transformation can be daunting. Sometimes it may feel that the systems we're critiquing, bad as they are, are too difficult to replace. At times we may ask, isn't something better than nothing?

The answer to this question is twofold. First, around the country, people are already building a whole lot of fruitful "somethings," devising non-carceral ways to confront conflict, violence, mental health problems, addiction, and other harms. The point is not to provide an alternative to electronic monitoring, an alternative to probation, an alternative to the registry, and so on—but to look instead at the actual problems we face, and to take lessons from projects around the country that are addressing these problems in effective ways. The second answer is that sometimes the best "alternative" is . . . nothing. Sometimes the most useful action is no action at all.

Nothing

For Patricia Howard, the Indiana mother of five who's been on house arrest for several years, her confinement—as with so many people subjected to prison or one of its alternatives—has proven to be anything but useful. In fact, it has been the opposite. As house arrest prevents her from doing the simplest things in her community—going to church, taking her kids to the park, attending their school events, visiting a friend's house—it has prevented her from living the fulfilling adult life she'd built for herself. In many ways, it has prohibited her from contributing meaningfully to her community.

"Dealing with the judicial system at that level, it fundamentally changes who you are—the person who I was, I was confident, I was smart, I was put together, I had my life together. I was for all intents and purposes a good person," Howard says. "Home confinement just completely ripped the carpet out from underneath everything we were trying to build. . . . It was such an unnecessary answer to the entire situation."

Similarly, for Monica Jones, the Arizona activist and student who was arrested and brought to a sex work rescue operation, the alternative to a forced rescue program is simple: no alternative. "Leave people alone," she says. "If they don't need your help, you leave them alone."

Jones says that rather than shoving sex workers into positions where they're being forcibly "helped," often by criminalizing them, a truly helpful step would be to remove the "criminal" label. "Make it more safe for them to exist in this world," she says.

Moving toward real freedom will mean taking criminalization out of the equation. As long as we retain the idea of a "criminal"—along with entrenched, racialized ideas about who a criminal is and what they look like—alternatives will always involve the idea of putting people Somewhere Else. As long as we are creating the category of a human being who is lesser, who is marked as unfit for regular society, there will always be a push to siphon off those individuals—to ensure they are not with the rest of us, on our streets, in our homes, in our societies.

But pushing back against the idea of criminality itself means building solutions that won't revolve around creating new Somewhere Elses to put people. Instead, it means building a future that revolves around shared community.

What would it look like for there to simply be no Somewhere Else?

Ending the Somewhere Else includes abolishing needless and harmful surveillance mechanisms that not only embolden police forces but also galvanize neighbors to police each other. Case in point: the sex offender registry. "They just need to get rid of the registry altogether," Robert Suttle, the Louisiana man who was convicted of "intentional exposure to AIDS virus" and now advocates against HIV criminalization, says. "The point of the registry is—for what?"

By looking more closely at these structures of surveillance and confinement, it becomes clear that the registry is not helping people. There is no evidence whatsoever that it prevents sexual violence. It actually foments both institutional and interpersonal violence against registered people, preventing them from accessing basic resources like housing and making them vulnerable to vigilante attacks. It does not do what it purports to do (reducing sexual harm). What it does do is make it very difficult for those in its clutches to work their way toward transformed lives in which they can support themselves and contribute to their communities.

A useful strategy for supporting people, enhancing safety, and preventing harm would effectively work itself out of existence. In contrast, tactics like house arrest and the registry—tactics of control and marginalization, instead of support—simply keep themselves going.

Ruth Wilson Gilmore compares the prison industrial complex to slavery in its success at reproducing itself. For example, most prison labor does not go toward manufacturing products that will be used in the outside world. Instead, it maintains the prison itself, keeping it operating, keeping it clean, keeping it ready for new inhabitants to cycle in and for older inhabitants to languish.[1] The same applies to mechanisms of control outside the prison—like the registry, probation, and the foster care system. The restrictions, heavy surveillance, and harsh consequences combine to successfully reproduce themselves. Under the state's watchful eye, it's so hard to meet requirements and stay within the bounds of the acceptable, especially when one is living in poverty and marked with a "criminal" label. People often end up incarcerated, or they lose their children, or they're locked in more restrictive treatment. Others, like Patricia Howard, still on house arrest at the time of this writing, are held indefinitely under the same mechanisms of control. The system feeds itself, and as it does, it grows, strengthens, and deepens its roots.

Thus, "nothing" becomes a powerful alternative to imagine. It stunts the growth of a self-feeding machine bent on expansion.

When it comes to mental-health-related "solutions," such as psychiatric institutions, forced drug treatment, and stringent mandatory outpatient regimens, the "nothing" option is a re-envisioning of our society's entire approach to psychiatric disability. This doesn't mean refusing help for people experiencing psychological pain; it means acknowledging that there are plenty of situations in which someone doesn't *want* help, or doesn't view their psychological difference as, in itself, a problem. Some advocates question the concept of diagnosis itself, much in the way that anti-prison activists are challenging the concept of criminality. (In fact, these groups of activists very often overlap.)

A diagnosis generally identifies a problem that should ideally be eradicated: when a person is diagnosed with an ear infection, or the flu, or cancer, the obvious assumption is that they'd be better off without it. However, when it comes to psychiatry, many diagnoses simply describe a way of thinking, acting, or being that differs from the norm. Mandated psychiatric treatment often assumes a goal of suppressing or eliminating those different ways of being in the world. Yet the overall goal of mental health treatment must not be to end mental and psychological difference. Of course, it's important to provide options for support and healing for those who seek them. But that's a very different phenomenon from *mandating* that people with certain mental health differences undergo elimination-oriented treatment. Organizations like the Hearing Voices Network, a national web of support and advocacy groups, are working to shift perceptions of people saddled with labels like "schizophrenia." Members of the network, which is made up of people who hear voices and see visions, reframe their experience to challenge the idea that mental differences are always problems to be fixed. The Hearing Voices Network's website explains:

> When we talk about voices and visions, we simply mean someone is hearing, seeing or sensing something that others around them aren't. For some, these experiences can be comforting. For example, someone who is lonely may really value a voice that becomes a trusted confidant. A person who has recently lost someone they care about may benefit from talking to them at the end of the day, or smelling their perfume/aftershave. Others find these experiences to be a source of inspiration. Authors, for example, sometimes talk about how the characters can come to life and write the story for them. However, for some people these voices and visions can be extremely distressing—criticising, threatening or causing confusion.[2]

In other words, in some cases, the experiences of hearing voices and seeing visions can be meaningful, revelatory, treasured. In other cases, they can be terrifying, painful, and inhibiting. Sometimes, in a single person, they are all of the above. Mental difference is complex and specific to individuals and their nuanced circumstances. The idea that there must *always* be treatment—a Somewhere Else, or at least a Something Else—ignores the fact that for some people, their different way of being isn't something they want to change, or isn't something for which they want outside help.

Similarly, many people can use illicit drugs without problem; only a small (albeit significant) percentage are actually addicted or in danger of overdose.[3] Yet the criminal legal system operates as if a person's choice to use a certain substance automatically necessitates an intervention—a "something" that brings them under state control.

Of course, not everyone is doing just fine. Plenty of people with addictions, disabilities, and health problems actually want and need support. But support does not always require a Somewhere Else. When a support-related idea is proposed, it's important to question whether it's simply another way of confining, controlling, and surveilling people—a strategy that causes more harm than help.

It's helpful to return to Sadie Ryanne Baker's litmus test for potential solutions: "We must examine every individual part of the mental health care system critically by asking, 'Does this specific thing help or hurt oppressed people?'" Forced medication, for example, is never ethical. Another strategy that does not pass the litmus test is pouring funding into police training to "improve" officers' responses to mental health crises. Calls for increased police training—instead of shifting first-response duties to real service providers—often push more resources into policing, ignoring officers' roles as purveyors of harm and fear. As Baker says, "I don't want my 'crisis counselor' to be open-carrying a gun."[4] Any authentic solution must work toward redefining safety as separate from policing and imprisonment.

However, just because the state shouldn't be making unilateral decisions or carting people off to Somewhere Else doesn't mean it has no responsibilities. The state holds an abundance of resources that can—and should—be redistributed in the service of true safety.

Pursuing real alternatives to prison must include acknowledging that harm and violence are often driven by poverty, economic injustice, and lack of access to basic necessities.[5] Mass incarceration, mass surveillance, and mass policing clearly have not ended murder, assault, or rape. Any real effort to prevent and address violence must involve an infusion of vital resources.

The role of the state needs to change. It needs to center on support instead of surveillance and control. That means that programs and assistance should be *offered* instead of deployed in the service of coercion and confinement. And these programs and support systems need to be radically reimagined to meet people's actual needs.

Actual Support: Building a Real Social Welfare System

We have mentioned a smattering of ingredients for what a non-carceral set of "alternatives" might look like. However, a true transformation in this direction would be much larger than the sum of its parts. At its core would be a new vision, one that leaves white supremacy, patriarchy, economic injustice, heteropatriarchy, ableism, and other structures of oppression in the dust. This vision would also recognize that any movement away from prisons and prison-like institutions must involve challenging capitalism and building an economically just system that provides actual support to those who need and want it.

For starters, within any realistic vision of a system built to meet people's needs rather than impose punishment, everyone must be able to access the health care they need, without a label or a charge imposed on them. "Right now, we *have* to diagnose clients to get reimbursed for services," notes Sadie Ryanne Baker, the Chicago activist who has been both a user and provider in the mental health system. "Removing insurance companies from the process altogether—which is a revolutionary idea because it would necessitate the radical transformation of our economy!—would stop the incentive for providers to over-diagnose." Moreover, she adds, "if services weren't dependent on income, everyone could have access to the types of treatment that are backed up by research but currently seen as luxuries of the ruling classes." In other words, removing financial incentives and impediments—and instead implementing access to mental health care for all—would drastically decrease unnecessary diagnoses, and the resulting consequences.

Food is another basic need that goes chronically unmet, particularly in low-income communities of color. Fundamentally changing that reality must be a key component of any true system of support. "In our neighborhoods, support looks like better food resources so people can eat healthy, something that will make their brain function," says Colette Payne, the Chicago mother who had been tethered to an electronic monitor. "I live in a neighborhood that doesn't even have a grocery store. It's been gone since 2013. . . . They took it down and now there's nothing there." Payne must ask her sister to drive her to the grocery store. She gets there about once a month and, when the food runs out, "I just have to eat restaurant food like everyone else."

When resources as basic as food are missing from a community, the search for real "alternatives to prison" must become a search for values and priorities instead. It's time to shift the conversation: instead of seeking an institution that can replace prisons—whether it be electronic monitors, psychiatric hospitals, probation, or heightened policing—we must focus on what people need in order to survive and thrive in their communities.

Shifting toward a model of actual support would mean *not* leaving people behind. Providing all students with access to school counselors, for example, would be a step toward reversing the systemic abandonment of communities of color and poor communities. Housing is another key component of this commitment to real support. For people on the sex offender registry, a lack of housing access is often the most insurmountable barrier to making their way in the world. With close to zero options, they end up homeless or housed in single-room-occupancy buildings under "pressure-cooker conditions," particularly difficult for people struggling with mental health issues.[6] How would society shift if, instead of "housing" millions of people in prisons, some of that money was spent on providing homes where people could truly live? This "alternative" might sound almost too simplistic, too basic—but maybe it *is* basic, or should be. Everyone should have decent shelter, as a human right.

The violence of tearing children from their parents and caregivers enacted through the child protective services and foster care systems can also be reimagined and transformed. It requires a radical rearrangement of resources accompanied by an ideological shift toward actual support instead of punishment and restriction. In other words, instead of widening the net of the prison industrial complex, we need to widen a different net—the safety net.

"If we had a completely different approach in which the child welfare system assists in providing for children, then there would be no problem . . . with expanding the net," Dorothy Roberts says. "It wouldn't be expanding the net of the carceral state, it would be expanding the net of families who were supported by the state." If the philosophy revolved around ensuring that individuals, families, and communities could access the resources they need, Roberts adds, "expanding the net would be fine. Expand it to every family in the country!"[7]

Along with expanding access to basic resources like food and housing, a transformative approach to child welfare might include parenting support that centers on accompaniment and assistance, not condescension and supervision. One hopeful example is the Minding the Baby initiative in New Haven, Connecticut.[8] In this program, low-income young mothers—who participate voluntarily—receive regular home visits from nurse practitioners and social workers.[9] The nurses and social workers provide health care (including mental health care) and offer expertise in understanding, bonding, and communicating with babies. They provide a sympathetic ear for the inevitable questions that arise during early parenting. The program also takes a critical stance toward child protective services and its separation-oriented bent, centering the parent-child relationship and focusing on strengthening and supporting that relationship rather than tearing it apart.

Programs like Minding the Baby are rare, but around the country, grassroots groups like Chicago's Black on Both Sides, Philadelphia's DHS Give Us Back Our Children, and Milwaukee's Welfare Warriors are organizing against the foster care system and for the construction of a *real* child welfare system. Welfare Warriors, for example, is mobilizing to demand that the state provide a "guaranteed child support" program that would cover children until they're eighteen, payment for "motherwork" (including caregiving for one's own children), welfare grants that are sufficient to cover all necessary parenting expenses, and post-secondary education access for mothers receiving welfare payments.[10] Members view a transformation of the welfare system as key to confronting the current system of "disappearing" children and destroying families. They say that many real child welfare problems— like inadequate food, shelter, and health care—stem from poverty and can only be confronted when people are actually supported in meeting their own needs and those of their children, free of the pressure of crushing surveillance.

Jobs with a living wage are another crucial form of support that would fuel real community safety and help to render prisons—and prison-like reforms—obsolete. Furthermore, in a social welfare system built around truly supporting people, everyone's skills and experiences would be utilized. People who've been involved with drug use, gang membership, and other activities that are currently criminalized should be able to use those experiences in ways that are useful to both themselves and the larger society. Angel Sanchez, the law student who spent many years on probation and house arrest, suggests that, on a large scale, people should have an opportunity to "professionalize" their roles as an "ex–drug user" or an "ex–gang member," sharing what they've learned and how they've moved forward.

Given the United States' vast resources, this new vision—of mass support and mass possibility, rather than mass surveillance, policing, and confinement—is not unrealistic. "We actually have enough in this world for everybody already," says Ruth Wilson Gilmore. "It's not like there's some rocket science math to be done to make it possible for everybody to live, to have nutritious foods, adequate shelter, pleasure in their lives, something to do."[11]

Viewed en masse, of course, this might seem like an enormous goal, but fortunately, it's a coalitional fight being fought on many different fronts simultaneously. "Overtime for farm workers is a step in the direction away from mass incarceration," Gilmore says. "Environmental justice is a step away from mass incarceration." At first, these struggles may seem unrelated to the abolitionist fight to end mass incarceration, but they are tied together in transforming the world into one in which people's needs are met and prisons become obsolete.[12]

As we allow ourselves to dream about what ending incarceration might look like, we're actually dreaming something much bigger: the world that all of us truly want to live in.

Grassroots Support and Healing

Building connections between movements is key to growing a world without prisons of any kind. Also crucial is the process of growing connections between individuals—creating community and building support systems from the ground up.

Elliott Fukui, who spent much of his youth confined in psychiatric institutions and mandated treatment programs, broke free when he turned eighteen. His parents tried to force him to sign over his right to attorney, meaning they'd have continued control over his treatment, but he refused. Instead, he began to piece together his own support system. He found the Icarus Project, an organization that describes itself as "a support network and education project by and for people who experience the world in ways that are often diagnosed as mental illness."[13]

Through the Icarus Project and the connections he's made there, Fukui has been figuring out what healing and survival mean outside of coercive measures and top-down mandates. This includes making plans to confront emergencies after they happen.

"I formed a safety chain of friends who were willing to support me when I was in an emotional state or an episodic state so I wouldn't have to go back to the hospital," he says. "I have a team of about twelve people across the country. . . . I've gotten to the point when I can recognize when I'm moving toward an episodic state. I can shoot out a text message or email and they coordinate among themselves as to who can come and sit with me until I move through it."[14]

Thanks to this network, Fukui hasn't been hospitalized since he was nineteen (he's now approaching thirty). Ever since his last hospitalization, he's been strengthening his network of support and drawing up his own instructions for what to do when a difficult situation arises.

The Icarus Project approaches mental health as a wider social justice issue. In addition to facilitating support networks and creating tools for healing, the project works on educational initiatives that challenge people to think in more liberatory ways about care, community, and disability, exploring their intersections with larger systems. For example, economic injustice not only impacts people's access to non-coercive mental health treatment—many simply can't afford it—but also underlies many of the problems that are diagnosed as mental illness. Money is the number one cause of stress among people in the United States.[15] The impact of this constant strain—the sense that one is always a step away from destitution—takes an emotional and psychological toll, and that toll is compounded for people simultaneously experiencing the effects of racism and other oppressions.[16]

"We have a responsibility to actually examine what the impacts of the intergenerational trauma are, the ways that capitalism and consumerism contribute to anxiety [and] depression across the board," notes Fukui. "We live in a culture that is not prepared to look at, acknowledge, and address the harms that have been caused, and that those impacts are still being felt and being passed down generationally through us. We have a responsibility to really look at what it means to build healing through acknowledging and addressing those systems." Instead of critiquing, or even acknowledging, the ways in which capitalism, racism, misogyny, homophobia, transphobia, and poverty negatively impact people's mental health, coercive psychiatric systems place the emphasis on altering individuals' behavior to conform to societal expectations.

In contrast, organizing toward social justice and building personal healing networks often means defying these expectations. It means forging connections amid, rather than conforming to, a society bent on isolation and confinement.

Even a small step like getting to know your neighbors can be a radical act as well as a means of survival. That's what Fukui—and countless others across the country—are currently doing in order to intentionally create safe communities outside of the systems of policing and incarceration. "I get to know my neighbors when I move somewhere so they're not inclined to call 911 right away if I do have an episode," explains Fukui. "I know that if I do go outside and I'm episodic, there's a chance I could be shot, there's a chance I could be committed, there's a chance that I could end up in jail or in prison."

It's not easy to build these types of support systems, but in working toward ways to love and protect each other in our own communities, we can begin to glean some vision for what a loving and safe society would look and feel like on a larger scale.

The Icarus Project isn't the only mental health support project that operates outside of traditional systems. The Hearing Voices Network centers people who hear voices, see visions, or regularly have other unusual experiences of this type.[17] The network, which has branches in twenty countries (including the United States), works to connect people who have these extremely pathologized experiences. Local groups meet regularly and provide an opportunity for people to find community around an experience that is usually relegated to spaces of isolation like doctors' offices, hospitals, and—so often—prisons.

In this way, organizing toward social justice and building personal healing networks are linked practices. Both involve forging connections within a society bent on isolation and confinement.

The Hearing Voices Network and the Icarus Project are just two examples of how bonds can be forged with the intertwined goals of personal healing and shifting societal consciousness. These networks, built by and among directly impacted people, demonstrate that creating community—connecting—is itself a political action in the face of systems meant to disconnect, confine, isolate, and silence.

This type of community-building is not limited to networks focused on mental illness. Visible Voices, the peer empowerment group Colette Payne coordinates, focuses on mutual support and healing while simultaneously working on legislative advocacy and education. Visible Voices is made up of formerly incarcerated women and is grounded in the power of storytelling. Members share their stories with each other as a way of finding support and strength. They also share their stories publicly to raise consciousness about the myriad injustices happening behind bars and within the web of reentry.[18] Payne first became involved in Visible Voices while living at a halfway house; members came in to facilitate a support group. She began to tell her story within the close-knit network of women in Visible Voices, then discovered that sharing that story publicly could have a powerful effect, changing the way people, including lawmakers, thought about policy.

Robert Suttle, who spent years on the sex offender registry after being criminalized for having HIV, is now assistant director of the Sero Project, a network of people with HIV who battle stigma and injustice, including criminalization laws.[19] His job is to be a connector of policy advocates, of grassroots organizers, and of people struggling with HIV criminalization who feel alone. Sometimes, he says, the most important act he can engage in is easing someone's mind by saying, "Hey, I've been through this, too."

As with Visible Voices, the process of creating connections between impacted people can translate into political action because, for people who have been criminalized, real healing often involves pushing back against the injustices that are harming them.

"Sero is big about HIV criminalization reform, but we're also big about self-empowerment of people living with HIV, establishing networks of people living with HIV, to voice their own concerns," Suttle says. The point, he says, is for people who are criminalized to "run the show, develop their own priorities and address things that they are passionate about," all within the context of a network that also prioritizes individual support.

The idea of "running the show" may seem daunting. Mass carceral systems reinforce the notion that we can't take care of ourselves and each other—that we need an authoritative system of control and punishment looming over our communities to be safe and secure. State punishment systems, and their all-powerful authority, may cause us to doubt our own ability to address our problems. In reality, however, we all have internal resources (and, if we work together with our communities, external resources) that we can bring to bear in times of crisis. People have been solving all kinds of problems for millennia without the prison industrial complex. "We have what we need to solve our problems," Mariame Kaba says. "We have to remind ourselves of that because so many of us feel so disempowered and so scared of other people. Because of that, here we are ceding all our power all the time to the police to do everything."[20]

We'll make mistakes, of course, on this path toward running our own show. Our networks will sometimes break down. Crises will persist. New ones will certainly emerge. We will have to sharpen our thinking, our community-building skills, and our imaginations.

The one mistake we cannot afford to make is to refuse to try.

Drug Treatment:
The Alternatives to the Alternatives

That process of trying—and sometimes making mistakes—includes grappling with the issues of drug addiction, abuse, and overdose. Even as "drug treatment" has emerged among many reformers as the obvious alternative to incarceration, the treatment on offer often looks like a prison. But the standardized treatment and abstinence models are not the only ways to address harmful drug use.

First, we need to get ourselves out of the habit of looking for a one-to-one replacement for any carceral institution, whether it be a prison or a prison alternative. That's part of the logic of Somewhere Else: *If we don't put them in prison, we'll put them in a treatment center. If we don't put them in a treatment center, we'll put them in [fill in the blank] as a solution.* The truth is that a solution that is not simply a Somewhere Else will not fit neatly in that blank. It won't even be able to be referred to as "a solution." Rather, it's about creating a whole range of new practices and new structures to reduce harm and suffering, facilitate healing, and support people as they work to confront the issues behind their addictions.

For instance, the primary causes of death among injection drug users are overdose and AIDS.[21] If the goal is to drastically decrease or eliminate both of these issues, creating avenues for harm reduction rather than advocating complete abstinence would be more successful.

There's no across-the-board definition or practice for reducing harm. Harm reduction includes a number of strategies aimed at decreasing negative consequences—for example, offering clean needles to injection drug users to help prevent new cases of HIV and hepatitis C. Unlike abstinence-only models, harm reduction methods don't shame, stigmatize, or penalize people who continue to use drugs.[22] This approach conveys a principle that is antithetical to the prison industrial complex: recognizing drug users as whole, complex human beings who are inherently entitled to their agency and their freedom. Some people may want to stop using a certain drug entirely. Others may be able to keep using drugs regularly while significantly reducing the harm their drug use can cause in their and their loved ones' lives. Intermittent drug use may feel all right as long as their basic needs, like health care and nutrition, are met.

At least ten countries around the world have established "drug consumption rooms" where people can go to use drugs (usually injection drugs or inhalants) under safer, sanitary conditions, supervised by medical staff and free of the fear of arrest or criminalization. Ninety such sites currently exist around the world.[23]

And they're working. Since opening its drug consumption rooms in 2003, Vancouver, Canada, has seen dramatic decreases in overdoses and increases in safety and disease-reducing hygiene. The sites bring users into contact with health care providers and make medical information and services more accessible.[24] It might seem counterintuitive, but providing spaces to use drugs safely has also led more people to voluntarily seek treatment. Studies of the initial Vancouver program showed that those who visited the drug consumption site regularly were more likely to seek treatment and ultimately stop using injection drugs.[25]

A few cities in the United States are currently considering establishing similar safe injection sites, a radical departure from current abstinence-based drug control policies.[26] But as of late 2018, efforts to open similar sites in New York City were blocked by the Department of Justice, which informed the mayor that such sites violate federal law.[27]

Drug consumption rooms are one manifestation of a larger set of values—the principle that each person has a right to figure out how to live and that it's impossible to achieve true health (individual or communal) without this freedom.

At the same time, we can't deny that for some, addiction and drug misuse are real, brutal, and sometimes deadly. In 2016, 64,000 people in the United States died of drug overdoses.[28] People who are *not* addicted—or don't use a particular drug regularly—are especially likely to overdose because their bodies aren't accustomed to the substance. If people do want to seek help for their drug use, must they enter a requirement-based program that limits their rights? Does "getting better" have to mean handing over your freedom?

On the contrary, treatment that works is grounded in the fact that drug users are people with their own minds who make decisions based on their realities. Many in the treatment field don't favor this approach, but some are vocal advocates. Dr. Carl Hart is one of them. Hart is a neuroscientist who's been studying drug addiction for more than two decades. He's discovered that even people who are experiencing drug dependency don't make choices based *only* on their relationship with a drug.[29] Like everyone, drug users are driven by a variety of factors. Hart's studies have found, time and again, that for many, basic needs like shelter, food, and housing take precedence over drugs.

Drugs and alcohol use can offer temporary respite from stress, strain, pain, and boredom. If a person has few other prospects for relief—including positive or meaningful aspects of their life—then frequent substance use can become the most appealing option, sometimes leading to misuse and addiction. The solution, then, is not to criminalize substance use or force people into treatment. Instead, it's crucial to provide other avenues for happiness, fulfillment, meaning, diversion, and fun. Hart points to the importance of opportunities for education, engaging jobs, community involvement, the arts, and sports—these resources, along with health care and other supports, can help prompt decisions that shift people away from harmful behaviors.[30]

That's what Susan Sered, a researcher at Suffolk University in Boston who specializes in women's health and human rights, has also found. She points to women who have stopped using certain drugs while they were pregnant or once their babies were born, or else have reduced their use to allow them to be attentive parents. The child welfare system often takes away people's children once there's been evidence of drug use, but once their children are gone, one of their motivations is gone and so drug use becomes even more likely.[31]

Sered talks about the motivation for—and against—ongoing drug misuse in the context of her own community, an upper-middle-class neighborhood where exercise is popular and knee replacement surgery is overwhelmingly common. Following such surgeries, most people are given serious pain medication, often opioids. But, she notes, the affluent middle-aged people and seniors who've had knee surgeries generally don't become addicted to these drugs. Why not?

"The people in my community had good interesting jobs that they like, they had nice houses, they had families and hobbies and all kinds of things that they're involved in and that they're respected for doing," she says. "When there was a choice, they stopped using drugs."

Sered has documented the day-to-day lives of women criminalized for their drug use, largely in low-income communities.[32] Two women completely stopped using without a formal treatment program. Instead, they found decent-paying, fulfilling jobs, comfortable housing situations, and strong support networks. One had a close family. The other found housing in an apartment building filled with older people and people with disabilities. Since the woman was younger and in good physical shape, she started assisting her neighbors with grocery shopping and cleaning; in return, they cooked for her, gave her gifts, offered praise. She developed close, caring friendships with the people she was surrounded by every day—and didn't use drugs again for ten years.

The alternative to prison in the latter woman's case was not a treatment institution. Instead, it consisted of "a decent apartment in a social context that gave her really good opportunities for building social networks, for being praised, for being accepted, for having real self-esteem . . . from people thanking her on a daily basis for helping them out." We should never underestimate the importance of respect and appreciation to the process of healing and recovering from addiction.

For many people, confronting trauma is another key to moving past harmful drug use. LeeAnn, the Florida mother who was placed on the sex offender registry for holding a young woman's money while she engaged in sex work, finally found a treatment program that helped her move beyond her addiction. The element that clicked, and ultimately facilitated her recovery, was uncovering the reasons behind her use. Once she did, she recognized that she was making a decision to use (in this case, to cope with trauma), as opposed to addiction simply happening *to* her. She was then able to wrestle with the roots of the problem instead of trying to follow a rule or a law wholly disconnected from herself as a person.

Transformative Justice and Community Accountability

The practice of digging deep and wrestling with a problem's roots instead of attempting to shove it in a cage can be used to address a wider range of problems, beyond addiction.

Plenty of people can get behind the idea that when it comes to drug addiction, a cage is not the answer. But as we advocate for a world in which cages are *never* the answer, the two of us routinely encounter the question "What about the rapists?" Even some people who are committed to ending mass incarceration may flinch when we mention that our book addresses sex offender registries and the problems with expanding the punishment of those who've caused sexual harm.

However, since prison does not solve sexual violence and in fact *promotes* sexual violence, that question can be turned on its head.[33] What *about* the rapists or, more centrally, the rape survivors? What are we doing to actually address rape and sexual assault?

There's no one answer to what it looks like to confront sexual violence outside of prison and prison-like alternatives, but people are already exploring how to do so in a variety of ways. One of those methods is community accountability (CA), a process by which a given community comes together to address a particular instance of harm, including the circumstances leading up to that harm. There's no prescribed pattern for community accountability; instead, each situation involves its own individualized process.

In late 2015, it came to light that Malcolm, a well-known Chicago activist and spoken-word artist, had sexually assaulted a young woman three years earlier. In a public letter, Kyra described how she'd gone on a date with Malcolm. She had been sexually assaulted several months earlier and was mired in a court process related to that assault—a process she found deeply traumatizing. Kyra mentioned feeling relieved to be spending time with Malcolm, an activist who spoke of caring profoundly about the prevention of sexual violence. Later that night, he assaulted her.

In her letter, Kyra wrote that she no longer felt safe in activist spaces, in her community, or in the world. She spoke of how some of the people she'd told had encouraged her to remain silent; she connected her struggle with that of many Black women who are told not to speak out about violence at the hands of Black men, lest those men become entrapped in the criminal legal system. She emphasized that she had no faith in the courts to deal with matters of sexual violence and sought some type of community accountability instead.

According to Creative Interventions, an online resource center that

creates and promotes community accountability practices, community accountability is

> a process in which a community such as family, friends,
> neighbors, coworkers or community members work
> together to transform situations of harm. This can also
> describe a process in which the community recognizes
> that they are impacted by violence even if it is primarily
> between individuals, that they may have participated in
> allowing the violence to happen or even causing the vio-
> lence, and are responsible for resolving the violence.[34]

Kyra approached the Chicago chapter of Black Youth Project 100
(BYP100), a nationwide group of Black organizers, of which Malcolm
was a member, and shared what he had done. None of the parties had
ever participated in a community accountability process to address sexual harm. Nonetheless, Kyra, BYP100 members, and Malcolm agreed
to engage in a community accountability process to address the harm.

People often use the term "transformative justice" in conjunction
with the concept of community accountability. Unlike the more popularly used term "restorative justice," transformative justice seeks not
only to restore people to the way that they were before the harm happened but actually to transform the conditions (both interpersonal
and societal) that enabled the violence or harm to occur in the first
place. The term was popularized by generationFIVE, a Bay Area organization founded with the goal of ending child sexual abuse. According to generationFIVE, transformative justice is "an approach to
respond to and prevent child sexual abuse and other forms of violence
that puts transformation and liberation at the heart of the change. It is
an approach that looks at the individual and community experiences
as well as the social conditions, and looks to integrate both personal
and social transformation."[35]

It's helpful to think of transformative justice as a wider framework or approach and community accountability as more of a strategy. Crucial to both community accountability and transformative justice is the principle that harm doesn't happen in a vacuum and that fully confronting an act of violence must go beyond addressing the specific situation. In addition to seeking healing for survivors and transformation for people who've caused harm, these ways of addressing violence seek to transform the larger structures and institutions—from the patriarchy to the psychiatric hospital, from white supremacy to the prison—that paved the path for their occurrence.[36] Unlike in the criminal legal process, in a transformative justice process, people who have been harmed have control over what information, if any, about the process or the harm that happened to them will be shared with the public. Some processes happen with little to no public recounting whatsoever. Other processes, like the one described below, result in the sharing of some details.

In Kyra and Malcolm's case, the accountability process was facilitated by members of some of Chicago's social justice communities. Mariame Kaba, who had done this kind of work for many years, served as the lead facilitator.

The process lasted fifteen months.[37] It began with the formation of a survivor support team, whose members met with Kyra regularly and determined how the process would play out. The team included Kaba, another facilitator chosen by Kyra, and a close friend of Kyra's.

The process, as led by the support team, wasn't only focused on determining what would happen to the person who caused harm. In contrast to a courtroom—where the response to sexual violence is focused entirely on the perpetrator and the punishment they will receive—this process centered the survivor's needs. Kyra's support team helped her figure out and access what she needed to heal. Team members also worked with Kyra to map out the steps she wanted Malcolm to take to hold himself accountable for the harm, then monitored how these steps were carried out. Given Malcolm's close involvement with BYP100, the survivor support team also worked to lay out steps for organizational accountability, recognizing that when sexual violence happens, it never affects *only* the survivor and the person who caused harm. Shifts in the community are necessary to respond to the harm and, hopefully, make such harm less likely in the future.

Another group played a key role: the accountability team, which worked with Malcolm to support him in complying with, understanding, and sustaining his commitment to the process. Headed by an experienced transformative justice practitioner, the team also included a fellow BYP100 member who knew Malcolm well and whom the survivor support team trusted.

Near the start of the process, the survivor support team called for Malcolm to issue a public acknowledgment of the harm he'd caused. After working with his team, Malcolm shared a statement on Facebook, which said in part: "When someone says I've harmed them, I do not believe I get to tell them how they've been harmed. I want to publically apologize to Kyra for the harm I caused her. I am committed to and am engaged in a survivor led transformative justice process. I have done wrong and I am committed to being held accountable for the harm I have done that centers the needs of the person I have done harm to."

Over the following months, Kyra and her team called for other measures, which Malcolm undertook. They asked for an intensive education process focused on sexual violence and enthusiastic consent, which took into account Malcolm's existing level of knowledge and political understanding. The accountability team held biweekly sessions with Malcolm, as well as regular phone conversations, in which they discussed readings about consent, sexual violence, patriarchy, and sexism. They engaged him in writing activities about his actions and what reparations could look like. Kyra also asked that Malcolm stop participating in women-led organizing spaces throughout the process. His accountability team ensured that he complied.

It wasn't just Malcolm who was undergoing a transformation; it was also BYP100 as an organization. In response to the survivor support team's call, BYP100 incorporated a curriculum on enthusiastic consent into its group orientation. The organization also strengthened its course of action for responding to harm, forming a national Healing and Safety Council. As part of the council, BYP100 members created a manual for preventing and intervening in harm, called *Stay Woke, Stay Whole: Black Activist Manual.*[38]

At the beginning of the process, Kyra set a goal that the process would culminate in a peace circle. Rooted in the practices of many Indigenous communities of North America, peace circles are spaces in which people come together, talk, and listen, turn by turn (usually sitting in an actual circle).[39] A circle can be used to simply strengthen and build community or for a particular goal—there are grief circles, celebration circles, and circles to discuss a particularly difficult issue that has arisen in the news. There are also circles that address a specific act of harm in the community. These circles often bring together a survivor, a person who has caused harm, impacted community members, and support people in an effort to move more deeply toward healing and accountability.

Kyra envisioned a circle in which she, Malcolm, and their support teams would meet. In February 2017, more than a year after the process began, the circle happened. Afterward, Kyra, Malcolm, the facilitators, and the support teams issued public statements reflecting on the process and serving as a rough blueprint for others interested in community accountability.

In her statement, Kyra wrote that she found the circle healing. The many months she'd spent immersed in the process had been hard on her, she said, and she sometimes questioned whether Malcolm deserved the generosity she was showing him by engaging. But in the circle, she wrote, she noticed a change in her own relationship to the situation:

While I don't think "forgiveness" is the word to describe what I feel because I personally don't believe forgiveness is something that can or necessarily should be given to abusers, I no longer feel the intense hatred for Malcolm that I used to. I spent a lot of energy being angry and scared (rightfully so) and feeling that way all the time was exhausting. It made day-to-day life difficult and my fear of running into Malcolm in Black organizing spaces made it practically impossible for me to engage politically in Chicago. After meeting with Malcolm and hearing from him firsthand about his end of the process, I've felt a noticeable shift in my energy for the better. And while being around Malcolm is still triggering and probably will be for the foreseeable future, I don't have the same debilitating fear of being in the same city as him.

In his own public statement, Malcolm spoke of the fourteen months he spent in this process as a journey that will never truly be complete. He discussed how, prior to being called out by Kyra, he'd been writing and speaking publicly about toxic masculinity, reading works by bell hooks, and participating in Black-women-led organizing spaces. He knew the analysis and the language; he regarded himself as an "ally." But the process served as a kind of self-reckoning:

It took me awhile to even name the harm. I saw myself become the narratives I shamed other men for creating. Replaying in my head all the reasons why this wasn't that big of a deal, making excuses for my past self, or claiming that I knew then what consent was but this was a misunderstanding. Everything except take responsibility for my actions. The journey to prioritizing Kyra over fears of damage to my career or wanting to just walk away to avoid any questions about my harm was a long road, to say the least. Though I am not some anomaly in the thread of Black men, I was one who learned and unlearned enough to stay committed to making amends to Kyra. Whether I intended to commit harm or not, I had to decide to take responsibility for the harm or avoid responsibility. I am grateful for the community around me that guided me to a place of growth. To see myself not only in theory but in practice.

It's important to remember that this process was specific to the people, organizations, times, and places involved—it cannot be exactly replicated in other instances. In her own statement, Mariame Kaba noted that the community accountability model itself cannot be applied as a universal alternative because it must be voluntary. "There is no coercion involved because that would replicate the oppressive forces that we seek to dismantle," she wrote.

Community accountability processes take significant work. "There is nothing 'soft' or 'easy' about this," Kaba wrote. "CA processes test everyone and can be some of the most difficult physical and emotional work that we can undertake. Healing requires an acknowledgment that there are wounds. Healing requires parties who actually want to heal."

Coming away from the circle, Kyra wrote that she hoped Malcolm would use what he'd learned to both inform his own actions and "educate other men about sexual violence and toxic masculinity." She described her goals as oriented toward the future as well as addressing past harm. "My process allowed me not only to hold Malcolm accountable for his actions but to also reeducate him so that he hopefully won't harm anyone else in the future," she said. "That was important to me." Additionally, Kyra's generosity in sharing her story publicly has made it possible for others facing similar situations to learn from her process as they work to build their own.

But to make community accountability a viable option for people who've faced harm, there need to be more people who know how to actually support and facilitate the process. That's why Kaba and Just Practice, a Chicago-based transformative justice group, are training a cohort of people in Chicago to facilitate community accountability processes around sexual harm.[40] The group hopes to make it more feasible for people to find routes toward healing and accountability. Similarly, the Bay Area Transformative Justice Collective, an all-volunteer collective that encourages and creates transformative justice responses to child sexual abuse, facilitates introductory workshops as well as events where community members and support networks can come together and practice these skills in their everyday lives.[41] After all, if we reject police and prisons, there must be other, radically different ways to answer that persistent question: What *are* we doing to address harm?

In addition to creating a range of effective responses to violence, the question of what we are doing also needs to be answered on the preventive end: What do we do to prevent violence from happening in the first place? One approach is to consider who is meant by "we." In recent years, with the rise of #MeToo, in which survivors of sexual abuse have been speaking out and naming the people who abused them, and an increased level of visibility around sexual violence, women, trans, and nonbinary people have continued to largely shoulder the burden of anti-violence organizing. A key aspect of prevention will be men taking the initiative to challenge and engage with other men to uproot sexual violence. We can see models for this in groups like Men Can Stop Rape, a national organization based in Washington, DC, which runs mentoring programs for young men in order to mobilize them to prevent gender-based violence, and Philly Stands Up, a collective of people of various gender identities that works with individuals who have caused harm to hold them accountable to survivors, as part of a multifaceted effort to prevent future violence.[42]

Another answer comes back to the necessity of structural supports. Erica Meiners, the researcher of civil commitment and sex offender registries, talks about a man named Julius who was diagnosed with schizophrenia, served thirty years in prison for sexual assault and armed robbery, was released, and then raped two women.

"There are so many junctures that could have stopped the sexual assaults of these women," Meiners says. "Julius . . . was released with essentially zero support: no access to treatment, very tight mobility, and essentially no plan. He had no family members and was in a decent but by no means well-resourced transition program. Imagine what would've happened if there had been some sort of plan to support Julius—radical thought!—with mental health services, with community, with some sort of socialization plan, with anything. I'm not saying that *would* have stopped the sexual assaults, but I think it *could have.*"[43]

The "could have" is important. Prison—a form of violence in itself—and harmful measures like the registry don't prevent violence. Redirecting resources away from these harmful practices provides enormous opportunities to build thoughtful, effective systems of support. Those systems will look different for different individuals and different communities, but many of the ingredients are the same. From adequate housing to real mental health services to opportunities for mutually supportive connections with other people, it's time to think creatively about what's actually needed to make harm less likely and to make violence less possible.

Community Safety

Another key component of making violence less possible—while moving beyond prisons, policing, and surveillance—is developing strategies for dealing with immediate crises. The truth is, there isn't yet a robust network of resources in every community that can be accessed in an immediate physical emergency. Given that current lack, even abolitionists faced with a violent crisis (say, an attack by an intimate partner) may feel the need to call the police or an ambulance, which can trigger the police being called, too, and they shouldn't be shamed for doing so.

However, calling 911 in a moment of crisis can lead to other dangers, particularly for marginalized people. Policing, and state apparatuses such as emergency room protocol, often intensify violence toward victims, especially Black, Brown, disabled, and trans victims. Elliott Fukui, who, as a mixed-race trans queer twelve-year-old had attempted suicide, and Peg Plews, the white disabled anti-policing organizer, both experienced physical violence—as well as the violence of forced medications and confinement in locked solitary cells—when they were brought to the emergency room. What, then, is the alternative? What would it look like for the members of a neighborhood, together, to feel confident in their ability to effectively and safely handle problems without calling the police?

In 2015, Rachel Herzing, co-founder of the abolitionist organization Critical Resistance, embarked on a project called Build the Block to pilot strategies for reducing calls to 911—and thus, police contact—in Oakland and San Francisco.[44] For one pilot, she focused on a particular Oakland neighborhood that already had a palpable sense of community and connectedness. She brought neighbors together to discuss instances in which they'd called the cops and asked, "What could you do instead next time that issue comes up?"

To begin answering that question, they created a neighborhood directory. They used an existing neighborhood directory as a starting point, but instead of only listing names and contact information, the new directory also included each household's particular needs. For example, one family might say, "We have three children." Another might say, "We live with an elderly person who has Alzheimer's." Another might note that their jobs take them out of town for weeks at a time. The directory also included each household's "assets"—ways in which they might be able to support their neighbors in addressing their needs.

"Through doing that," Herzing says, "we learned that one neighbor was trained as an EMT and could provide emergency medical assistance if somebody just called him; he was willing to do that. We learned about the variety of language and translation skills in the community. We learned that there were trained conflict mediators in the community. We learned that they actually had a bunch of resources they could leverage toward solving their own issues." In addition to looking at the needs and resources in the community, they discussed the physical layout of the neighborhood, including where each person lived and spent their time, and how these factors might affect the ways in which they'd respond to an emergency.

The directory, and the process of creating it, helped to cement an infrastructure for responding to crises without calling in potentially harmful outside forces. As that experiment continues to grow, Herzing hopes that it will become a template that others can share and adapt for their own neighborhoods and needs.

A neighborhood directory won't immediately take the place of police in all scenarios in which they're called, but Herzing sees it as part of the process of developing a "logic of not calling the cops"— forming structures and learning skills that will reduce police presence and enable new, more connected, more effective systems to take hold.

In this sense, there's something to be said for starting small. Maybe people won't wholeheartedly commit to not calling the police if an intruder with a gun is in their home, but could they stop calling the police about their neighbors' loud music? Could they stop calling the police when they see a fight erupting between young people?

"Maybe I don't have all the remedies for the worst-case scenario right now," Herzing says. "But if we deal with all the rinky-dink things people are already calling the cops for and we build up our skills incrementally to be able to deal with those things, then we know that when people build more skills and more confidence, they're able to take more on the next time."

This goal of taking things on—learning and using skills that so many of us have forgotten because we've been encouraged to rely on the police—is especially urgent for those who have never felt they can rely on police to address actual acts of violence. For many LGBTQ people of color, the police have never been an option for "safety"; on the contrary, they're widely known to be a danger.

The Audre Lorde Project (ALP) is an organization of trans and queer people of color organizing in New York City. Safe OUTside the System (SOS) is an ALP initiative in Brooklyn that works to challenge interpersonal and police violence by using community-based strategies rather than relying on the police.[45] SOS began as a response to a crisis. In 2005, Rashawn Brazell, a Black gay man, left home. Parts of his body were later found throughout Brooklyn.

Ejeris Dixon, a Black queer organizer who'd recently started working at the Audre Lorde Project, began to gather residents together for community meetings to collectively answer the question: "If we want to address violence without relying on the criminal legal system, what could that look like?"[46]

It was a slow process partially because there were few models for what they were trying to do. Most abolitionist projects for addressing violence focus on incidents between people who knew each other. Dixon found very few organizations working to address violence, or the threat of violence, from strangers—a situation in which people are more likely to call the police. The key to addressing this type of harm, Dixon says, lies in strengthening ties between neighbors, so that more people *do* know each other. She refers to Safe OUTside the System's approach as "community safety."

After a year and a half of community conversations—"trying to figure out the link between strangers," as Dixon puts it—the group came up with a plan. They would do outreach to local businesses and other institutions like community centers and churches. They'd ask each institution to become a "safe space" (designated as such with a sticker) that would serve as a refuge from violence, a place that could intervene in acts of violence, and a support for survivors, with a focus on LGBTQ people of color. SOS members started by approaching the businesses where they already knew people and offering to train them in violence de-escalation. But first, they had to learn those skills themselves.

They went to community board meetings, learned what other local groups working on violence were up to, and connected with people who taught de-escalation tactics. They talked to bouncers, security workers, and self-defense trainers. They discussed how the skills that were being used to keep people safe during events, actions, and protests could translate into addressing violence that might happen on the street or in a bar or in a store.

When SOS began to approach businesses about becoming safe spaces, the group discovered that although many didn't specifically address homophobic or transphobic violence, many businesses were already using creative ways to de-escalate situations and cope with tough circumstances.

"The most fascinating thing I remember seeing when we first started engaging with a space [was that] even if they said they didn't have a way of addressing violence, they had a way," Dixon says. "Even if it was a way that we didn't agree with, they had a way to deal with it."

This is an important lesson for everyone struggling to forge paths to safety and justice outside the criminal legal system: whether or not they identify as prison abolitionists, people are already figuring out how to deal with problems without the police. Some of the most interesting and powerful abolitionist projects build upon that reality. The Bay Area–based StoryTelling and Organizing Project (STOP), an initiative of Creative Interventions, compiles the stories of people who have faced, intervened in, prevented, and addressed violence.[47] Many have done so entirely without police involvement. Some of the project's narratives are "success stories," while others are more complicated. The project also recognizes that no story is ever over—interventions that don't "work" in the moment may have impacts years later in terms of a survivor's healing or a person who caused harm finally acknowledging what they did and wanting to be accountable.

Mimi Kim, the founder of Creative Interventions, worked predominantly in immigrant communities where calling the police was often not seen as an option because of the accompanying risk of detention and deportation for undocumented community members. In one STOP story, a California survivor of domestic violence fled an abusive marriage by taking refuge at a friend's house. Once she was there, her friends and family assembled a support network of people to help her access the immediate resources she needed—for example, setting up a schedule for people to bring over food. Her mother assisted in persuading her abusive husband to leave their house, so she could live there. The survivor says that the route she chose worked for her because people listened and responded to the particular needs she expressed.[48]

By compiling these types of stories, Kim wanted to challenge the assumption that certain situations, such as gender-based violence, *necessitate* police intervention. Such strategies and stories are rarely spotlighted. "We are building a long, long history of everyday people trying to end violence in ways that don't play into oppressive structures," she wrote in 2008, four years after founding Creative Interventions.[49]

Herzing, who also works with Creative Interventions, agrees. "We're so inundated with messages about how we can't do anything or try anything . . . how we should just leave it to the 'professionals,' we shouldn't 'stick our nose in other people's business.' So people are really afraid to engage and intervene."

That's why learning and practicing are essential. "You build your muscles up, build your muscle memory, and figure out different strategies," says Herzing, making an analogy: "I practice playing some game on my phone, and I learn, 'Oh! This is how this thing works.' But you only learn to do these things by trying them over and over and learning a little more each time."

Dixon describes a similar learning curve with SOS. In addition to training with people versed in established intervention strategies, the group crowdsourced ideas that had worked for community members, then created a manual based on those steps.

Sometimes SOS saw those strategies emerge from unexpected places. Dixon recalls meeting a woman who owned a coffee shop in the neighborhood. The woman expressed some interest in the project but was wary of its focus on LGBTQ people. "I like you," she told Dixon. "I don't know if I like gay people." A long conversation ensued, but by the end, Dixon couldn't convince her to become part of the project. Dixon gave the shop owner SOS's materials—a description of the project, a tip sheet for interventions, and a Safe Space sticker—and moved on.

A month or two later, the owner called Dixon. "Hey, I safe-spaced today! Is it okay if I didn't know if the person was gay?" she asked.

She described seeing a young woman fleeing a group of boys who were chasing her down the street. "I could tell she was not safe, I didn't know where her family was, she ran past my coffee shop, and I let her in and I locked the door," the woman told Dixon. "I gave her some tea, and we kept them outside, and we got in touch with her parents and we made sure she got home safe. This is what you wanted me to do, right?" She felt good about the experience, she said—and she'd do it again.

Dixon reflects that it wasn't just their initial conversation or the SOS materials that contributed to the shop owner's decision to intervene that day. It was the simple fact of alerting someone to their own potential in preventing and addressing violence. "There's something just in the power of asking and inviting people into a project that was bigger than them," she says. "Maybe you're a bodega or you sell coffee or you're a bakery, but you care about these issues, and there's a space for you."

As SOS expanded, people with all kinds of skills and backgrounds started looking for ways to contribute. Dixon describes another way that community members engaged in building safety utilizing their own strengths and talents. Since people in the community risked violence as they traveled to and from parties, SOS members created a Safe Party Toolkit (a collection of party-safety strategies), which they made available online and as a print zine. They hosted safe parties, where they practiced putting strategy into action. They arranged for people to walk each other to the train, give people rides home, and ensure that people were traveling in groups. DJs and performers who were excited about SOS's work provided entertainment for the parties, creating another opportunity to build community—and have fun. (After all, building community can and should be fun, at least some of the time!)

In the world we currently live in, it's not always possible to avoid a police presence. If someone's facing a life-threatening health problem, those around them often do have to call 911. The SOS team hosted a workshop to acknowledge this reality, and to strategize around how to deal with emergencies. The workshop, entitled "There's No Movement Ambulance," was led by a lawyer and a paramedic. It addressed the questions "What are instances in which you do have to call 911?" and "How do we reduce violence and harm if that happens?"[50]

As their work grew and gained recognition in the community, members of SOS began to face another set of challenges: people approaching them with needs they didn't yet know how to fill. People called with myriad requests: "I just got attacked last week. You guys work on violence, help me." "My son got killed due to homophobic violence. Help me." "I'm being harassed every time I walk home. Help me."

"We had to learn counseling skills," Dixon says. "How do you help someone in the middle of being traumatized? What does trauma look like?"

They searched for resources, figured out which resources required extra support (such as counseling services that require low-income people to jump through hoops to receive care), and thought through how to interact with people who needed help but didn't understand SOS's abolitionist politics or wanted to involve the police.

When they realized how little financial support was available to people whose family members had been killed, especially for those who hadn't reported the murder to the police, SOS members started a fund to raise money for survivors, to pay for necessities like medical bills, therapy, and time off work.

As they built these new support systems, SOS members were also exchanging knowledge and skills with others in their community. Dixon talks about the long process—what she calls the "slow build"— of engaging with business owners and staff about the importance of addressing the harassment of trans and queer people in their establishments. Sometimes proprietors would express reluctance to address homophobia and transphobia. Dixon would respond with the question "Do you think people deserve to die?" She then explained how verbal harassment can escalate to physical and sometimes deadly violence.

In addition to the slow build of developing a network of safe spaces, SOS members concentrated on getting to know their neighbors. That included simply saying hi more often and making friends with people on their routes home.

"If you're seven blocks from the train, and you walk down the street on this street and that street, are you saying hi to people? Do you know people?" Dixon asked. "We just kept seeing more and more, the more people were engaged with people in general, especially people on their common routes, the more that those people would really look out for them and rely on each other."

Like Elliott Fukui, who worked to make deeper connections with his neighbors so that if they saw him in an episodic state they'd be less likely to call the cops and more able to support him, SOS members discovered that neighborhood relationships themselves were a form of protection.

This isn't always easy. Dixon recalled experiencing constant sexual harassment near her apartment; her roommates encountered transphobic violence. At a community meeting, she made an effort to get to know some of the guys who sold drugs near her building—people who were always there and whom she passed every day. She'd already been saying hello to them for a while, and after the meeting they started to chat. Though the conversation was light and about nothing in particular, they started talking more when they saw each other on the street, and Dixon noticed a shift. She felt comfortable telling them about the harassment that she and her roommates experienced. They reassured her, "No one's gonna mess with you." The harassment decreased after that.

Building relationships takes time, of course. It takes effort and sometimes requires discomfort. It's not as automatic as dialing 911. It's a way of life.

As Dixon puts it, "You've got to be committed to being in community with people and not just having your house be the place you live."

Building Toward Transformation

The "slow build" that Dixon describes is a thread that runs across the gamut of real alternatives to prison—that is, alternatives that don't look like cages. Unlike the fantasies woven by politicians and practitioners of prison-like solutions, these projects don't come premade and perfectly packaged, ready to slip in to replace prisons. Instead, they all require a process of ongoing building: a process that's collaborative and doesn't depend on a hierarchical power to put it in place. It can't because, in order to truly move beyond prisons, we need to move beyond relying on all-powerful institutions.

There is not a readymade abolitionist solution available for every problem that might arise. There's no abolitionist constitution, no abolitionist sentencing guidelines, no abolitionist rulebook, no abolitionist president issuing abolitionist executive orders, no list of abolitionist Supreme Court decisions. Abolition recognizes that problems happen within the context of specific communities and must be solved within that context as well—there are no universal experts who know the answer to every question or the salve for every harm. That puts the responsibility on each of us to co-create, co-build, and co-dedicate ourselves to growing new ways of addressing our problems.

Once that responsibility shifts back to ourselves, it becomes clear that one of the greatest problems *is* those all-powerful, hierarchical institutions that claim to solve them. The institutions of the prison industrial complex reinforce rather than dismantle societal inequalities and oppressions. As new alternatives appear, one way to assess whether they are truly different is to ask whether they are actively working *against* oppression. Are they challenging racism, capitalism, transphobia, patriarchy, ableism, and heterosexism? To move past the notion that certain categories of people must be placed Somewhere Else, we must root out the structures of oppression that are putting them in these categories in the first place.

We also recognize that new roots need to be planted, watered, and given sunlight. We recognize that building a world in which mental health care doesn't mean more cages and more police-like figures will have to mean strengthening networks and services of mutual support, and funding those services. We recognize that basic needs like good food and good housing are non-negotiables. We recognize that educational resources not only must be moved away from policing and punitive disciplinary practices but also need to be redirected toward practices that foster collective learning, growth, and healing—perhaps requiring a shift in the American model of education itself. We recognize that not only must we pressure politicians to abolish oppressive sex offender registries, but we must invest in real sex education for all, education that recognizes and confronts misogyny, homophobia, and transphobia and prioritizes a deep understanding of consent. Not only must we push elected officials and policymakers to decriminalize drug use, sex work, and HIV exposure, but we must also foster a social world in which people are supported and honored in making their own choices about what to do with their bodies and minds.

Fortunately, none of these goals must be approached from scratch. Abolition is not a theoretical wish for the future. From the Icarus Project to Build the Block, from Just Practice to Visible Voices, from the Sero Project to Safe OUTside the System and Creative Interventions, people are already building toward transformation. Moreover, in our individual lives and communities, we often seek justice and healing without police and prisons, whether we're calling a friend to mediate a conflict, gathering our block together to discuss issues facing the neighborhood, or simply saying hi to people on the street.

As Ruth Wilson Gilmore puts it, we should "talk about abolition not as an aspirational adventure" but as a growing body of "already-accumulated encounters and awarenesses and activities."[51]

The journey has begun. In a sense, we have always been on it. Humans have always searched for solutions—for ways to support each other, defend each other, hold each other accountable, heal each other, and heal ourselves. This quest was part of humanity's work long before the rise of the prison, and we will still be doing it long after the prison is behind us.

Maybe, then, it's less useful to think about "alternatives" and more useful to think of that journey, that practice, that slow build. Along the way, not only will we learn new approaches, but we'll also be supporting each other, solving problems, and building the world we want to see.

Abolition is not aspirational, but it is an adventure. It may feel daunting to have no rulebook, no constitution, and no prescription. But it is also exciting! When you're on a quest, anything is possible. It's up to all of us to create new possibilities, new routes, new pathways, and new visions, together.

ACKNOWLEDGMENTS

THIS BOOK WOULD NOT HAVE BEEN POSSIBLE IF NOT FOR THE MANY people who were willing to share their experiences, insights, and analyses with us through interviews. Thank you to Sadie Ryanne Baker, Liat Ben-Moshe, Davonda Buck, Ejeris Dixon, Etan, Harvey Fair, Elliott Fukui, Ruth Wilson Gilmore, Rebecca Harris, Rachel Herzing, Rachel Hoffman, Patricia Howard, Jesse, Joe, Monica Jones, K, Mariame Kaba, Oumou Kaba, James Kilgore, Kyra, Crystal Laura, LeeAnn, Lynda Lopez, Malik, Gregory McKelvey, Erica Meiners, MG Tabitha Minson, Pat, Colette Payne, Peg Plews, Patrick Reilly, Dorothy Roberts, Angel Sanchez, Susan Sered, Robert Suttle, Stacey Thompson, Josmar Trujillo, Ethan Viets-Vanlear, Jennifer Viets, Alex Vitale, and Angela Willard.

Thank you to DHS Give Us Back Our Children, Girls for Gender Equity, the Red Hook Initiative, the Sadie Nash Leadership Project, and the Women and Justice Project for connecting us with members willing to share their experiences with us.

We owe much gratitude to Michelle Alexander for writing an incredible foreword, and for your much-needed encouragement, motivation, and advice. For taking the time to read our manuscript and offer invaluable feedback, support, and/or reassurance, we also owe special thanks to Craig Gilmore, Mimi Kim, Peter Wagner, and Derecka Purnell. Thanks to Ava Kofman for sharing her research with us. Thanks to Diane Wachtell and zakia henderson-brown for encouraging us to collaboratively explore this issue and write this book, and for your developmental edits and feedback. Thank you to Tom Engelhardt for editing and publishing Maya's 2015 TomDispatch article, "Prison by Any Other Name," that planted the initial seed for this book idea. And a huge thank-you to our agent Hannah Bowman for believing in this project, and for your wise guidance, edits, knowledge, and support.

For Maya, the journey of writing this book intersected with another wild journey: pregnancy and the first year of my infant's life. Between my work at *Truthout* and my work as Kai's mom, creating the time for this book project sometimes felt like an exercise in advanced physics. It would've been impossible without Ryan Croken, my partner and co-parent, and my own parents, Clara Sheffer and Jerry Schenwar, who provided invaluable childcare. You all deserve a colossal thank-you! Thanks also to all the friends who kept me grounded and helped me fight isolation in various ways during this time in which baby, work, and book collided, including Andie Baker, Claudia Garcia-Rojas, Jenn Sodini, Hina Mahmood, and Naomi Milstein. Gratitude goes to my healing circle, convened by Jennifer Viets—a reminder of how to live abolition in everyday life—and my Dino's Bar karaoke crew (the Frank Fan Club) for feeding my soul and allowing me to turn every song I sing into an abolitionist anthem, at least in my head. Thank you to everyone on the *Truthout* team for your support, and your dedication to writing in the service of justice, which inspires my own. In particular, Ziggy West Jeffery and Alana Price, thanks for your incredible co-leadership and mission-driven brilliance. Thank you to everyone in Love & Protect for embodying a transformative vision of abolition, and for being my organizing home in Chicago. Thank you to my sister Keeley Schenwar for cheering me on and believing in me; I believe in you. Thank you to my niece, Aniela, for your spirit, your sense of fun, and all of your beautiful drawings that line the wall next to the table where I worked on this book. And thank you to Kai for always reminding me that the future is real and that joy is real, and for sometimes taking a nap at just the right time.

For Vikki, writing a book while parenting frequently feels like an isolating experience. Doing so while parenting a teenager as well as freelancing full-time makes it feel even more so. This makes me even more grateful for community and encouragement. Vikki gives many thanks and much appreciation to Steven Englander for his never-ending support as well as for listening to my endless thinking-aloud, letting me bounce half-formed ideas off him, and encouraging me to live life outside of reading, writing, and research; Siuloong Englander, who, when I first told her that we were looking at how alternatives to incarceration can expand the carceral net, asked, "Why would you want to do that?" and for (sometimes) listening to her mother's thought processes, tolerating my takeover of every communal surface in the house with books and notes, and whipping up delicious vegan food during the grueling revision process; Renee Feltz for talking me through book- and freelance-related conundrums; Jeanne Theoharis for always challenging me to think deeper and look further (sometimes while looking at art and sometimes while eating Yemeni food); George Francisco for providing books and, just as importantly, food, drink, and fun; and the wonderful folks from ABC No Rio for creating pockets of culture and community even without a physical building. During our final revisions, Steven had a (life-saving) lung transplant, which required months of round-the-clock care. Many friends, neighbors, and community members stepped up to help with ongoing food and respite care (including Parker, Tauno, Marisa, Melissa, Jason,

Mike and Vandana, Wendy, Nanda and Jose, Miguel and Antigona, Eric and Jenna, Renee, Cale, Maya, Malav, Mark, Dan, Christine, English Daniel, Marta, English Steve, Miranda, Brian and Christina, Robert Thorn, Jen and Ari, and Julie and Rich). Thank you to everyone for showing us what community looks like.

Finally, our gratitude and appreciation goes out to all the people who are working, day by day, to build movements for liberation and justice.

NOTES

Introduction: Everybody Loves Prison Reform

1. J. Fontaine, D. Gilchrist-Scott, M. Denver, and S.B. Rossman, "Families and Reentry: Unpacking How Social Support Matters," Urban Institute, June 2012, www.urban.org/research/publication/families-and-reentry-unpacking -how-social-support-matters.

2. S. Fahy, A. Gelb, J. Gramlich, and P. Stevenson, "Use of Electronic Offender-Tracking Devices Expands Sharply," Pew Charitable Trusts, 2016, www.pewtrusts.org/en/research-and-analysis/issue-briefs/2016/09/use-of -electronic-offender-tracking-devices-expands-sharply.

3. P. Wagner and W. Sawyer, "States of Incarceration: The Global Context," Prison Policy Initiative, June 2018, www.prisonpolicy.org/global/2018 .html; D. Stemen, "The Prison Paradox: More Incarceration Will Not Make Us Safer," Vera Institute of Justice, July 2017, www.vera.org/publications/for-the -record-prison-paradox-incarceration-not-safer.

4. M. Alper, M.R. Durose, and J. Markman, "2018 Update on Prisoner Recidivism: A 9-Year Follow-Up Period (2005–2014)," Bureau of Justice Statistics, US Department of Justice, May 2018, www.bjs.gov/content/pub/pdf /18upr9yfup0514.pdf.

5. Throughout this book, we use "Brown" as a broad term that includes

Native and Latinx people, as well as some Arab, South Asian, Pacific Islander, and other people who identify as Brown.

An overwhelming number of studies show that not only are Black and Brown people incarcerated at higher rates than white people in the United States, but that this stems from systemic racism, including higher rates of targeting by police. (The discrepancies in incarceration can't be explained by the racist assumption that there are significantly higher crime rates among marginalized groups.) This article provides a catalog of a number of studies illustrating this evidence: R. Balko, "There's Overwhelming Evidence That the Criminal-Justice System Is Racist. Here's the Proof," *Washington Post*, September 18, 2018.

6. P. Wagner and B. Rabuy, "Following the Money of Mass Incarceration," Prison Policy Initiative, January 25, 2017, www.prisonpolicy.org/reports /money.html.

7. K. Whitlock, "Endgame: How 'Bipartisan Criminal Justice Reform' Institutionalizes a Right-wing, Neoliberal Agenda," Political Research Associates, June 6, 2017, www.politicalresearch.org/2017/06/06/endgame-how-bipartisan -criminal-justice-reform-institutionalizes-a-right-wing-neoliberal-agenda.

8. G. Hulse, "Unlikely Cause Unites the Left and the Right: Justice Reform," *New York Times*, February 18, 2015.

9. N. Gingrich and B.W. Hughes Jr., "What California Can Learn from the Red States on Crime and Punishment," *Los Angeles Times*, September 16, 2014.

10. White House, Office of the Press Secretary, "Remarks by the President After Visit at El Reno Federal Correctional Institution," July 16, 2015, obamawhitehouse.archives.gov/the-press-office/2015/07/16/remarks-president -after-visit-el-reno-federal-correctional-institution.

11. 115th Congress, U.S. Senate Committee on the Judiciary, S. 3649, The First Step Act, Section-by-Section Summary, 2018.

12. National Fraternal Order of Police, "FOP Partners with President Trump on Criminal Justice Reform," press release, November 9, 2018, www .fop.net/CmsDocument/Doc/FOP%20on%20First%20Step%20Act.pdf.

13. The White House, "President Donald J. Trump Secures Landmark Legislation to Make Our Federal Justice System Fairer and Our Communities Safer," December 21, 2018, www.whitehouse.gov/briefings-statements/president -donald-j-trump-secures-landmark-legislation-to-make-our-federal-justice -system-fairer-and-our-communities-safer.

14. Y. Nair, "Beth Richie on Race, Gender and the 'Prison Nation,'" *Windy City Times*, May 22, 2013.

15. B. Richie, *Arrested Justice: Black Women, Violence, and America's Prison Nation* (New York: New York University Press, 2012), 3–4.

16. A. Davis, "Masked Racism and the Prison Industrial Complex," Color-Lines, 1998, www.colorlines.com/articles/masked-racism-reflections-prison-industrial-complex.

17. "The Conservative Case for Reform," Right on Crime, www.rightoncrime.com/the-conservative-case-for-reform.

18. In "Smoke and Mirrors," a series of articles about criminal legal system reform, writers and activists Nancy A. Heitzeg and Kay Whitlock urge us to question these diversions. Are people simply thrust under a different type of control, like probation or monitoring? Do they eventually end up in prison for violating the terms of these milder alternatives? Are the numbers of people targeted by these "diversions" actually expanding beyond those who would have otherwise ended up incarcerated? Heitzeg and Whitlock warn that bipartisan reform's narrow emphasis on reducing "overincarceration" leaves the door wide open—sometimes blatantly, sometimes stealthily—to all kinds of long-term expansions of the system. For more, see K. Whitlock and N.A. Heitzeg, "'Bipartisan' Criminal Justice Reform: A Misguided Merger," *Truthout*, February 24, 2015.

19. "The production of surplus is necessary, or else there's no profit, while the overaccumulation of surplus is crisis," writes Gilmore in *Golden Gulag: Prisons, Surplus, Crisis, and Opposition in Globalizing California* (Berkeley: University of California Press, 2007), 57. Gilmore discusses surplus populations—workers at the extreme edges of, or completely outside of, the restructured labor markets of the late twentieth century—as one of the contributing factors to California's prison building boom: "Capital must be able to get rid of workers whose labor power is no longer desirable—whether permanently, by mechanical or human replacement, or temporarily by layoffs—and have access to new or previously idled labor as the need arises" (71). Thus, California's incarceration boom served to remove surplus populations from outside society.

20. "History of the Death Penalty," timeline, ProCon.org, www.deathpenalty.procon.org/view.timeline.php?timelineID=000025.

21. M. Morris, ed., *Instead of Prisons: A Handbook for Abolitionists* (Syracuse, NY: Prison Research Education Action Project, 1976), ch. 2.

22. Abbé Petigny, *Allocution Adressée aux Prisoners*, quoted in M. Foucault, *Discipline and Punish: The Birth of the Prison* (New York: Pantheon Books, 1977), 239.

23. A.Y. Davis, "Racialized Punishment and Prison Abolition," in *The Angela Y. Davis Reader*, ed. J. James (Malden, MA: Blackwell, 1998).

24. Davis, "Racialized Punishment and Prison Abolition."

25. "Prisons: Prisons for Women—History," Law Library: American Law

and Legal Information, www.law.jrank.org/pages/1799/Prisons-Prisons-Women-History.html.

26. R.G. Shelden, "Slavery in the 3rd Millennium Part II—Prisons and Convict Leasing Help Perpetuate Slavery," *Black Commentator* 142 (2005).

27. Davis, "Racialized Punishment and Prison Abolition."

28. M. Alexander, *The New Jim Crow: Mass Incarceration in the Age of Colorblindness* (New York: The New Press, 2010).

29. A. Nellis, "The Color of Justice: Racial and Ethnic Disparity in State Prisons," The Sentencing Project, 2016, www.sentencingproject.org/publications/color-of-justice-racial-and-ethnic-disparity-in-state-prisons.

30. J. Rothwell, "How the War on Drugs Damages Black Social Mobility," Brookings Institution, 2014, www.brookings.edu/blog/social-mobility-memos/2014/09/30/how-the-war-on-drugs-damages-black-social-mobility.

31. J. Kilgore, "Mass Incarceration Since 1492: Native American Encounters with Criminal Injustice," *Truthout*, February 7, 2016.

32. L. Ross, *Inventing the Savage: The Social Construction of Native American Criminality* (Austin: University of Texas Press, 1998).

33. "The Counted: People Killed by the Police in the U.S.," *The Guardian*, June 1, 2015.

34. C. Petitjean, "Prisons and Class Warfare: An Interview with Ruth Wilson Gilmore," *Verso*, August 2, 2018.

35. For more, see Gilmore, *Golden Gulag*; C. Parenti, *Lockdown America: Police and Prisons in the Age of Crisis* (New York: Verso, 2000).

36. Interview with Ruth Wilson Gilmore, summer 2016.

37. G. Gavett, "Map: The U.S. Immigration Detention Boom," *Frontline*, PBS, October 18, 2011, www.pbs.org/wgbh/frontline.

38. T. Robbins, "Little-Known Immigration Mandate Keeps Detention Beds Full," National Public Radio, November 19, 2013.

39. U.S. Department of State, Bureau of International Information, "White House Outlines President's Immigration Reform Proposal," 2005.

40. S. Horsley, "5 Things to Know About Obama's Enforcement of Immigration Laws," National Public Radio, August 31, 2016.

41. S. Ackerman, "ICE Is Imprisoning a Record 44,000 People," *Daily Beast*, November 11, 2018.

42. D. Lind, "It's Official: The Trump Administration Has Replaced Family Separation with Indefinite Family Detention," *Vox*, June 30, 2018. While we won't be covering immigration policy in depth in this book, we recommend following the work of groups like Mijente, Familia: TQLM, MPower Change,

Asian Americans Advancing Justice, and other organizations advocating for immigrant justice in ways that eschew incarceration.

43. D. Berger, "How Prisons Serve Capitalism," Public Books, August 18, 2018, www.publicbooks.org/how-prisons-serve-capitalism.

44. C.W. Ostrom, B.J. Ostrom, and M. Kleiman, "Judges and Discrimination: Assessing the Theory and Practice of Criminal Sentencing," research report submitted to the U.S. Department of Justice, February 2004, www.ncjrs.gov/pdffiles1/nij/grants/204024.pdf.

45. Interview with Mariame Kaba, August 2016. Kaba is a longtime anti-prison and anti-violence activist who founded Project NIA, an effort to end youth incarceration, as well as the Chicago Freedom School, We Charge Genocide, Survived and Punished, the Chicago Taskforce on Violence Against Women and Girls, and many other efforts to combat the prison nation as well as racial and gender-based oppression.

46. P. Cullors-Brignac and D. Zuñiga, "A Mental Health Jail Is an Oxymoron; Diversion Is What's Needed," *Los Angeles Daily News*, June 24, 2014.

47. S. Fahy, A. Gelb, J. Gramlich, and P. Stevenson, "Use of Electronic Offender-Tracking Devices Expands Sharply," Pew Charitable Trusts, September 2016, www.pewtrusts.org/en/research-and-analysis/issue-briefs/2016/09/use-of-electronic-offender-tracking-devices-expands-sharply.

48. J. Kilgore, "The First Step Act Opens the Door to Digital Incarceration," *Truthout*, December 18, 2018.

49. "Law Enforcement," Right on Crime, www.rightoncrime.com/category/priority-issues/law-enforcement.

50. "About Us," Families Against Mandatory Minimums, www.famm.org/about.

51. "Sentencing," Coalition for Public Safety, www.coalitionforpublicsafety.org/issues/sentencing; "Corrections," Coalition for Public Safety, www.coalitionforpublicsafety.org/issues/corrections.

52. We encourage readers to explore the works and words of Angela Davis, Ruth Wilson Gilmore, Assata Shakur, Beth Richie, Debbie Kilroy, Mariame Kaba, Luana Ross, Mumia Abu-Jamal, Mimi Kim, Miss Major, Karlene Faith, Dean Spade, Rachel Herzing, Ejeris Dixon, Liat Ben-Moshe, Dylan Rodriguez, and many more.

53. For more on the ineffectiveness of prison and confinement in addressing harm and violence, see Maya's previous book: M. Schenwar, *Locked Down, Locked Out: Why Prison Doesn't Work and How We Can Do Better* (Oakland, CA: Berrett-Koehler, 2014). In addition to the ways in which prison perpetuates violence outside of prisons, it is important to note the prevalence of violence within prisons, including physical abuse, sexual abuse, and torture such

as solitary confinement.

54. "What Is the PIC? What Is Abolition?" Critical Resistance, www
.criticalresistance.org/about/not-so-common-language.

55. A. Shakur, "Women in Prison: How It Is with Us," *Black Scholar* 9, no. 7
(1978): 8–15.

56. In her landmark book *Are Prisons Obsolete*, Angela Davis writes of what
a leap toward freedom—a prison abolitionist strategy—might look like. "Positing decarceration as our overarching strategy," she writes, "we would try
to envision a continuum of alternatives to imprisonment—demilitarization
of schools, revitalization of education at all levels, a health system that provides free physical and mental care to all, and a justice system based on
reparation and reconciliation rather than retribution and vengeance." For
more, see A.Y. Davis, *Are Prisons Obsolete?* (New York: Seven Stories Press,
2003).

57. B. Harro, "The Cycle of Liberation," in *Readings for Diversity and Social
Justice: An Anthology on Racism, Anti-Semitism, Sexism, Heterosexism, Ableism, and Classism*, ed. M. Adams et al. (New York: Routledge, 2000), 469.

58. Thank you to Mariame Kaba for pointing us toward Harro's definition
of liberation.

1: Your Home Is Your Prison

1. Interviews with Patricia Howard, September and October 2015.

2. P.E. Gobry, "Abolish Prisons," *The Week*, May 9, 2015.

3. "Policy: Electronic Monitoring Program," no. 4028, Corrections Center of Northwest Ohio, September 22, 2014, www.ccnoregionaljail.org/images
/4208%20%20Electronic%20Monitoring%20Program.pdf.

4. Interviews with Angel Sanchez, September 2015 and August 2016.

5. We would urge everyone to remember that restrictive, punitive measures are not the only options; more on that in Chapter 7.

6. R. Corbett and G.T. Marx, "Critique: No Soul in the New Machine:
Technofallacies in the Electronic Monitoring Movement," *Justice Quarterly* 8,
no. 3 (1991): 399–414.

7. T. Wright, "Electronic Monitoring Isn't Helping People on Parole, It's
Sending Them Back to Prison," *In These Times*, October 10, 2018.

8. S. Fahy, A. Gelb, J. Gramlich, and P. Stevenson, "Use of Electronic
Offender-Tracking Devices Expands Sharply," Pew Charitable Trusts, 2016,
www.pewtrusts.org/en/research-and-analysis/issue-briefs/2016/09/use-of
-electronic-offender-tracking-devices-expands-sharply. Some advocates esti

mate that the number could be as high as 200,000, or even higher, but there's so little transparency around monitoring that an exact national total of people bound by EM remains unavailable.

9. Fahy et al., "Use of Electronic Offender-Tracking Devices Expands Sharply."

10. J. Kilgore, "The Spread of Electronic Monitoring: No Quick Fix for Mass Incarceration," *Truthout*, July 30, 2014.

11. R. Ellis, "Oklahoma Prison System to Release Some Inmates Early to Ease Overcrowding," *NewsOK*, September 27, 2017.

12. 115th Congress, U.S. House Committee on the Judiciary, H.R. 5682, First Step Act, 2018. At the time we were finishing the book, the First Step Act had been introduced and widely praised by legislators on both sides of the aisle. It passed both House and Senate and was signed into law by Trump.

13. "One in 31: The Long Reach of American Corrections," Public Safety Performance Project, Pew Center on the States, 2009, www.pewtrusts.org /en/research-and-analysis/reports/2009/03/02/one-in-31-the-long-reach-of -american-corrections.

14. M. Carney, "Correction Through Omniscience: Electronic Monitoring and the Escalation of Crime Control," *Washington University Journal of Law and Policy* 40, no. 1 (2012): 279–305. It's worth noting that this net-widening tendency has long been typical of EM in contexts beyond the United States. According to the John Howard Society of Alberta, which studies Canada's monitoring practices, "There is considerable evidence suggesting that electronic monitoring widens the corrections net in terms of increasing both the number of correctional personnel and the number of offenders given formal sanctions." John Howard Society of Alberta, "Electronic Monitoring," 2000, www.johnhoward.ab.ca/pub/A3.htm.

15. F. Main, "Dart Sees 'Alarming' Rise in Gun Defendants Freed on Electronic Monitoring," *Chicago Sun-Times*, February 22, 2018.

16. Chicago Community Bond Fund, "Money for Communities, Not Cages: Why Cook County Should Reduce the Sheriff's Bloated Budget," October 2018, 4, chicagobond.org/wp-content/uploads/2018/10/money-for -communities-not-cages-why-cook-county-should-reduce-the-sheriffs -bloated-jail-budget.pdf.

17. R. McQuaid, "Marion County Jail at Capacity Again, Sheriff's Office Says," Fox 59 (Indianapolis, IN), August 14, 2018, fox59.com/2018/08/14 /marion-county-jail-at-capacity-again-sheriffs-office-says; Marion County Sheriff's Office, "In Custody Report: April 2019," www.co.marion.or.us/SO /Operations/programs/Documents/Monthly%20Stats/201904/Cust.pdf.

18. A. Kofman, "Digital Jail: How Electronic Monitoring Drives Defendants

into Debt," ProPublica, July 3, 2019, www.propublica.org/article/digital-jail -how-electronic-monitoring-drives-defendants-into-debt.

19. J. Sabatini, "Number of Inmates Released on Electronic Monitoring Triples Following Bail Ruling," *San Francisco Examiner*, March 20, 2019.

20. Z. Kligler, "Trump's Turn to Electronic Monitoring Isn't a Humane Solution," *In These Times*, July 24, 2018.

21. C. Long, F. Bajak, and W. Weissert, "ICE Issuing More Immigrant Ankle Monitors. But Do They Work?," Associated Press, August 25, 2018.

22. J. Fernandes, "Alternatives to Detention and the For-Profit Immigration System," Center for American Progress, www.americanprogress.org /issues/immigration/news/2017/06/09/433975/alternatives-detention-profit -immigration-system.

23. J. Kilgore and D. Gonzalez, "How GPS Is Playing a Critical Role for ICE," *Medium*, August 30, 2019.

24. M. Sidahmed, "Rudy Giuliani Suggests Muslims on US Watchlists Should Wear GPS Bracelets," *The Guardian*, September 22, 2016.

25. M.R. Dickey, "Jay-Z's Roc Nation and First Round Capital Invest $3 million in Bail Reform Startup Promise," TechCrunch, March 19, 2018.

26. J. Kilgore, E. Sanders, and M. Hayes, "No More Shackles: Why We Must End the Use of Electronic Monitors for People on Parole," Center for Media Justice, 2018, www.centerformediajustice.org/wp-content/uploads/2018/10 /NoMoreShackles_ParoleReport_UPDATED.pdf.

27. W. Sweet, "Jeremy Bentham (1748–1832)," in *Internet Encyclopedia of Philosophy: A Peer-Reviewed Academic Resource*, ed. J. Fieser and B. Dowden, www.iep.utm.edu/bentham.

28. It should be noted that under dictator Gerardo Machado, a prison extremely closely modeled on the Panopticon, the Presidio Modelo, was built in Cuba. Both Fidel and Raul Castro were later incarcerated there. N.G. Torres, "Uncovering a Dark Secret at 'Model Prison,'" *Miami Herald*, October 26, 2014.

29. R.W. Schwitzgebel, "A Belt from Big Brother," *Psychology Today* 2, no. 11 (1969): 45–65.

30. E. Anderson, "The Evolution of Electronic Monitoring Devices," National Public Radio, May 24, 2014.

31. Schwitzgebel himself recently lamented, "Unfortunately, electronic technology has gone to punishment." Anderson, "The Evolution of Electronic Monitoring Devices."

32. National Institute of Justice, "Electronic Monitoring Reduces Recidivism," 2011, www.ncjrs.gov/pdffiles1/nij/234460.pdf; B.R. McCarthy, "Palm

Beach County's In-House Arrest Work Release Program," National Institute of Justice, 1987, www.ncjrs.gov/App/publications/abstract.aspx?ID=105345.

33. For more on the history of mass incarceration, see this book's introduction. For a more in-depth exploration of this history, see A.Y. Davis, *Are Prisons Obsolete?* (New York: Seven Stories Press, 2003); C. Parenti, *Lockdown America: Police and Prisons in the Age of Crisis* (New York: Verso, 2000); and R.W. Gilmore, *Golden Gulag: Prisons, Surplus, Crisis and Opposition in Globalizing California* (Berkeley: University of California Press, 2007).

34. R.K. Gable and R.S. Gable, "Electronic Monitoring: Positive Intervention Strategies," *Federal Probation* 69, no. 1 (2005): 21–25.

35. Corbett and Marx, "Critique: No Soul in the New Machine."

36. Cook County Sheriff's Office, Bureau of Information and Technology Business Intelligence Unit, "Cook County Stats of People Placed on EM," 2016, www.eff.org/document/cook-county-stats-people-placed-em.

37. B.K. Payne, M. DeMichele, and N. Okafo, "Attitudes About Electronic Monitoring: Minority and Majority Racial Group Differences," *Journal of Criminal Justice* 37 (2009): 155–162.

38. "Offender Monitoring Solution Improves Efficiencies and Cuts Costs," 2015, www.sierrawireless.com/products-and-solutions/sims-connectivity-and -cloud-services/managed-iot-solutions/omnilink-offender-monitoring-solution.

39. J.L. Doleac, "Study After Study Shows Ex-Prisoners Would Be Better Off Without Intense Supervision," blog post, Brookings Institution, July 2, 2018, www.brookings.edu/blog/up-front/2018/07/02/study-after-study-shows-ex -prisoners-would-be-better-off-without-intense-supervision.

40. S. Lustbader and V. Gullapalli, "How Electronic Monitoring Sets People on Parole Up to Fail," *The Appeal,* March 4, 2019, theappeal.org/how -electronic-monitoring-sets-people-on-parole-up-to-fail.

41. J. Fontaine, D. Gilchrist-Scott, M. Denver, and S.B. Rossman, "Families and Reentry: Unpacking How Social Support Matters," Urban Institute, June 2012, www.urban.org/research/publication/families-and-reentry-unpacking -how-social-support-matters.

42. "Friends Say Lindsay Lohan Called the Judge a F-king Bitch; Kyron's Dad Says Stepmom Is Involved," *Nancy Grace,* CNN, July 8, 2010, www.cnn .com/TRANSCRIPTS/1007/08/ng.01.html.

43. S.L. Sklaver, "The Pros and Cons of Using Electronic Monitoring Programs in Juvenile Cases," *Juvenile Justice Committee Newsletter,* July 2015, s3 .documentcloud.org/documents/1155251/american-bar-associations-report -on-the-pros-and.txt.

44. National Institute of Justice, "Electronic Monitoring Reduces Recidivism."

45. T. Ho, K. Knutson, S. Lockwood, and J.M. Nally, "The Post-release Employment and Recidivism Among Different Types of Offenders with a Different Level of Education: A 5-Year Follow-Up Study in Indiana," *Justice Policy Journal* 9, no. 1 (2012): 16–34.

46. Interview with Pat, 2015. Pat prefers to keep her last name private in talking about matters related to her time on monitoring.

47. M. Nellis, "Surveillance and Confinement: Explaining and Understanding the Experience of Electronically Monitored Curfew," *European Journal of Probation* 1, no. 1 (2009): 41–65, doi.org/10.1177/206622030900100104.

48. Interview with James Kilgore, August 2016.

49. National Institute of Justice, "Electronic Monitoring Reduces Recidivism."

50. L. High, "Boulder's BI Incorporated Has Earned More Than Half-Billion Dollars from ICE Contracts," *Daily Camera*, July 14, 2018; S. Phelan, "Who Profits from ICE's Electronic Monitoring Anklets?," *San Francisco Bay Guardian*, March 16, 2010.

51. "The GEO Group Awarded Contract by U.S. Immigration and Customs Enforcement for the Continued Provision of Services Under Intensive Supervision and Appearance Program," press release, Business Wire, September 10, 2014, www.businesswire.com/news/home/20140910005643/en/GEO-Group-Awarded-Contract-U.S.-Immigration-Customs#.VKd3zivF8nc.

52. The GEO Group, Inc., *2014 Annual Report*, 2015, www.materials.proxyvote.com/Approved/36162J/20150310/AR_237329/#/2.

53. BI Incorporated, "BI Incorporated Celebrates 40 Years of Innovation in Offender Monitoring Technology," October 15, 2018, www.officer.com/command-hq/corrections/offender-monitoring/press-release/21027349/bi-inc-bi-incorporated-celebrates-40-years-of-innovation-in-offender-monitoring-technology.

54. J. Holland, "Private Prisons Are Embracing Alternatives to Incarceration," *The Nation*, August 23, 2016; Kilgore, Sanders, and Hayes, "No More Shackles."

55. "About Us," Offender Management Services, 2015, offender-management.com/about-us.

56. J. Shapiro, "As Court Fees Rise, the Poor Are Paying the Price," National Public Radio, May 19, 2014.

57. Sklaver, "Pros and Cons."

58. "Electronic Home Monitoring Program," City of Mountlake Terrace, www.cityofmlt.com/faq.aspx?TID=18.

59. "Electronic Home Monitoring Program," City of Mountlake Terrace.

60. A. Jungen, "County Uses GPS Units to Monitor Defendants, and It Works . . . Until They Cut Them Off," *La Crosse Tribune*, May 2, 2016.

61. "EHM Application," Offender Monitoring Solutions, www .ehmonitoring.com/forms/ehm-application.

62. Interview with Etan, August 2016. Etan, who was preparing to take the bar exam when he agreed to be interviewed, asked not to be publicly identified.

63. R.D. LaCourse Jr., "Three Strikes, You're Out: A Review," Washington Policy Center, 1997, www.washingtonpolicy.org/publications/detail/three -strikes-youre-out-a-review.

64. Interview with Harvey Fair, November 2015.

65. Interview with James Kilgore, August 2016.

2: Locked Down in "Treatment"

1. The name of this center has been changed.

2. Interview with Stacey Thompson, May 2017.

3. "Governor Christie Marks Opening of New Jersey's First Licensed Substance Use Disorder Treatment Prison," *New Jersey Business and Industry Association Magazine*, April 10, 2017.

4. K. Jaeger, "How Trump's 'Drug Czar' Pick Wants to Tackle Addiction," Attn:, April 12, 2017, archive.attn.com/stories/16385/trumps-drug-czar-pick -wants-tackle-addiction.

5. J. Katz, "Drug Deaths in America Are Rising Faster Than Ever," *New York Times*, June 5, 2017; "The Lancet: Experts Call for Global Drug Policy Reform as Evidence Shows 'War on Drugs' Has Harmed Public Health and Human Rights," press release, EurekaAlert, March 24, 2016, www.eurekalert .org/pub_releases/2016-03/tl-tle032216.php.

6. D.F. Maron, "Drug Courts Appeal to Democrats and Republicans," *Newsweek*, October 6, 2009.

7. N. Walsh, "Addicted to Courts: How a Growing Dependence on Drug Courts Impacts People and Communities," Justice Policy Institute, March 2011, www.justicepolicy.org/uploads/justicepolicy/documents /addicted_to_courts_final.pdf.

8. According to the *Diagnostic and Statistical Manual of Mental Disorders*, 5th ed., substance use disorder is classified as a mental health condition.

9. O. Khazan, "Trump's Call for Mental Institutions Could Be Good," *The Atlantic*, February 23, 2018.

10. G. Panetta, "Trump Said People with Mental Illness Should Be 'Involuntarily Confined' If Necessary to Prevent Mass Shootings, Despite Research Showing a Lack of Connection Between Mental Illness and Gun Violence," *Business Insider*, August 5, 2019.

11. D. Sisti and C. Baum-Baicker, "Commentary: Is President Trump Causing Toxic Stress?," Scattergood Program for Applied Ethics of Behavioral Health Care, www.scattergoodethics.org/is-president-trump-causing-toxic -stress.

12. D. Sisti, "Psychiatric Institutions Are a Necessity," *New York Times*, May 9, 2016.

13. M. De Young, *Madness: An American History of Mental Illness and Its Treatment* (Jefferson, NC: McFarland, 2014), ch. 6.

14. B.E. Harcourt, "Reducing Mass Incarceration: Lessons from the Deinstitutionalization of Mental Hospitals in the 1960s," *Ohio State Journal of Criminal Law* 9, no. 1 (2011): 53–87.

15. E. Walters, "State Spending More on Mental Health Care, but Waitlist Grows," *Texas Tribune*, May 1, 2016; M. Hadro, "Prison Instead of Treatment? U.S. Fails the Mentally Ill," Catholic Online, February 22, 2017, www.catholic .org/news/national/story.php?id=73701; D.A. Fuller, E. Sinclair, H.R. Lamb, J.D. Cayce, and J. Snook, "Emptying the 'New Asylums': A Beds Capacity Model to Reduce Mental Illness Behind Bars," Treatment Advocacy Center, 2017, www.treatmentadvocacycenter.org/storage/documents/emptying-new -asylums-exec-summary.pdf.

16. Interview with Rachel Herzing, August 2016.

17. U.S. Department of Justice, "Drug Courts," May 2018, www.ncjrs.gov /pdffiles1/nij/238527.pdf.

18. M. Szalavitz, "How America Overdosed on Drug Courts," *Pacific Standard*, May 18, 2015.

19. Walsh, "Addicted to Courts."

20. R.S. King and J. Pasquarella, "Drug Courts: A Review of the Evidence," The Sentencing Project, January 2016, 3, www.sentencingproject.org/wp -content/uploads/2016/01/Drug-Courts-A-Review-of-the-Evidence.pdf.

21. Substance Abuse and Mental Health Services Administration, "Adult Drug Courts and Medication-Assisted Treatment for Opioid Dependence," *In Brief* 8, no. 1 (Summer 2014), www.atforum.com/wp-content/uploads/Adult -Drug-Courts.pdf.

22. W.G. Meyer, "Constitutional and Legal Issues in Drug Courts," in *The Drug Court Judicial Benchbook*, ed. D.B. Marlowe and W.G. Meyer (Alexandria, VA: NDCI, 2011).

23. Alcoholics Anonymous, 2014 Member Survey, www.aa.org/assets /en_US/p-48_membershipsurvey.pdf.

24. A. Goodman, "'Drugs Aren't the Problem': Neuroscientist Carl Hart on Brain Science and Myths About Addiction," *Democracy Now!*, January 6, 2014.

25. When Maya interviewed Hart in 2012, he noted, "The stories say [drug users'] situations are fucked up because of those drugs, instead of looking at everything else going on in their lives." And when Vikki interviewed Hart in 2014, he noted, "Drugs can be used safely if we educate people about them. That part is usually missing from these discussions." M. Schenwar, "There Is No Good Drug War," *Truthout*, July 31, 2013; V. Law, "'Government, Not Gangsters, Should Control the Drug Market': But Will That Stop Mass Incarceration?," *Truthout*, September 30, 2014.

26. Boston University Medical Center. "Mandatory Treatment Not Effective at Reducing Drug Use, Violates Human Rights, Researchers Say," press release, *ScienceDaily*, June 21, 2016.

27. J. Strang, J. McCambridge, D. Best, T. Beswick, J. Bearn, S. Rees, and M. Gossop, "Loss of Tolerance and Overdose Mortality After Inpatient Opiate Detoxification: Follow Up Study," *BMJ (Clinical Research Ed.)* 326, no. 7396 (2003): 959–960.

28. P.P. Christopher, D.A. Pinals, T. Stayton, K. Sanders, and L. Blumberg, "Nature and Utilization of Civil Commitment for Substance Abuse in the United States," *Journal of the American Academy of Psychiatry and the Law Online* 43, no. 3 (2015): 313–320.

29. Drug Policy Alliance, "Drug Courts Are Not the Answer: Toward a Health-Centered Approach to Drug Use," 2011, www.drugpolicy.org /sites/default/files/Drug%20Courts%20Are%20Not%twentiethe%20 Answer_Final2.pdf.

30. M.B. Hoffman, "The Drug Court Scandal," *North Carolina Law Review* 18, no. 5 (2000): 1439–1534.

31. Walsh, "Addicted to Courts."

32. Drug Policy Alliance, "Drug Courts Are Not the Answer."

33. T. Ho, S.M. Carey, and A.M. Malsch, "Racial and Gender Disparities in Treatment Courts: Do They Exist and Is There Anything We Can Do to Change Them?," *Journal for Advancing Justice* 1 (2018).

34. Drug Policy Alliance, "Drug Courts Are Not the Answer."

35. Drug Policy Alliance, "Drug Courts Are Not the Answer."

36. Szalavitz, "How America Overdosed on Drug Courts."

37. V. Law, "Why Are So Many Women Behind Bars in Oklahoma?," *The Nation*, September 29, 2015.

38. T.C. Wild, "Social Control and Coercion in Addiction Treatment: Towards Evidence-Based Policy and Practice," *Addiction* 101, no. 1 (2006): 40–49, doi: 10.1111/j.1360-0443.2005.01268.x; A.R. Pasareanu, J.K. Vederhus, A. Opsal, Ø. Kristensen, and T. Clausen, "Improved Drug-Use Patterns at 6 Months Post-Discharge from Inpatient Substance Use Disorder Treatment: Results from Compulsorily and Voluntarily Admitted Patients," *BMC Health Services Research* 16 (2016): 291.

39. Interview with Elliott Fukui, March 2017.

40. E.F. Torrey, "How Many Psychiatric Beds Does America Need?," March 2016, www.treatmentadvocacycenter.org/storage/documents/backgrounders /how-many-psychiatric-beds-does-america-need.pdf.

41. T.C. Lutterman, A. Berhane, R. Shaw, B.E. Phelan, P. Wu, and J. Atay, *Funding and Characteristics of State Mental Health Agencies, 2009* (Rockville, MD: Substance Abuse and Mental Health Services Administration, 2011).

42. M. Pellot-Hernandez, "U.S. Civil Confinement Clashes with U.K. and E.U. Human-Rights Laws," blog post, University of North Carolina School of Law, December 15, 2015, www.blogs.law.unc.edu/ncilj/2015/12/15/us-civil -confinement-clashes-with-uk-and-eu-humanrights-laws.

43. K. Kim, M. Becker-Cohen, and M. Serakos, "The Processing and Treatment of Mentally Ill Persons in the Criminal Justice System: A Scan of Practice and Background Analysis," Urban Institute, 2015, www.urban.org/sites /default/files/publication/48981/2000173-The-Processing-and-Treatment-of -Mentally-Ill-Persons-in-the-Criminal-Justice-System.pdf.

44. Fuller et al., "Emptying the 'New Asylums.'"

45. E. Tibbetts, "SBH Breaks Ground on New Psychiatric Hospital," *Quad-City Times*, April 12, 2018; T. Leys, "Controversial Psychiatric Hospital, First of Its Kind in Iowa, Approved for Quad Cities," *Des Moines Register*, July 21, 2017.

46. C. Isaacs, "The Treatment Industrial Complex: How For-Profit Prison Corporations Are Undermining Efforts to Treat and Rehabilitate Prisoners for Corporate Gain," American Friends Service Committee, 2014, www.afsc.org /document/treatment-industrial-complex-how-profit-prison-corporations -are-undermining-efforts-treat-a.

47. M. Ollove, "Amid Shortage of Psychiatric Beds, Mentally Ill Face Long Waits for Treatment," *Stateline* (blog), Pew Charitable Trusts, August 2, 2016, www.pewtrusts.org/en/research-and-analysis/blogs/stateline/2016/08/02 /amid-shortage-of-psychiatric-beds-mentally-ill-face-long-waits-for -treatment.

48. J. Aleccia, "State's Psychiatric Care Changes Still Not Enough, Say Some Experts," *Seattle Times*, March 21, 2015.

49. J. O'Sullivan, "Gov. Inslee Pushes to Add Psychiatric Beds Around Washington State," *Seattle Times*, May 11, 2018.

50. J. Goldstein-Street, "How a New UW Teaching Hospital Might Help Washington State's Mental-Health Crisis," *Seattle Times*, March 25, 2019.

51. Fuller et al., "Emptying the 'New Asylums.'"

52. T. Beck, "Asylum, Again: Why We Need to Stop Punishing the Mentally Ill," *Los Angeles Review of Books*, October 15, 2018.

53. H. Hussock and C.D. Gorman, "The Case to Bring Back the Asylum," *Wall Street Journal*, May 18, 2018.

54. F. Butterfield, "Asylums Behind Bars: A Special Report—Prisons Replace Hospitals for the Mentally Ill," *New York Times*, March 5, 1998; "The New Asylums," *Frontline*, PBS, May 10, 2005; M. Clark, "Prisons Are the New Asylums," MSNBC, April 8, 2014; A. Shin, "Prisons and Jails: The Not-So-New Asylums," *Washington Post*, April 8, 2014.

55. "Serious Mental Illness Prevalence in Jails and Prisons," Treatment Advocacy Center, September 2016, www.treatmentadvocacycenter.org /evidence-and-research/learn-more-about/3695.

56. Interview with Liat Ben-Moshe, March 2017. Ben-Moshe elaborated: "This pervasive narrative reduces a much more complex process and puts the blame on an easy target, deinstitutionalization, and away from discussions of neoliberal policies that led simultaneously to the growth of the prison system and to lack of financial support for people with disabilities to live in the community. Blaming deinstitutionalization for the rise in incarceration makes it look as if psych hospitals were places of quality care and treatment, and that they were neutral and needed. But they were none of those things."

57. J.D. Wright, "The Mentally Ill Homeless: What Is Myth and What Is Fact?," *Social Problems* 35, no. 2 (1988): 182–191.

58. L. Ben-Moshe, C. Chapman, and A. Carey, "Reconsidering Confinement: Interlocking Locations and Logics of Incarceration," in *Disability Incarcerated: Imprisonment and Disability in the United States and Canada*, ed. L. Ben-Moshe, C. Chapman, and A. Carey (New York: Palgrave Macmillan, 2014).

59. Ben-Moshe, Chapman, and Carey, "Reconsidering Confinement."

60. Ben-Moshe, Chapman, and Carey, "Reconsidering Confinement."

61. D. Petersen, *A Mad People's History of Madness* (Pittsburgh: University of Pittsburgh Press, 1982).

62. Ben-Moshe, Chapman, and Carey, "Reconsidering Confinement"; K. Whitlock and M. Bronski, *Considering Hate: Violence, Goodness, and Justice in American Culture and Politics* (Boston: Beacon Press, 2015). Whitlock and Bronski note that people labeled insane were seen to be "helpless individuals"

in *need* of confinement.

63. Whitlock and Bronski, *Considering Hate.*

64. M. Foucault, *Lectures at the Collège de France, 1974–1975,* trans. G. Burchell (London: Picador, 2007).

65. Interview with Peg Plews, June 2017.

66. D.L. Braddock and S.L. Parish, "Social Policy Toward Intellectual Disabilities in the Nineteenth and Twentieth Centuries," in *The Human Rights of Persons with Intellectual Disabilities: Different but Equal,* ed. S.S. Herr, L.O. Gostin, and H.H. Koh (Oxford: Oxford University Press, 2003).

67. Braddock and Parish, "Social Policy Toward Intellectual Disabilities."

68. K. Gorwitz, "Census Enumeration of the Mentally Ill and the Mentally Retarded in the Nineteenth Century," *Health Service Reports* 89, no. 2 (March–April 1974), 181.

69. P. Wagner and W. Sawyer, "Mass Incarceration: The Whole Pie: 2018," Prison Policy Initiative, www.prisonpolicy.org/reports/pie2018.html.

70. C. Graziani and E. Cole, "InCorrect Care: A Prison Profiteer Turns Care into Confinement," Treatment Industrial Complex Series, 2016, www .grassrootsleadership.org/reports/incorrect-care-prison-profiteer-turns-care -confinement; C. R. Yung, "Civil Commitment for Sex Offenders," *Virtual Mentor* 15, no. 10 (2013): 873–877.

71. E. Horowitz, "Timeline of a Panic: A Brief History of Our Ongoing Sex Offense War," *Southwestern Law Review* 47 (2017): 33–48.

72. E. Meiners, "How 'Risk Assessment' Tools Are Condemning People to Indefinite Imprisonment," *Truthout,* October 6, 2016.

73. G. Steptoe and A. Goldet, "Why Some Young Sex Offenders Are Held Indefinitely," The Marshall Project, January 27, 2016, www.themarshallproject .org/2016/01/27/why-some-young-sex-offenders-are-held-indefinitely.

74. A. Stahl, "Why Sex Criminals Get Locked Up Forever," *Vice,* April 13, 2016.

75. Steptoe and Goldet, "Why Some Young Sex Offenders Are Held Indefinitely."

76. A. Harris, E. Phenix, R.K. Hanson, and D. Thornton, "Static-99 Coding Rules. Revised—2003," www.static99.org/pdfdocs/static-99-coding-rules_e .pdf. This assessment is used extensively in the United States, Canada, Australia, and United Kingdom.

77. A. Phenix, Y. Fernandez, A.J.R. Harris, M. Helmus, R.K. Hanson, and D. Thornton, "Static-99R Coding Rules, Revised," November 14, 2016, www .static99.org/pdfdocs/Coding_manual_2016_v2.pdf. This point was initially made in E. Meiners and T. Meronek, "The Prison-Like Public Hospital Sys-

tems Disproportionately Packed with Gay Men," *The Advocate*, May 23, 2018.

78. Interview with Meiners, September 2017.

79. Stahl, "Why Sex Criminals Get Locked Up Forever."

80. R. Prentky and S. Righthand, "Juvenile Sex Offender Assessment Protocol-II (J-SOAP-II), Manual," The Marshall Project, 2003, www.themarshallproject.org/documents/2698306-JSOAP-II-User-Manual-1#.drix5vDzV; Steptoe and Goldet, "Why Some Young Sex Offenders Are Held Indefinitely."

81. Interview with Meiners, September 2017.

82. Stahl, "Why Sex Criminals Get Locked Up Forever"; D. Post, "Minnesota's Egregious Sex Offender Confinement Statute Held Unconstitutional," *Washington Post*, June 18, 2015; G. Hamilton-Smith, "The Endless Punishment of Civil Commitment," *The Appeal*, September 4, 2018, theappeal.org/the-endless-punishment-of-civil-commitment.

83. M. Clarke, "Texas Uses Failed Private Prison to Hold Civilly Committed Sex Offenders," *Prison Legal News*, September 3, 2018, www.prisonlegalnews.org/news/2018/sep/3/texas-uses-failed-private-prison-hold-civilly-committed-sex-offenders.

84. The Adam Walsh Act defines a "sexually dangerous person" as a person who "engaged or attempted to engage in sexually violent conduct or child molestation and is sexually dangerous to others." The text about release is from 18 U.S.C. §4248, "Civil Commitment of a Sexually Dangerous Person."

85. R. Przybylski, "Recidivism of Adult Sexual Offenders," policy brief, Office of Sex Offender Sentencing, Monitoring, Apprehending, Registering, and Tracking, 2015, www.smart.gov/pdfs/RecidivismofAdultSexualOffenders.pdf.

86. "Sex Offender Recidivism Lower Than for Other Released Prisoners: BJS Study," The Crime Report, May 31, 2019, thecrimereport.org/2019/05/31/sex-offender-recidivism-lower-than-for-other-released-prisoners-bjs-study; S. Orchowsky and J. Iwama, "Improving State Criminal History Records: Recidivism of Sex Offenders Released in 2001," Justice Research and Statistics Association, November 2009, www.jrsa.org/pubs/reports/sex_offender_final.pdf; P.A. Langan, E.L. Schmitt, and M.R. Durose, "Recidivism of Sex Offenders Released from Prison in 1994," Bureau of Justice Statistics, November 2003, www.bjs.gov/content/pub/pdf/rsorp94.pdf; State of Connecticut Office of Policy and Management, Criminal Justice Policy and Planning Division, "Recidivism Among Sex Offenders in Connecticut," February 15, 2012, www.ct.gov/opm/lib/opm/cjppd/cjresearch/recidivismstudy/sex_offender_recidivism_2012_final.pdf.

87. I.M. Ellman and T. Ellman, "'Frightening and High': The Supreme

Court's Crucial Mistake About Sex Crime Statistics," University of Minnesota Law School, 2015, hdl.handle.net/11299/188087; R. Balko, "The Big Lie About Sex Offenders," *Washington Post*, March 9, 2017.

88. A. Young, "Madness and Lived Experience: An Analysis of the Icarus Project," *Social Justice and Community Engagement* 31 (August 2018).

89. Y. Paradies, J. Ben, N. Denson, A. Elias, N. Priest, A. Pieterse, et al., "Racism as a Determinant of Health: A Systematic Review and Meta-analysis," *PLoS ONE* 10, no. 9 (2015): e0138511; S. Williams, "Racism and the Invisible Struggle of Mental Health in the Black Community," *Self*, May 22, 2017; L. Marrast, D.U. Himmelstein, and S. Woolhandler, "Racial and Ethnic Disparities in Mental Health Care for Children and Young Adults: A National Study," *International Journal of Health Services* 46, no. 4 (2016): 810–824, doi:10.1177/0020731416662736.

90. B. Berger, "Power, Selfhood, and Identity: A Feminist Critique of Borderline Personality Disorder," The Advocates' Forum, 2014, www.ssa.uchicago.edu/power-selfhood-and-identity-feminist-critique-borderline-personality-disorder.

91. F. Pride, "Schizophrenia as Political Weapon," *The Root*, January 25, 2010, www.theroot.com/schizophrenia-as-political-weapon-1790878403.

92. R.C. Schwartz and D.M. Blankenship, "Racial Disparities in Psychotic Disorder Diagnosis: A Review of Empirical Literature," *World Journal of Psychiatry* 4, no. 4 (2014): 133–140, doi:10.5498/wjp.v4.i4.133.

93. Braddock and Parish, "Social Policy Toward Intellectual Disabilities."

94. Interview with Liat Ben-Moshe, March 2017.

3: Confined in "Community"

1. Interview with Pat, September 2015.

2. D. Kaeble, "Probation and Parole in the United States, 2016," Bureau of Justice Statistics, April 2018, www.bjs.gov/content/pub/pdf/ppus16.pdf.

3. D. Kaeble and T.P. Bonczar, "Probation and Parole in the United States, 2015," Bureau of Justice Statistics, 2016, www.bjs.gov/content/pub/pdf/ppus15.pdf.

4. M. Friedman, "Just Facts: The Probation Nation," Brennan Center for Justice, March 29, 2016, www.brennancenter.org/blog/probation-nation.

5. P. Wagner and W. Sawyer, "Mass Incarceration: The Whole Pie 2019," Prison Policy Initiative, www.prisonpolicy.org/reports/pie2019.html.

6. "Confined and Costly: How Supervision Violations Are Filling Prisons and Burdening Budgets," Council of State Governments, 2019, csgjusticecen-

ter.org/confinedandcostly.

7. M.P. Jacobson, V. Schiraldi, R. Daly, and E. Hotez, "Less Is More: How Reducing Probation Populations Can Improve Outcomes," Papers from the Executive Session on Community Corrections, Harvard Kennedy School Program in Criminal Justice Policy and Management, 2017, www.hks.harvard.edu/sites/default/files/centers/wiener/programs/pcj/files/less_is_more_final.pdf.

8. Kaeble and Bonczar, "Probation and Parole in the United States, 2015."

9. "Probation and Parole Systems Marked by High Stakes, Missed Opportunities," Pew Charitable Trusts, September 25, 2018, www.pewtrusts.org/research-and-analysis/issue-briefs/2018/09/probation-and-parole-systems-marked-by-high-stakes-missed-opportunities.

10. E. Swavola, K. Riley, and R. Subramanian, "Overlooked: Women and Jails in an Era of Reform," Vera Institute of Justice, 2016, www.vera.org/publications/overlooked-women-and-jails-report.

11. Jacobson et al., "Less Is More."

12. M. Finkel, "New Data: Low Incomes—but High Fees—for People on Probation," Prison Policy Initiative, April 9, 2019, www.prisonpolicy.org/blog/2019/04/09/probation_income.

13. Finkel, "New Data."

14. R.P. Corbett Jr., "The Burdens of Leniency: The Changing Face of Probation," *Minnesota Law Review* 99, no. 5 (2015): 1697–1732.

15. "Non-academic Admissions Clearance," Student Development and Enrollment Services, Office of Student Rights and Responsibilities, University of Central Florida, www.osrr.sdes.ucf.edu/admissions.

16. R.J. Miller and A. Alexander, "The Price of Carceral Citizenship: Punishment, Surveillance, and Social Welfare Policy in an Age of Carceral Expansion," *Michigan Journal of Race and Law* 21, no. 2 (Winter 2016): 6.

17. "Profiting from Probation: America's 'Offender-Funded' Probation Industry," Human Rights Watch, 2014, www.hrw.org/report/2014/02/05/profiting-probation/americas-offender-funded-probation-industry.

18. "'Set Up to Fail': The Impact of Offender-Funded Private Probation on the Poor," Human Rights Watch, 2018, www.hrw.org/report/2018/02/20/set-fail/impact-offender-funded-private-probation-poor.

19. While private prisons incarcerate between 8 and 8.5 percent of the U.S., prison population, private prison corporations have expanded to confine 73 percent of people in immigrant detention. For more, see the Sentencing Project's "Capitalizing on Mass Incarceration: U.S. Growth in Private Prisons," 2018, www.sentencingproject.org/wp-content/uploads/2018/07/Capitalizing

-on-Mass-Incarceration.pdf. See also A. Geiger, "U.S. Private Prison Population Has Declined in Recent Years," Pew Research Center, April 11, 2017, www.pewresearch.org/fact-tank/2017/04/11/u-s-private-prison-population -has-declined-in-recent-years.

20. "Profiting from Probation," Human Rights Watch.

21. K. Whitlock, "Community Corrections: Profiteering, Corruption and Widening the Net," *Truthout*, November 20, 2014.

22. Interview with Monica Jones, December 2017.

23. R.B. Turner, "Project ROSE and Oppression as 'Rescue,'" Human Trafficking Center, April 10, 2014, www.humantraffickingcenter.org/project-rose -and-oppression-as-rescue.

24. M.G. Grant, "'I Have a Right to My Own Body': How Project ROSE Tries to 'Save' Sex Workers," *Rewire News*, March 14, 2014.

25. M. Cassidy, "Phoenix Pilot Program Offers Aid to Those in Life of Prostitution," *Arizona Republic*, January 27, 2015.

26. Global Health Justice Partnership of the Yale Law School and Yale School of Public Health, "Diversion from Justice: A Rights-Based Analysis of Local 'Prostitution Diversion Programs' and Their Impacts on People in the Sex Sector in the United States," 2018, www.law.yale.edu/sites/default/files/area /center/ghjp/documents/diversion_from_justice_pdp_report_ghjp_2018rev .pdf.

27. Global Health Justice Partnership of the Yale Law School, Yale School of Public Health, and the Sex Workers Project of the Urban Justice Center, "Un-Meetable Promises: Rhetoric and Reality in New York City's Human Trafficking Intervention Courts," September 2018, law.yale.edu/sites/default/files/area /center/ghjp/documents/un-meetable_promises_htic_report_ghjp_2018rev .pdf.

28. M. Chen, "Are New York's Sex Workers Getting Their Fair Day in Court?," *The Nation*, October 6, 2014.

29. Global Health Justice Partnership and Yale School of Public Health, "Diversion Sex Sector in the United States."

30. Global Health Justice Partnership and Yale School of Public Health, "Diversion from Justice."

31. Global Health Justice Partnership and Yale School of Public Health, "Diversion from Justice."

32. Project Safe, archive of blog posts tagged with "activism," www .projectsafephilly.org/tag/activism.

33. Project ROSE, Fact Sheet, www.scribd.com/document/210590059 /Project-ROSE-Fact-Sheet.

34. "New Study: Assisted Outpatient Treatment Saves More Taxpayer Money Than It Costs," press release, Cision PRWeb, February 18, 2015, www .prweb.com/releases/2015/02/prweb12524187.htm.

35. E. Fuller Torrey and J.D. Snook, "Assisted Outpatient Treatment Enters the Mainstream," *Psychiatric Times* 34, no. 4 (April 29, 2017).

36. C.H. Rodriguez, "With Hospitalization Losing Favor, States Allow Outpatient Mental Health Treatment," *Governing*, November 13, 2018.

37. T. Burns, J. Rugkåsa, A. Molodynski, J. Dawson, K. Yeeles, M. Vazquez-Montes, M. Voysey, J. Sinclair, and S. Priebe, "Community Treatment Orders for Patients with Psychosis (OCTET): A Randomised Controlled Trial," *The Lancet* 381, no. 9878 (2013): 1627–1633.

38. S. Kisely, L.A. Campbell, and N. Preston, "Compulsory Community and Involuntary Outpatient Treatment for People with Severe Mental Disorders," *Cochrane Database Systematic Reviews* 3 (2005), doi:10.1002/14651858. CD004408.pub2.

39. E. Fabris, *Tranquil Prisons: Chemical Incarceration Under Community Treatment Orders* (Toronto: University of Toronto Press, 2011).

40. Fabris, *Tranquil Prisons*. Fabris himself notes, "I am not against medicine or drugs on the whole. I like science and reason."

41. D.M. Perry, "The Pills Have Eyes," *Pacific Standard*, February 1, 2018.

42. Council on Recovery and Empowerment, "Position Paper on MA House Bill 1792 and Senate Bill 906, Assisted Outpatient Treatment," 2013, www.westernmassrlc.org/images/stories/CORE_position_re_AOT_Bill __7_12_2013.pdf.

43. Interview with Robert Suttle, September 2017.

44. K.K. Bonnar-Kidd, "Sexual Offender Laws and Prevention of Sexual Violence or Recidivism," *American Journal of Public Health* 100, no. 3 (2010): 412–419.

45. K.M. Zgoba and K. Bachar, "Sex Offender Registration and Notification: Limited Effects in New Jersey," NCJ 225402, U.S. Department of Justice, Office of Justice Programs, National Institute of Justice, April 2009, www .ncjrs.gov/pdffiles1/nij/225402.pdf 2009; Criminal Courts Committee and the Corrections and Community Reentry Committee of the NYC Bar, "Report on an Act to Amend the Correction Law in Relation to Enacting 'Brittany's Law': This Bill Is Opposed," 2012, www2.nycbar.org/pdf/report/uploads/20072258 -BilltoCreateViolentFelonyOffenderRegistry.pdf.

46. J.J. Prescott and J.E. Rockoff, "Do Sex Offender Registration and Notification Laws Affect Criminal Behavior?," *Journal of Law and Economics* 54, no. 1 (2010): 161–206, doi:10.1086/658485.

47. "Map of Registered Sex Offenders in the United States," National Center for Missing and Exploited Children, 2018, www.missingkids.com/content /dam/pdfs/SOR%20Map%20with%20Explanation.pdf; "Registries in the U.S. Has Climbed to over 900,000," Arizona Chapter of Women Against Registry, 2018, www.az.womenagainstregistry.org/registries-in-the-u-s-has-climbed -to-over-900000.

48. B. Schwartzapfel, "Congress Acts to Mark Passports of Sex Offenders," The Marshall Project, February 2, 2016.

49. Office of Justice Programs, Office of Sex Offender Sentencing, Monitoring, Apprehending, Registering, and Tracking, "Sex Offender Management Assessment and Planning Initiative," 2017, www.smart.gov/SOMAPI/pdfs /SOMAPI_Full%20Report.pdf.

50. J. Fifield, "Despite Concerns, Sex Offenders Face New Restrictions," *Stateline* (blog), Pew Charitable Trusts, May 6, 2016, www.pewtrusts.org /en/research-and-analysis/blogs/stateline/2016/05/06/despite-concerns-sex -offenders-face-new-restrictions.

51. Bonnar-Kidd, "Sexual Offender Laws and Prevention."

52. B. Schwartzapfel, "Banished," The Marshall Project, October 3, 2018, www.themarshallproject.org/2018/10/03/banished.

53. C. Thompson, "For Some Prisoners, Finishing Their Sentences Doesn't Mean They Get Out," The Marshall Project, May 24, 2016.

54. Office of Justice Programs, "Sex Offender Management Assessment and Planning Initiative"; Bonnar-Kidd, "Sexual Offender Laws and Prevention."

55. P.A. Zandbergen, J.S. Levenson, and T.C. Hart, "Residential Proximity to Schools and Daycares: An Empirical Analysis of Sex Offense Recidivism," *Criminal Justice and Behavior* 37, no. 5 (2010): 482–502, doi:10.1177/0093854810363549.

56. Interview with LeeAnn, March 2017.

57. Interview with Erica Meiners, September 2017.

58. "More children are abused by a caregiver or someone they know, than abused outside of the home by a stranger." American Academy of Pediatrics, "Child Abuse and Neglect," April 13, 2018, www.healthychildren.org/English /safety-prevention/at-home/Pages/What-to-Know-about-Child-Abuse.aspx.

59. Center for Sex Offender Management, "Myths and Facts," www .criminaljustice.ny.gov/nsor/som_mythsandfacts.htm.

60. E. Horowitz, *Protecting Our Kids? How Sex Offender Laws Are Failing Us* (Santa Barbara, CA: ABC-CLIO, 2015), 51.

61. E. Dexheimer, "Program to Corral Ballooning Sex Offender Registry Failing," *Austin American-Statesman*, September 3, 2016.

62. Horowitz, *Protecting Our Kids?*, 62.

63. Alliance for Constitutional Sex Offense Laws, "Registrants Sue CA Dept of Justice—Demand Improvements to, or End of, Megan's Law Website," November 10, 2015, www.all4consolaws.org/2015/11/registrants-sue-ca-dept -of-justice-demand-improvements-to-or-end-of-megans-law-website.

64. J. McFadden, "SC Couple Pleads Guilty to Killing Convicted Sex Offender; Has No Regrets," *Rock Hill* (SC) *Herald*, May 6, 2014.

65. M. Baran and J. Vogel, "Sex-Offender Registries: How the Wetterling Abduction Changed the Country," American Public Media, October 4, 2017.

66. Horowitz, *Protecting Our Kids?*, xviii.

67. "About Us," Women Against Registry, www.womenagainstregistry.org /page-1730782.

68. "Innocent Victims Videos," Women Against Registry, www .womenagainstregistry.org/Innocent-Victim-Videos.

4: Policing Parenthood

1. Interview with Tabitha Minson, April 2018.

2. L. Haney, "Motherhood as Punishment: The Case of Parenting in Prison," *Women, Gender, and Prison: National and Global Perspectives* 39, no. 1 (2013): 105–130.

3. A. Lieberman and L. Burt, "Babies in Prison? It's Not What You Think," New America, August 4, 2016, www.newamerica.org/education-policy /edcentral/babies-prison.

4. C.K. Villanueva, S.B. From, and G. Lerner, "Mothers, Infants and Imprisonment: A National Look at Prison Nurseries and Community-Based Alternatives," Women's Prison Association, 2009, www.prisonlegalnews.org /news/publications/womens-prison-assoc-report-on-prison-nurseries-and -community-alternatives-2009.

5. Haney, "Motherhood as Punishment."

6. V. Jackson, "Residential Treatment for Parents and Their Children: The Village Experience," *Science and Practice Perspectives* 2, no. 2 (2004): 44–53.

7. Interview with Dorothy Roberts, December 2017.

8. Interview with Mariame Kaba, August 2016.

9. Interview with Angela Willard, December 2017.

10. L. Radel, M. Baldwin, G. Crouse, R. Ghertner, and A. Waters, "Substance Use, the Opioid Epidemic, and the Child Welfare System: Key Findings from a Mixed Methods Study," Office of the Assistant Secretary for Planning

and Evaluation, U.S. Department of Health and Human Services, 2018, www
.aspe.hhs.gov/system/files/pdf/258836/SubstanceUseChildWelfareOverview
.pdf.

11. C. Wildeman, F.R. Edwards, and S. Wakefield, "The Cumulative Prevalence of Termination of Parental Rights for U.S. Children, 2000–2016," *Child Maltreatment* (online), May 21, 2019, doi:10.1177/1077559519848499.

12. S. Clifford and J. Silver-Greenberg, "Foster Care as Punishment: The New Reality of 'Jane Crow,'" *New York Times*, July 21, 2017.

13. National Coalition for Child Protection Reform, "Who Is in the System—and Why," Issue Paper 5, National Coalition for Child Protection Reform, September 7, 2015, drive.google.com/file /d/0B291mw_hLAJsT00wNkk5R1c1dWM/view.

14. Interview with Dorothy Roberts, December 2017.

15. "Child Welfare in America—An Overview," National Coalition for Child Protection Reform, March 11, 2018, www.nccpr.org/the-nccpr-quick -read.

16. "Children and Families of the Incarcerated Fact Sheet," National Resource Center on Children and Families of the Incarcerated, 2014, www .nrccfi.camden.rutgers.edu/files/nrccfi-fact-sheet-2014.pdf.

17. 115th Congress, U.S. Senate Committee on Finance, "An Examination of Foster Care in the United States and the Use of Privatization," 2017, Executive Summary, www.govinfo.gov/content/pkg/CPRT-115SPRT26354/html /CPRT-115SPRT26354.htm.

18. "Foster Care vs. Family Preservation: The Track Record on Safety and Well-being," Issue Paper 1, National Resource Center on Children and Families of the Incarcerated, 2015, www.nccpr.org/issue-papers-family -preservation-foster-care-and-reasonable-efforts.

19. C.H. Tolliver, "About," *Black on Both Sides* (blog), 2013, www .blackbothsides.wordpress.com/about.

20. A. Brown, A. Dworsky, C. Cary, K. Love, M.E. Courtney, and V. Vorhies, "Midwest Evaluation of the Adult Functioning of Former Foster Youth: Outcomes at Age 26," Chapin Hall at the University of Chicago, 2012, www.issuelab.org/resource/midwest-evaluation-of-the-adult-functioning-of -former-foster-youth-outcomes-at-age-26.html.

21. S. McCarthy and M. Gladstone, "State Survey of California Prisoners: What Percentage of the State's Polled Prison Inmates Were Once Foster Care Children?," California Senate Office of Research, December 2011, sor.senate .ca.gov/sites/sor.senate.ca.gov/files/State Survey of California Prisoners.pdf.

22. Citizens for Juvenile Justice, "Missed Opportunities: Preventing Youth in the Child Welfare System from Entering the Juvenile Justice System," Citi-

zens for Juvenile Justice, 2015, www.cfjj.org/missed-opp, Executive Summary.

23. R. Greenstein, "Welfare Reform and the Safety Net," Center on Budget and Policy Priorities, 2016, www.cbpp.org/research/family-income-support /welfare-reform-and-the-safety-net.

24. L.H. Shaefer and K. Edin, "The Rise of Extreme Poverty in the United States," *Pathways: A Magazine on Poverty, Inequality, and Social Policy*, Stanford Center on Poverty and Inequality, Summer 2014, https://inequality .stanford.edu/sites/default/files/media/_media/pdf/pathways/summer_2014 /Pathways_Summer_2014_ShaeferEdin.pdf.

25. H. Koball and Y. Jiang, "Basic Facts About Low-Income Children: Children Under 18 Years, 2016," National Center for Children in Poverty, Columbia University Mailman School of Public Health, 2018, www.nccp.org /publications/pub_1194.html.

26. R. Wexler, "30 Streams and a Lot of Weeds: Making Sense of Child Welfare Finance," Fighting for Family: Organizing and Advocacy at the Intersection of the Criminal and Family Punishment System, Drexel Law School, July 12, 2019.

27. D. Ginther and M. Johnson-Motoyama, "Do State TANF Policies Affect Child Abuse and Neglect?," October 27, 2017, pdfs.semanticscholar.org/fd31 /a0ce1ff65da9f078b869bdfd1c58dfd496b3.pdf.

28. U.S. Department of Health and Human Services, Administration for Children and Families, Administration on Children, Youth and Families, Children's Bureau, "Foster Care Statistics 2016 (Numbers and Trends)," 2018, www .childwelfare.gov/pubPDFs/foster.pdf; Kids Count Data Center, "Child Population by Race, 2012–2016," dataset, Annie E. Casey Foundation, 2018, www .datacenter.kidscount.org/data/tables/103-child-population-by-race#detailed /1/any/false/870,573,869,36,868/68,69,67,12,70,66,71,72/423,424.

29. E. Meiners and C. Tolliver, "Refusing to Be Complicit in Our Prison Nation: Teachers Rethinking Mandated Reporting," *Radical Teacher* 106 (2016): 106–114.

30. D. Roberts, *Shattered Bonds: The Color of Child Welfare* (New York: Basic Books, 2001).

31. M.D. O'Sullivan, "More Destruction to These Family Ties: Native American Women, Child Welfare, and the Solution of Sovereignty," *Journal of Family History* 41, no. 1 (2015): 19–38, doi:10.1177/0363199015617476.

32. B.J. Jones, M. Tilden, and K. Gaines-Stoner, *The Indian Child Welfare Act Handbook: A Legal Guide to the Custody and Adoption of Native American Children* (Chicago: American Bar Association, 2008).

33. Jones, Tilden, and Gaines-Stoner, *The Indian Child Welfare Act Handbook.*

34. Northern Plains Reservation Aid, "History and Culture, Boarding Schools," www.nativepartnership.org/site/PageServer?pagename=airc_hist_boardingschools.

35. Child Welfare League of America, "South Dakota's Children 2017: South Dakota's Children at a Glance," 2017, www.cwla.org/wp-content/uploads/2017/03/SOUTH-DAKOTA.pdf.

36. S. Woodward, "Native Americans Expose the Adoption Era and Repair Its Devastation," *Indian Country Today*, December 6, 2011.

37. National Council on Disability, "Rocking the Cradle: Ensuring the Rights of Parents with Disabilities and Their Children," 2012, www.ncd.gov/sites/default/files/Documents/NCD_Parenting_508_0.pdf.

38. Kids Count Data Center, "Child Population by Race, 2012–2016."

39. N. Martin, "When the Womb Is a Crime Scene," ProPublica, September 23, 2015, www.propublica.org/article/when-the-womb-is-a-crime-scene.

40. C. Lippy, C. Burk, and M. Hobart, "There's No One I Can Trust: The Impact of Mandatory Reporting on the Help-Seeking and Well-Being of Domestic Violence Survivors," National LGBTQ DV Capacity Building Learning Center, May 2016, www.idvsa.org/wp-content/uploads/2016/05/TheresNoOneICanTrust-MandatoryReporting.pdf.

41. J. Tabachnick and A. Klein, "A Reasoned Approach: Reshaping Sex Offender Policy to Prevent Child Sexual Abuse," Association for the Treatment of Sexual Abusers, 2011, www.atsa.com/pdfs/ppReasonedApproach.pdf; S. Roan, "Effectiveness of Making Therapists Report All Child Abuse Questioned," *Los Angeles Times*, July 17, 1991.

42. S.M. Krason, "Mondale Act and Its Aftermath: An Overview of Forty Years of American Law, Public Policy, and Governmental Response to Child Abuse and Neglect," in *Child Abuse, Family Rights, and the Child Protective System: A Critical Analysis from Law, Ethics, and Catholic Social Teaching*, ed. S.M. Krason (Lanham, MD: Scarecrow Press, 2013).

43. M. Raz, "Unintended Consequences of Expanded Mandatory Reporting Laws," *Pediatrics* 139, no. 4 (2017).

44. U.S. Department of Health and Human Services, Administration for Children and Families, Administration on Children, Youth and Families, Children's Bureau, "Child Maltreatment 2015," 2017, www.acf.hhs.gov/sites/default/files/cb/cm2015.pdf.

45. T. Tracy, "Administration of Children's Services Staffers Now Being Sent to NYPD Investigator Course," New York *Daily News*, September 24, 2017.

46. Tracy, "Administration of Children's Services Staffers."

47. M. Chilton, "Jazmine Headley's Arrest Exposes the Punitive Design of

Public Assistance," *The Nation*, December 14, 2018.

48. E. Meiners and M. Schenwar, "'Stop-and-Frisk' for Caregivers: How Expanded Mandated Reporting Laws Hurt Families," *Truthout*, June 29, 2017.

49. U.S. Department of Health and Human Services, Administration for Children and Families, Administration on Children, Youth and Families, Children's Bureau, "Mandatory Reporters of Child Abuse and Neglect," 2015, www.childwelfare.gov/pubPDFs/manda.pdf.

50. As political scholar Stephen Krason writes of the results of mandated reporting, "We now have a situation where a massive state bureaucracy with sweeping coercive power is having millions upon millions of dollars being poured into it each year even though perhaps 85% of its actions are completely unnecessary." Krason, "Mondale Act and Its Aftermath," 9.

51. Center for the Study of Social Policy, "Disparities and Disproportionality in Child Welfare: An Analysis of the Research," Annie E. Casey Foundation, 2011, www.aecf.org/resources/disparities-and-disproportionality-in-child-welfare.

52. J. Katz, "Penn State Case Should Prompt Smart Action," *Hartford Courant*, November 21, 2011.

53. H. Kim, C. Wildeman, M. Jonson-Reid, and B. Drake, "Lifetime Prevalence of Investigating Child Maltreatment Among US Children," *American Journal of Public Health* 107, no. 2 (2017): 274–280, doi:10.2105/AJPH.2016.303545.

5: Communities as Open-Air Prisons

1. Interview with K, August 2018. K, who still lives in the Red Hook housing projects where he grew up and is continually targeted by police, asked to withhold his full name to protect his and his family's privacy.

2. Office of the Mayor, City of New York, "Mayor de Blasio, Commissioner Bratton Unveil New, Groundbreaking Neighborhood Policing Vision," June 25, 2015, www1.nyc.gov/office-of-the-mayor/news/440-15/mayor-de-blasio-commissioner-bratton-new-groundbreaking-neighborhood-policing-vision#/0.

3. New York Police Department, "Neighborhood Policing," www1.nyc.gov/site/nypd/bureaus/patrol/neighborhood-coordination-officers.page.

4. In August 2018, Vikki observed these billboards in the subway in the East Village, Crown Heights, Washington Heights, Union Square, Greenwich Village, and other parts of New York City.

5. New York Police Department, "Neighborhood Policing."

6. N. Venugopal, "Map: How Red Hook's White Population Surge Is Changing the Neighborhood," DNAinfo, November 18, 2016, https://www .dnainfo.com/new-york/20161118/red-hook/red-hook-demographics-white -population-real-estate.

7. N. Prakash, "Why These Activists Think the Exit of New York's Top Cop Isn't Nearly Enough to Change Policing," *Splinter*, August 2, 2016, splinternews.com/why-these-activists-think-the-exit-of-new-yorks-top-cop -1793860801.

8. New York Police Department, "Neighborhood Policing."

9. J. Byrne, "Emanuel Floats $24M in New Police Training, Community Policing Money in '18 Budget," *Chicago Tribune*, October 13, 2017; J. Trujillo, "1,000 More Cops: The Last Thing We Need," New York *Daily News*, February 20, 2015; C. Chang, "LAPD Veteran Michel Moore Promises 'Compassion and Partnership' While Sworn In as Police Chief," *Los Angeles Times*, June 28, 2018.

10. M. Ford, "A Blueprint to End Mass Incarceration," *The Atlantic*, December 16, 2016. Other reform organizations that advocate decreased incarceration but encourage community policing include Families Against Mandatory Minimums and Right on Crime.

11. G. Lopez, "How More and Better Police Could Lead to Less Incarceration, Explained by an Expert," *Vox*, November 30, 2015.

12. White House, Office of the Press Secretary, "Remarks by the President at the 122nd Annual IACP Conference," October 27, 2015, www .obamawhitehouse.archives.gov/the-press-office/2015/10/27/remarks -president-122nd-annual-iacp-conference.

13. U.S. Department of Justice, Office of Public Affairs, "Department of Justice Awards Nearly $9 Million to Advance Community Policing Efforts and Increase First Responder Safety Through Active Shooter Training," press release, October 23, 2017, www.justice.gov/opa/pr/department-justice-awards -nearly-9-million-advance-community-policing-efforts-and-increase.

14. "About Us," Red Hook Initiative, www.rhicenter.org/aboutus.

15. E. Elizalde, "Red Hook Youth and Cops Unite For First Annual Basketball Tournament," *Bklyner*, August 1, 2016.

16. Interview with Joe, August 2018. Joe chose to withhold his full name to protect his and his family's privacy.

17. G. Rayman, "Caught on Video: Detective Allegedly Uses Banned Chokehold on Man During Routine Noise Complaint Call," New York *Daily News*, August 10, 2018.

18. Abolition Research Group, "The Problem with Community Policing," October 8, 2017, www.aworldwithoutpolice.org/2017/10/08/the-problem-with -community-policing.

19. K.B. Howell, "Broken Lives from Broken Windows: The Hidden Costs of Aggressive Order-Maintenance Policing," *New York University Review of Law and Social Change* 33 (2009): 271–329.

20. A.J. Ritchie, "Black Lives over Broken Windows: Challenging the Policing Paradigm Rooted in Right-Wing 'Folk Wisdom,'" *The Public Eye*, July 6, 2016, www.politicalresearch.org/2016/07/06/black-lives-over-broken-windows -challenging-the-policing-paradigm-rooted-in-right-wing-folk-wisdom; Police Reform Organizing Project, "The Human and Economic Cost of Broken Windows Policing in NYC," 2014, www.policereformorganizingproject .org/cost-broken-windows-policing.

21. Abolition Research Group, "The Problem with Community Policing."

22. "Community Policing, Bratton Style" (editorial), January 31, 1994, *New York Times*.

23. J. Eig, "Eyes on the Street: Community Policing in Chicago," *American Prospect*, November/December 1996.

24. A. Aguilera and A.S. Vitale, "The Limits of Community Policing, NYPD City Council," *Gotham Gazette*, March 2, 2015.

25. Office of the Mayor, City of Chicago, "Mayor Emanuel and CPD Superintendent Johnson Celebrate Graduation," press release, April 10, 2018, www .cityofchicago.org/city/en/depts/mayor/press_room/press_releases/2018 /april/PoliceGraduation.html; Office of the City Clerk, City of Chicago, "Mayor Rahm Emanuel's 2018 Budget Address," www.chicityclerk.com/sites /default/files/pages/Mayor%20Rahm%20Emanuel%202018%20Budget%20 Address.pdf.

26. Office of Reform Management, Chicago Police Department, "Community Policing," www.home.chicagopolice.org/office-of-reform-management /community-policing; Office of the Mayor, City of Chicago, "Community Policing Advisory Panel Releases Draft Recommendations," press release, August 10, 2017, www.cityofchicago.org/city/en/depts/mayor/press_room /press_releases/2017/august/CPAPRecommendations.html.

27. V.E. Kappeler and L.K. Gaines, *Community Policing: A Contemporary Perspective* (New York: Routledge, 2010).

28. Kappeler and Gaines, *Community Policing*; O.B. Waxman, "How the U.S. Got Its Police Force," *Time*, May 18, 2017.

29. A.S. Vitale, *The End of Policing* (Brooklyn, NY: Verso Books, 2017); A.M.

Cantu, "The Chapparal Insurgents of South Texas," *New Inquiry*, April 7, 2016.

30. E. Sweeney, "Civilians on Patrol," *Boston Globe*, July 6, 2008.

31. "Our History," National Neighborhood Watch, a Division of the National Sheriffs' Association, www.nnw.org/our-history.

32. R. Abraham and A. Mercado, "NYPD's Neighborhood Meetings Aren't Reaching Intended Audience," City Limits, April 24, 2018, citylimits.org/2018/04/24/nypds-neighborhood-policing-meetings-arent-reaching-intended-audience.

33. New York Police Department, "Build the Block," video file, May 16, 2017, www.youtube.com/watch?v=oQVxzzX-Tp0.

34. Interview with Alex Vitale, July 2018.

35. Sweeney, "Civilians on Patrol."

36. Interview with Josmar Trujillo, July 2018.

37. S. Herbert, *Citizens, Cops, and Power: Recognizing the Limits of Community* (Chicago: University of Chicago Press, 2006); W.G. Skogan, S.M. Hartnett, J. DuBois, J.T. Comey, K. Twedt-Ball, and J.E. Gudel, "Public Involvement: Community Policing in Chicago," NIJ Research Report, Center for Urban Affairs and Policy Research, 2000, www.ncjrs.gov/App/Publications/abstract.aspx?ID=179557.

38. Department of the Army, Headquarters, *FM 3-24, MCWP 3-33.5, Insurgencies and Counterinsurgencies*, field manual, 2014, www.hqmc.marines.mil/Portals/135/JAO/FM%203_24%20May%202014.pdf.

39. Y. Alcindor, "Trial Turns to Zimmerman's Neighborhood-Watch Role," *USA Today*, June 25, 2013.

40. L. Alvarez, "Running, a Fight and Then a Shot, a Witness Testifies in Zimmerman's Trial," *New York Times*, June 25, 2013.

41. New York Police Department, July 10, 2018, "Overall Crime Continues to Decline in New York City Through the First Half of 2018," www1.nyc.gov/site/nypd/news/pr0710/overall-crime-continues-decline-new-york-city-the-first-half-2018#/0; B. Mueller and A. Baker, "Drop in Gang Violence Drove New York City Shootings Below 1,000 in 2016," *New York Times*, January 3, 2017; New York Police Department, 48th Precinct, "NYPD Gang Squad and 48 Neighborhood Coordination Officers will host a parental gang awareness meeting at Mt. Carmel Recreation Center-Wed June 27th 7:00PM. The best way to combat this growing problem is to become as knowledgeable about it as possible. JOIN US! #NYPDprotecting," June 13, 2018, www.twitter.com/NYPD48Pct/status/1007007564029136898.

42. C. Gill, D. Weisburd, C.W. Telep, Z. Vitter, and T. Bennett, "Community-Oriented Policing to Reduce Crime, Disorder and Fear and Increase Satisfac-

tion and Legitimacy Among Citizens: A Systematic Review," *Journal of Experimental Criminology* 10, no. 4 (2014): 399–428, doi:10.1007/s11292-014-9210-y.

43. Interview with Malik, August 2018. Malik asked that we not use his real name, especially given his brother's incarceration after Operation Tidal Wave.

44. Interview with Vitale, July 2018.

45. We Charge Genocide, "Counter-CAPS Report: The Community Engagement Arm of the Police State," 2015, www.wechargegenocide.org/wp-content/uploads/2015/10/CAPSreport-final.pdf.

46. We Charge Genocide, "Counter-CAPS Report."

47. Interview with Lynda Lopez, July 2018.

48. This example of the impact of neighborhood watch was noted by Chicago activists Rachel Hoffman and Rebecca Harris in a June 2018 interview.

49. Albany Park Neighbors, "January 2018—APN Member Meeting Notes," Facebook, February 1, 2018, www.facebook.com/notes/albany-park-neighbors/january-2018-apn-member-meeting-notes/1055023924638800.

50. Statistical Atlas, "West Rogers Park (Neighborhood), Chicago: Race and Ethnicity," www.statisticalatlas.com/neighborhood/Illinois/Chicago/West-Rogers-Park/Race-and-Ethnicity.

51. "WBEZ Mischaracterizes Neighborhood Watch," *50th Ward Follies* (blog), May 26, 2017, www.50thwardfollies.com/category/neighborhood-watch-program.

52. Interview with Jennifer Viets, October 2018.

53. N. Kensinger, "Red Hook's Long, Inevitable Gentrification Divides Community," *Curbed*, January 28, 2016.

54. W.T. Lyons, *The Politics of Community Policing: Rearranging the Power to Punish* (Ann Arbor: University of Michigan Press, 1999), 4.

55. Lyons, *The Politics of Community Policing*, 172.

56. C. Moraff, "Community Policing: Promise and Failure," *The Crime Report*, May 15, 2015, www.thecrimereport.org/2015/05/15/2015-05-community-policing-promise-and-failure.

57. Interview with Patrick Reilly, July 2018. Reilly elaborated on the significance of the CANS/CAPS history: "I think if we had a greater awareness of the history of police reform, people might be more skeptical of attempts to patch up community-police relations. . . . For me, the priority is to move the conversation from cooperating/repairing relations with the police to confronting them for their role in society."

58. A. A. Braga, "Better Policing Can Improve Legitimacy and Reduce Mass

Incarceration," *Harvard Law Review Forum* 129 (7): 233–241, March 10, 2016.

59. A. Papachristos, "Use of Data Can Stop Crime by Helping Potential Victims," *New York Times*, November 18, 2015.

60. D. Robinson and L. Koepke, "Stuck in a Pattern: Early Evidence on 'Predictive Policing' and Civil Rights," Center for Media Justice, 2016, www .centerformediajustice.org/resources/stuck-in-a-pattern, Executive Summary. The term "predictive policing" was coined by the company PredPol, founded by a professor who'd done research predicting killings in Iraq and used his experience to develop "preventative" tools for police in the United States.

61. Robinson and Koepke, "Stuck in a Pattern."

62. A.G. Ferguson, *The Rise of Big Data Policing: Surveillance, Race and the Future of Law Enforcement* (New York: New York University Press, 2017).

63. B.C. Anderson, "William Bratton on "Precision Policing," *City Journal*, August 1, 2018, www.city-journal.org/html/william-bratton-precision -policing-16084.html.

64. City of New York, Office of the Mayor, "Transcript: Mayor de Blasio and Commissioner O'Neill Host Press Conference to Discuss Crime Statistics," October 3, 2016, www1.nyc.gov/office-of-the-mayor/news/792-16/transcript -mayor-de-blasio-commissioner-o-neill-host-press-conference-discuss -crime#/0.

65. H. Bruinius, "At Crossroads of Policing and Murder, a Long Push for Accountability," *Christian Science Monitor*, February 15, 2018.

66. A. Winston and I. Burrington, "A Pioneer in Predictive Policing Is Starting a Troubling New Project," *The Verge*, April 26, 2018.

67. G. Joseph, "Has 'Gang Policing' Replaced Stop-and-Frisk?," *CityLab*, February 28, 2017.

68. K.B. Howell, "Gang Policing: The Post Stop-and-Frisk Justification for Profile-Based Policing," *University of Denver Criminal Law Review* 5 (2015): 1–31.

69. S. Gaskell, "NYPD Ready to Make Even Bigger 'Impact,'" *New York Post*, January 13, 2004.

70. Joseph, "Has 'Gang Policing' Replaced Stop-and-Frisk?"

71. Vikki was a peripheral part of a gang during her brief stint as a teenage armed robber. During the drafting of this book, she filed a Freedom of Information request to learn whether she was in the gang database. Her request was denied, and to this day she has no idea whether she is listed.

72. A. Muniz, "Maintaining Racial Boundaries: Criminalization, Neighborhood Context, and the Origins of Gang Injunctions," *Social Problems* 61,

no. 2 (2014): 216–236, doi:10.1525/sp.2014.12095.

73. W. Ruderman, "To Stem Juvenile Robberies, Police Trail Youths Before the Crime," *New York Times*, March 3, 2013.

74. J. Kemp, "Hood Starz and Wave Gang of Brooklyn Not :) After Getting Busted for Using Web for Crime," New York *Daily News*, January 19, 2012.

75. J. Goldstein, "43 in Two Warring Gangs Are Indicted in Brooklyn," *New York Times*, January 19, 2012.

76. Ferguson, *Rise of Big Data Policing*.

77. Ferguson, *Rise of Big Data Policing*.

78. M. Dumke, "Chicago's Gang Database Is Full of Errors—And Records We Have Prove It," ProPublica, April 19, 2018, www.propublica.org/article /politic-il-insider-chicago-gang-database.

79. J. Saunders, P. Hunt, and J.S. Hollywood, "Predictions Put into Practice: A Quasi-Experimental Evaluation of Chicago's Predictive Policing Pilot," *Journal of Experimental Criminology* 12, no. 3 (2016): 347–371, doi:10.1007/ s11292-016-9272-0.

80. R. Kinsella, S. Joseph, and J. Chausow, "BDS Testifies Before the NYC Council on the NYPD's Gang Takedown Efforts," Brooklyn Defender Services, June 13, 2018, www.bds.org/bds-testifies-before-the-nyc-council-on -nypds-gang-takedown-efforts.

81. Robinson and Koepke, "Stuck in a Pattern."

82. M. Dumke, "Chicago's Gang Database Isn't Just About Gangs," ProPublica, April 20, 2018, www.propublica.org/article/chicago-gang-database -is-not-just-about-gangs.

83. National Gang Center, "Compilation of Gang-Related Legislation," 2017, www.nationalgangcenter.gov/Legislation/Prosecution.

84. Ferguson, *Rise of Big Data Policing*.

85. M. Rivlin-Nadler, "How a Group Policing Model Is Criminalizing Whole Communities," *The Appeal*, January 12, 2018.

86. Rivlin-Nadler, "How a Group Policing Model Is Criminalizing Whole Communities."

87. Ferguson, *Rise of Big Data Policing*.

88. A. Southall, "Crime in New York City Plunges to a Level Not Seen Since the 1950s," *New York Times*, December 27, 2017.

89. R. Parascandola and G. Rayman, "Advocates Suspicious of NYPD's Gang Database Standards," New York *Daily News*, June 12, 2018.

90. A. Speri, "New York Gang Database Expanded by 70 Percent Under

Mayor Bill de Blasio," *The Intercept*, June 11, 2018.

91. Policing in Chicago Research Group, University of Illinois at Chicago, "Chicago Gang Database: Facts and Figures," 2017, www.docs.google.com /document/d/1Ft_41wtKLU2NVKGSiN2hMHFmHaSRkIS3rNatZVvAnOk /edit.

92. Robinson and Koepke, "Stuck in a Pattern."

93. C. O'Neil, "How Data Can Make Immigrants Look Like Criminals," *Bloomberg News*, March 8, 2017.

94. C. Thompson, "How ICE Uses Secret Police Databases to Arrest Immigrants," The Marshall Project, August 28, 2017, www.themarshallproject.org /2017/08/28/how-ice-uses-secret-police-databases-to-arrest-immigrants.

95. Autonomous Tenants Union, "Policing and Gentrification Mass Displacement and the 'Community Watch,'" *Medium*, May 24, 2018.

96. Interview with Rebecca Harris and Rachel Hoffman, June 2018.

6: Your School Is Your Prison

1. Editorial Staff of the Eagle Eye, "Our Manifesto to Fix America's Gun Laws," *The Guardian*, March 23, 2018.

2. E. King and A. Cynic, "Community Investment, Safety Without Cops: Good Kids Mad City Organizes Against Gun Violence," *Shadow Proof*, April 23, 2018.

3. M. Hogan, "Sheriff Reminds Deputies of Oath, Active Shooter Policy in Response to Parkland," *Cherokee Tribune and Ledger-News*, February 28, 2018.

4. R. Petersen, "Our Police Need Better Training. Florida School Shooting Failures Make This More Imperative," Fox News, March 13, 2018.

5. U.S. Department of Justice, Office of Public Affairs, "Attorney General Sessions Announces New Actions to Improve School Safety and Better Enforce Existing Gun Laws," press release, March 12, 2018, www.justice.gov /opa/pr/attorney-general-sessions-announces-new-actions-improve-school -safety-and-better-enforce.

6. E.L. Mahoney and C. Wright, "Gov. Scott Requests School Safety Money Shuffle to Add More Campus Officers," *Tampa Bay Times*, August 22, 2018; H. Russ and L. Kearney, "After Parkland Shooting, U.S. States Shift Education Funds to School Safety," Reuters, April 10, 2018.

7. M. Sykes, "New for School Year: Armed Marshals," *Axios*, August 19, 2018.

8. M. Howell and J. Moore, "Police Officers in Schools, Metro Funding, Speed Cameras: A Look at Bills Approved by Md. General Assembly," WTOP

(Chevy Chase, MD), April 10, 2018.

9. D. Andone, "They Led a National March. Now Parkland Students Return to a School They Say 'Feels Like Jail,'" CNN, April 2, 2018.

10. M. Allen, "Student and Activist David Hogg on Gun Policy and Safety," C-SPAN, March 23, 2018.

11. This chapter is not meant to be an explainer on the school-to-prison pipeline, but rather an exploration of the recent ways in which calls to reform have exacerbated conditions for marginalized students and intensified different forms of surveillance, policing, and incarceration. For more information on the school-to-prison pipeline, we recommend reading C. Laura's *Being Bad: My Baby Brother and the School-to-Prison Pipeline* (New York: Teachers College Press, 2014) as well as M.W. Morris's *Pushout: The Criminalization of Black Girls in Schools* (New York: The New Press, 2016).

12. Congressional Research Service, "School Resource Officers: Issues for Congress," 2018, www.everycrsreport.com/files/20180705_R45251_db54923 70a04c7e3b39f27ce52416d229a0ac17d.pdf.

13. Interview with Gregory McKelvey, February 2019.

14. Youth Accountability Team, Riverside County Probation Department, www.probation.co.riverside.ca.us/resources/yat.aspx.

15. S. Torres-Guillen, "Class Action: Complaint for Declaratory and Injunctive Relief and Nominal Actions," Case No. 5:18-cv-01399, ACLU of Southern California, July 1, 2018, www.aclu.org/sites/default/files/field_document /yat_complaint_filed_copy.pdf.

16. E. Blad and A. Harwin, "Black Students More Likely to Be Arrested at School," *Education Week*, January 24, 2017.

17. Project NIA, "Policing Chicago Public Schools: Gateway to the School-to-Prison Pipeline (2011–2012)," 2013, www.cpdincps.com/infogrpahic.

18. New York Civil Liberties Union, "New Data: Police Disproportionately Target Black and Latino Students in NYC Schools," press release, April 30, 2018, www.nyclu.org/en/press-releases/new-data-police-disproportionately -target-black-and-latino-students-nyc-schools?utm.

19. Interview with Oumou Kaba, January 2019.

20. A. Campbell, "Police Handcuff 6-Year-Old Student in Georgia," CNN, April 17, 2012.

21. A. Onyeka-Crawford, K. Patrick, and N. Chaudhry, "Let Her Learn: Stopping School Pushout for Girls of Color," National Women's Law Center, 2017, nwlc-ciw49tixgw5lbab.stackpathdns.com/wp-content/uploads/2017/04 /final_nwlc_Gates_GirlsofColor.pdf.

22. Morris, *Pushout*.

23. Interview with MG, December 2018. (MG chose to withhold her

full name.)

24. R. Epstein, J.J. Blake, and T. Gonzales, "Girlhood Interrupted: The Erasure of Black Girls' Childhood," Georgetown Law Center for Poverty and Inequality, 2017, www.law.georgetown.edu/poverty-inequality-center/wp-content/uploads/sites/14/2017/08/girlhood-interrupted.pdf.

25. S.A. Annamma, Y. Anyon, N.M. Joseph, J. Farrar, E. Greer, B. Downing, and J. Simmons, "Black Girls and School Discipline: The Complexities of Being Overrepresented and Understudied," *Urban Education* 54, no. 2 (2016): 211–242, doi:10.1177/0042085916646610.

26. Morris, *Pushout.*

27. U.S. Department of Education Office for Civil Rights, "Data Snapshot: School Discipline," Issue Brief No. 1., March, 2014, https://www2.ed.gov/about/offices/list/ocr/docs/crdc-discipline-snapshot.pdf.

28. H. Greensmith, "LGBTQ Girls Are Much More Likely to Face Discipline in School," *Rewire News*, May 11, 2018.

29. T. Fabelo, M.D. Thompson, M. Plotkin, D. Carmichael, M.P. Marchbanks III, and E.A. Booth, "Breaking Schools' Rules: A Statewide Study of How School Discipline Relates to Students' Success and Juvenile Justice Involvement," Council of State Governments Justice Center, July 2011, www.csgjusticecenter.org/wp-content/uploads/2012/08/Breaking_Schools_Rules_Report_Final.pdf.

30. J.M. Nowicki, "K-12 Education: Discipline Disparities for Black Students, Boys, and Students with Disabilities," GAO-18-258, U.S. Government Accountability Office, 2018, www.gao.gov/assets/700/690828.pdf.

31. S.D. Sparks and A. Klein, "Discipline Disparities Grow for Students of Color, New Federal Data Show," *Education Week*, April 24, 2018.

32. Onyeka-Crawford, Patrick, and Chaudhry, "Let Her Learn."

33. C. Na and D.C. Gottfredson, "Police Officers in Schools: Effects on School Crime and the Processing of Offending Behaviors," *Justice Quarterly* 30, no. 4 (2013): 619–650.

34. R. Klein, "The Other Side of School Safety: Students Are Getting Tasered and Beaten by Police," *Huffington Post*, September 8, 2018.

35. Interview with Crystal Laura, August 2018.

36. Education scholar David Stovall argues that for many Black and Brown students, school actually operates like a type of part-time incarceration: "If you think about a place where students are punished if they do not walk on demarcated lines in the floor, are required to remain silent during lunch, required to wear uniforms (including clear backpacks), subject to random searches, and are fined for being out of uniform, this place is not 'leading' you to prison. Instead, we should understand that space as an operative prison,

with the main difference being that you are allowed to go home every afternoon." D. Stovall, "Are We Ready for 'School' Abolition? Thoughts and Practices of Radical Imaginary in Education," *Taboo: The Journal of Culture and Education* 17, no. 1 (2018): 51–61, doi:10.31390/taboo.17.1.06.

37. P.A. Noguera, "Schools, Prisons, and Social Implications of Punishment: Rethinking Disciplinary Practices," *Theory into Practice* 42, no. 4 (2003): 341–350, doi: 10.1207/s15430421tip4204_12.

38. National Association of School Resource Officers, "Increase Current Funding for Specially Trained School Resource Officers, NASRO Tells DOJ," press release, February 16, 2018, www.nasro.org/news/press-releases/increase -current-funding-specially-trained-school-resource-officers-nasro-tells-doj.

39. M. Icsman, "Justice Department Pushes for Putting More Officers in Schools," *USA Today*, March 12, 2018.

40. "Public Schools Tackle Students' First Offense with Warning Cards," *Spectrum News*, NY1, September 14, 2018.

41. D.J. Losen and A. Whitaker, "Race, Discipline, and Safety at U.S. Public Schools," American Civil Liberties Union, 2018, www.aclu.org/issues/juvenile -justice/school-prison-pipeline/race-discipline-and-safety-us-public-schools.

42. K. Terenzi, K. Foster, and M. Kilpatrick, "The $746 Million a Year School-to-Prison Pipeline: The Ineffective, Discriminatory, and Costly Process of Criminalizing New York City Students," Center for Popular Democracy, 2017, www.populardemocracy.org/sites/default/files/STPP_layout_web_final .pdf.

43. A. Whitaker, S. Torres-Guillén, M. Morton, H. Jordan, S. Coyle, A. Mann, and W. Sun, "Cops and No Counselors: How the Lack of School Mental Health Staff Is Harming Students," American Civil Liberties Union, 2019, www.aclu .org/sites/default/files/field_document/030419-acluschooldisciplinereport .pdf.

44. Dignity in Schools, "Counselors Not Cops," dignityinschools.org/take -action/counselors-not-cops.

45. B. Chapman, "NYC Students Rally for More Guidance Counselors, Fewer Cops in Schools," New York *Daily News*, April 5, 2018.

46. Chapman, "NYC Students Rally."

47. D. Katch, "NYC Students Get Metal Detectors Expelled," *Socialist Worker*, January 19, 2018.

48. C. McCrory, "Student Protesters March in Phoenix, Call for Removal of School Resource Officers," *Cronkite News*, Arizona PBS, February 23, 2018; N. Gotlieb, "Group Protests Police in Schools at School Board Member's Home," *Southwest Journal*, February 5, 2018.

49. L. Graves, "Some PPS Students Plan to Protest Presence of Officers in Schools," KATU (Portland, OR), May 8, 2017.

50. H. Zehr, *The Little Book of Restorative Justice* (Intercourse, PA: Good Books, 2002).

51. Community Initiatives, "Restorative Justice for Oakland Youth," 2017, www.communityin.org/leader_voices/restorative-justice-oakland-youth.

52. S. Pavelka, "Restorative Justice in the States: A National Assessment of Legislation and Policy," *Justice Policy Journal* 13, no. 2 (2016).

53. Interview with Jesse, September 2018. This name has been changed to protect privacy and prevent retaliation.

54. CMAP, "Community Data Snapshot: North Lawndale, Chicago Community Area," June 2019, www.cmap.illinois.gov/documents/10180/126764 /North+Lawndale.pdf.

55. State of Illinois, Circuit Court of Cook County, "Restorative Justice Community Court Arrives in North Lawndale," press release, July 20, 2017, www.cookcountycourt.org/MEDIA/ViewPressRelease/tabid/338/ArticleId /2564/Restorative-Justice-Community-Court-arrives-in-North-Lawndale .aspx.

56. J. Simeone-Casas, S. Conway, and R. Cox, "Justice, Restored? New North Lawndale Court Aims to Change Punitive System," *Chicago Defender*, September 21, 2017.

57. Interview with Mariame Kaba, August 2016.

7: Beyond Alternatives

1. Interview with Ruth Wilson Gilmore, September 2016.

2. "About Voices and Visions," Hearing Voices Network, www.hearing -voices.org/voices-visions/about.

3. M. Griffel and C. Hart, "Is Drug Addiction a Brain Disease?," *American Scientist*, May 2018.

4. Interview with Sadie Ryanne Baker, March 2017.

5. W.A. Pridemore, "Poverty Matters: A Reassessment of the Inequality-Homicide Relationship in Cross-National Studies," *British Journal of Criminology* 51, no. 5 (2011): 739–772, doi:10.1093/bjc/azr019.

6. Interview with Erica Meiners, September 2017.

7. Interview with Dorothy Roberts, December 2017.

8. "Welcome! Minding the Baby National Office," Yale School of Medicine Child Study Center, Community Partnerships, www.medicine.yale.edu

/childstudy/communitypartnerships/mtb.

9. J. Lepore, "Baby Doe," *New Yorker*, February 1, 2016.

10. Mother Warriors Voice, "Time to Create a Mothers Movement?," 2008, www.welfarewarriors.org/mwv_archive/sp08/sp08_movement.htm.

11. Interview with Ruth Wilson Gilmore, September 2016.

12. Here we are alluding to Angela Davis's pathbreaking abolitionist text, *Are Prisons Obsolete?* (New York: Seven Stories Press, 2003), which envisions a world in which prisons become unthinkable and have no place in society.

13. The Icarus Project, www.theicarusproject.net.

14. Interview with Elliott Fukui, March 2017.

15. E. Martin, "Americans Are More Stressed About Money Than Work or Relationships—Here's Why," CNBC, June 26, 2018.

16. J. Wortham, "Racism's Psychological Toll," *New York Times Magazine*, June 24, 2015.

17. Hearing Voices Network USA, www.hearingvoicesusa.org.

18. Visible Voices, Cabrini Green Legal Aid, www.cgla.net/programs.

19. "Sero Project: About Us," www.seroproject.com/about-us.

20. Interview with Kaba, August 2016.

21. B.M. Mathers, L. Degenhardt, C. Bucello, J. Lemon, L. Wiessing, and M. Hickman, "Mortality Among People Who Inject Drugs: A Systematic Review and Meta-analysis," *Bulletin of the World Health Organization* 91, no. 2 (2013): 102–123.

22. "Principles of Harm Reduction," Harm Reduction Coalition, www .harmreduction.org/about-us/principles-of-harm-reduction.

23. K. Stone and G. Sander, "The Global State of Harm Reduction 2016," Harm Reduction International, www.hri.global/files/2016/11/14/GSHR2016_14nov .pdf.

24. European Monitoring Centre for Drugs and Drug Addiction, "Drug Consumption Rooms: An Overview of Provision and Evidence," 2018, www.emcdda.europa.eu/system/files/publications/2734/POD_Drug%20 consumption%20rooms.pdf.

25. K. DeBeck, T. Kerr, L. Bird, R. Zhang, D. Marsh, M. Tyndall, J. Montaner, and E. Wood, "Injection Drug Use Cessation and Use of North America's First Medically Supervised Safer Injecting Facility," *Drug and Alcohol Dependence* 113, nos. 2–3 (2010): 172–176.

26. B. Allyn, "Desperate Cities Consider 'Safe Injection' Sites for Opioid Users," National Public Radio, January 10, 2018.

27. N. Manskar, "NYC Heroin Injection Sites Get Thumbs Down from

Feds," Patch.com, September 18, 2018.

28. J. Katz, "The First Count of Fentanyl Deaths in 2016: Up 540% in Three Years," *New York Times*, September 2, 2017.

29. C. Hart, *High Price: A Neuroscientist's Journey of Self-Discovery That Challenges Everything You Know About Drugs and Society* (New York: HarperCollins, 2013).

30. M. Schenwar, "There Is No Good Drug War," *Truthout*, July 31, 2013.

31. Interview with Susan Sered, December 2017.

32. For more, see S. Sered and M. Norton-Hawk, *Can't Catch a Break: Gender, Jail, Drugs and the Limits of Personal Responsibility* (Berkeley: University of California Press, 2014).

33. M. Curzer, "Prison Rape Is Not a Punchline," Bitch Media, April 30, 2019, www.bitchmedia.org/article/prison-rape-not-punchline.

34. Creative Interventions, "Creative Interventions Toolkit: A Practical Guide to Stop Interpersonal Violence," sec. 5, "Other Resources," 2012, www .creative-interventions.org/wp-content/uploads/2012/06/5.CI-Toolkit-Other -Resources-Pre-Release-Version-06.2102.pdf.

35. The term "transformative justice" was coined by Ruth Morris in her book *Stories of Transformative Justice* (Toronto: Canadian Scholars' Press and Women's Press, 2000). It was later popularized by generationFIVE, a Bay Area organization that aimed to end child sexual abuse in five generations.

36. "Transformative Justice," Generation FIVE, www.generationfive.org /the-issue/transformative-justice.

37. *Transforming Harm* (blog), www.transformharm.tumblr.com.

38. O.N. Perlow, D.I. Wheeler, S.L. Bethea, and B.M. Scott, eds., *Black Women's Liberatory Pedagogies: Resistance, Transformation, and Healing Within and Beyond the Academy* (Basingstoke, UK: Palgrave Macmillan, 2017).

39. "The Indigenous Origins of Circles and How Non-Natives Learned About Them," Living Justice Press, www.livingjusticepress.org/index .asp?SEC=0F6FA816-E094-4B96-8F39-9922F67306E5&Type=B_BASIC.

40. Just Practice was co-founded by Shira Hassan, former director of the Young Women's Empowerment Project, and other Chicago activists. For more, see S. Hassan, "About Just Practice," www.shirahassan.com/about-just -practice.

41. Bay Area Transformative Justice Collective, batjc.wordpress.com.

42. Men Can Stop Rape, "Our Mission and History," www.mencanstoprape .org/Our-Mission-History/our-history.html; Esteban Kelly, "Philly Stands Up: Inside the Politics and Poetics of Transformative Justice and Community Accountability in Sexual Assault Situations," Mada, December 9, 2018,

madamasr.com/en/2018/12/09/feature/society/philly-stands-up-inside-the
-politics-and-poetics-of-transformative-justice-and-community-accountability
-in-sexual-assault-situations.

43. Interview with Meiners, September 2017.

44. Interview with Herzing, August 2016.

45. "Safe Outside the System," Audre Lorde Project, www.alp.org/programs
/sos.

46. Interview with Ejeris Dixon, March 2018.

47. StoryTelling and Organizing Project (STOP), Creative Interventions,
www.creative-interventions.org/about/ci-projects/storytelling-organizing
-project-stop.

48. "Community Responds to Domestic Violence," StoryTelling and Organizing Project, Creative Interventions, www.stopviolenceeveryday.org/wp
-content/uploads/community%20responds%20to%20domestic%20violence
.pdf.

49. V. Huang, "Transforming Communities: Community-Based Responses
to Partner Abuse," in *The Revolution Starts at Home: Confronting Partner
Abuse in Activist Communities*, ed. C.I. Chen, J. Dulani, and L. Piepzna-
Samarasinha (Oakland, CA: n.p., 2008).

50. While there is still no movement ambulance, some local projects have
cropped up around the country that aim to fill gaps in the emergency medical
system with grassroots work. For example, on Chicago's South Side, an area
where access to ambulances and hospitals falls short, a group called Ujimaa
Medics works to train youth to treat gunshot wounds.

51. Interview with Gilmore, September 2016.

INDEX

ABOUT THE AUTHORS

Maya Schenwar is the editor-in-chief of *Truthout*. She is the author of *Locked Down, Locked Out* and the co-editor of the anthology *Who Do You Serve, Who Do You Protect?* She lives in Chicago.

Victoria Law is a freelance journalist, the author of *Resistance Behind Bars*, and co-editor of *Don't Leave Your Friends Behind*. She is a co-founder of NYC Books Through Bars and lives in New York.

PUBLISHING IN THE PUBLIC INTEREST

Thank you for reading this book published by The New Press. The New Press is a nonprofit, public interest publisher. New Press books and authors play a crucial role in sparking conversations about the key political and social issues of our day.

We hope you enjoyed this book and that you will stay in touch with The New Press. Here are a few ways to stay up to date with our books, events, and the issues we cover:

- Sign up at www.thenewpress.com/subscribe to receive updates on New Press authors and issues and to be notified about local events
- Like us on Facebook: www.facebook.com/newpressbooks
- Follow us on Twitter: www.twitter.com/thenewpress

Please consider buying New Press books for yourself; for friends and family; or to donate to schools, libraries, community centers, prison libraries, and other organizations involved with the issues our authors write about.

The New Press is a 501(c)(3) nonprofit organization. You can also support our work with a tax-deductible gift by visiting www.thenewpress.com/donate.